I SHARED
THE DREAM

GEORGIA DAVIS POWERS

I SHARED THE DREAM

THE PRIDE, PASSION AND POLITICS OF THE FIRST BLACK WOMAN SENATOR FROM KENTUCKY

New Horizon Press   Far Hills, New Jersey

Copyright Acknowledgments

The author and publisher gratefully acknowledge permission to quote from
the following copyrighted material:

"The Country Preacher's Folk Prayer" by Leonard A. Slade, Jr., Professor
of English and Africana Studies, State University of New York at Albany.
Copyright © *Another Black Voice: A Different Drummer*, Winston-Derek
Publishers Inc. Used with permission.

Requests for permission should be addressed to:
New Horizon Press
P.O. Box 669
Far Hills, NJ 07931

Powers, Georgia Davis.
        I Shared the Dream: The Pride, Passion, and Politics of the
        first Black Senator from Kentucky

Library of Congress Catalog Card Number: 94-66756

ISBN: 0-88282-127-X
New Horizon Press

Manufactured in the U.S.A.

1999 1998 1997 1996 1995 / 5 4 3 2 1

This book is dedicated to the cherished memory of
my mother, Frances Walker Montgomery;
my father, Ben Gore Montgomery;
and their descendants.

—G.D.P.

CONTENTS

ACKNOWLEDGMENTS ix
AUTHOR'S NOTE x
PROLOGUE 1

I THE EARLY YEARS 7

1   GEORGIA, WON'T YOU PLEASE SIT DOWN? 9
2   STORMY WEATHER 23
3   GROWING PAINS 33

II THE UNSETTLED YEARS 43

4   DREAMS DEFERRED 45
5   THE PHILADELPHIA LAWYER 59

III THE CIVIL RIGHTS YEARS 81

6   FATEFUL CHOICES 83
7   A MEETING 91

IV THE POLITICAL YEARS 107

8   SMALL STEPS, BIG CHOICES 109
9   SELMA 123
10   MOVING AHEAD 131
11   CROSSING THE LINE 145
12   MARCHES AND PRIMARIES 163
13   M.L. 169
14   PREMONITIONS 179
15   SWEET VICTORY 187
16   SENATOR GEORGIA M. DAVIS 195
17   THE LADY FROM JEFFERSON 33 205
18   R & R 217
19   THE LAST NIGHT 227

V THE SUNSET YEARS 237

20 AFTER THE NIGHTMARE 239
21 HARD WORK AND DESPAIR 255
22 TAKING MY PLACE 263
23 IN THE FRAY 273
24 HATRED'S UGLY HEAD 281
25 PUBLIC SUCCESS, PRIVATE SORROW 293
26 MOSES, THE ORATOR 297
27 THE LAST FEW PLAYS 305

EPILOGUE 313

ACKNOWLEDGMENTS

I thank the following people and organizations for their help and belief in me:

Maxine Brown, CEO and president of the Fund for Women, Inc., for presenting me with a personal computer upon my retirement.

The Kentucky Foundation for Women, Inc., founded by Sallie Bingham, for the grant given to a person (who requests anonymity) to assist me.

James L. Powers for his encouragement, patience, and love.

AUTHORS' NOTE

These are the actual experiences and personal history of Georgia Davis Powers and this book reflects her opinions of the past, present, and future. The personalities, events, actions, and conversations portrayed within the story have been reconstructed from her memory, documents, letters, personal papers, press accounts, and the memories of other participants. In an effort to safeguard the privacy of certain individuals, the author has changed their names and, in some cases, altered otherwise identifying characteristics. Events involving the characters happened as described; only minor details have been changed.

PROLOGUE

I was standing in front of the dresser mirror patting my hair when I heard the shot. A woman screamed, "Oh my God! They've shot Dr. King!" I rushed to the door of my motel room and flung it open. Uniformed policemen were entering the courtyard. Where had they come from so fast, I wondered? Later I learned that the police station was just seconds away on the corner.

Someone was pointing to the second floor. I looked up to my left and gasped. One of Dr. King's knees stuck straight up in the air and I could make out the bottom of one foot. People in the courtyard had scattered to take cover. Without pausing, I hurried up the stairs closest to my room. Reaching King's room, I stepped inside and saw Andy Young and Ralph Abernathy, their faces grim, feverishly telephoning for an ambulance. They hardly noticed me, and I went out on the balcony.

Alone, I walked over and looked at Dr. King. He was lying in a pool of blood that was widening as I stood there staring. The bullet had pierced the right side of his neck. His tie had been severed from the knot. Both the knot and an inch of tie were sticking up. It is a picture permanently imprinted in my mind.

A siren wailed. I went over to the iron railing and looked down. A black ambulance, looking more like a patrol car, was making its way in. By this time the courtyard was crowded with people, many crying or praying.

Two medics from the ambulance hurried upstairs. They lifted Dr. King onto a stretcher, then brought him down to the courtyard. I hurried after them. Andy Young and Ralph Abernathy did the same.

I had always been terrified of being exposed. Only once did I put such thoughts aside. When they put Dr. King into the ambulance, I instinctively began climbing in to go with him. Andy Young gently pulled me back. "No, Senator," he said, "I don't think you want to do that."

A decision—perhaps not even consciously made—had placed me at the side of Martin Luther King Jr., the leader of the civil rights movement, on the day he died. Suddenly, the memory of our last telephone call accosted me. "Senator, please come to Memphis, I need you," he had said. I had come, but it hadn't helped. Nothing had.

Again the vision of his body flashed through my mind. I am descending into hell, I thought. I remembered all the preachers I had ever heard, describing the fiery furnaces of hell. I knew they were wrong; hell is not hot. Hell is cold.

As icy cold as I was now. Was I condemned to live forever shaking, unable to get warm, I wondered, while he lies colder still, in his grave? The thought was unbearable. I would gladly have suffered what I had feared for so long—

public exposure and the threat to my political career—to have him here beside me now as he had been last night.

There were times I knew we were under surveillance by the FBI when we were together. Later, when I tried to get copies of any information the FBI had relating to me, it took four years of repeated requests before I received anything. Officials finally sent me fifty-five of the eighty-two pages in which my name was mentioned. I was unable to get any information about the time period of my involvement with Dr. King. The first entry on the papers I received was dated April 1968, after King's death. Typed lines on about three-quarters of the pages I received were blacked out. The official explanation for the deletions was that the information was: (1) related solely to the internal personnel rules and practices of an agency, (2) could reasonably be expected to constitute an unwarranted invasion of personal privacy, or (3) could reasonably be expected to disclose the identity of a confidential source. I do not accept the FBI's explanations.

Why am I telling all this now? If Dr. King had been an ordinary man, the telling of my story wouldn't make much difference. However, Dr. King was no ordinary man. His life will be studied by scholars long after I'm gone.

Others have written about me, and the FBI has files relating to my life. Some published accounts differ from what I know to be the truth. In Carl Rowan's book, *Breaking the Barriers*, he refers to a 1977 official Justice Department task force report which he said included what was purported to be Mrs. Georgia Davis's account of what happened the night before King was killed. No one from a Justice Department task force ever interviewed me. I have not made any public statements about what happened until now.

In Ralph David Abernathy's autobiography, *And The Walls Came Tumbling Down*, he refers to my relationship with King. I was surprised when I received a call from the

Associated Press after Abernathy's book was released. It had always been my constant fear that one of King's close associates would talk about our relationship, but I couldn't believe it was Ralph who had actually done it. Then, when I finally read the account, I was further discouraged that he had not told the truth. Ralph was King's closest friend and confidant. Perhaps, due to his own illness and the toll the intervening years had taken on him, he was no longer able to remember things as they had happened.

When Dr. King's life is researched, I want the part relating to me to be available in my own words. It is my own history as well, both the good and the bad.

I am writing my story now as honestly as I know how, because I am the only living person who knows exactly what happened.

I

THE EARLY
YEARS

1

GEORGIA, WON'T YOU PLEASE SIT DOWN?

"Jimmie, do you see those dark clouds? The world is coming to an end," I warned my three-year-old brother one day. I was eight.

He looked up, saw the stormy sky, and began to scream, then to run. I was taking care of him and every day when we took our walk, he would dawdle, stopping to pick up glittering rocks, playing in the pudding-like mud, moving at his own slow pace. That day, since I had grown more and more restless, I decided he would move at my pace.

It was the first time, but certainly not the last, that I made such a decision. Of course, I felt ashamed of having scared my little brother, but I never have been a patient person.

Many years later, while seeking election to the Kentucky State Senate, my need to navigate my own course according to my own time table became immediately apparent to friend and foe alike.

I had three big negatives to overcome in my bid for the Senate. Kentucky is largely a rural state and I was from the city of Louisville. I was also Black and no person of color had ever been elected. Finally, Kentucky government was run in the tradition of the Good Ole Boys Club, and I was a woman. However, I was undaunted and plunged ahead.

During my twenty-one years in the Senate, my inability to suffer idle talk was reflected in an admonition very much like the one I had given my little brother: *Don't you see those dark clouds over Kentucky? Why are we wasting so much time when there are so many problems, so much to be done?*

I realize now that these are the questions which have dominated and illuminated my life, in and out of politics, from the very beginning.

I was born in a two room wooden shack built by my father in Jimtown, formerly Jim Crow Town, a colored settlement one mile east of Springfield, Kentucky. Poor Black people, mostly sharecropping field hands and by-the-day farm workers, lived in the rural county on small plots of land. Most, like us, had tiny green gardens toward the back of the property where they could raise their own vegetables.

My parents, Ben and Frances Montgomery, had both grown up in rural Kentucky—he in Bloomfield, and she sixteen miles away in Springfield. They were married when he was nineteen and she fifteen; her father had given them the land by dividing his own small plot.

While Pop went out and worked on nearby farms to support us, Mom had babies. First came my brother Joseph Ben, and then me. My parents named me "Georgia Lee," but the doctor wrote "George" on my birth certificate. This confusion over the male and female versions of my name seems ironic now, an omen of things that were to come. In truth, I never wanted to be a man. I did, however, always want the position, the control, and the power I saw that only men enjoyed. With this mind-set, I was driven by pride and ambition and sometimes tortured by the passions of my heart until, finally, I was validated by a successful career in the White, male-dominated field of politics.

Pop's mother, Grandma Annie, was married to Joseph Montgomery when Pop was born, but Joseph was not Pop's father. The truth is, we don't know for sure who Pop's father was, but we do know he was a White man. Pop's Black heritage didn't show. He had fine, chiseled features and straight, ash-blond hair.

Grandma Annie worked as a cook for Charley Thompson, a prosperous farmer. Some said he was Pop's father. Others said it was Dr. Ben Gore, a medical doctor for whom Grandma Annie had also worked. Still others said his father was Hal Muir, a wealthy banker who lived in Bloomfield. Grandma Annie never would discuss who actually was Pop's father, not even with Pop.

Because of the events which followed, I tend to believe that Hal Muir was my grandfather. After Joseph Montgomery died, Grandma Annie couldn't support her children alone, so she placed them around wherever she could. It tore Grandma Annie apart to give up her children, but poor people, then as now, do what they have to in order to survive.

Pop was seven at the time. He was sent to live with Hal Muir in the Muir's large, red brick home which sat on acres of land. Pop's room was in the basement; he lived there until he married my mother.

By the time Pop was twelve, he had learned to fix an automobile and to drive the Muir's big black sedan. For the next seven years, he drove the Muirs and their four daughters around Bloomfield, where people gossiped that he was Hal Muir's son.

Though they never lived together as a family again, there was a strong bond of love between Pop and his mother, and he didn't lose touch with her even though he was living with the Muirs. When I knew Grandma Annie, she was a cook at the old Talbott Tavern Hotel in Bardstown. She wore a white-bibbed apron all the time, at work and on the streets. When we came for a visit, we often found her rocking in her worn mahogany chair on the porch of her little house. Of course, when we went to look for her at the hotel, Pop would go to the back door. Blacks didn't go through the lobby, and even though other people thought he was White, Pop always knew what he was.

Although Grandma's own life was hard, her sister, Celia Mudd, was prosperous. Aunt Celia had been a slave owned by the Lankester family. When the Emancipation Proclamation freed the slaves, Aunt Celia was only twelve years old. She stayed with the Lankesters and worked for them until they all died. The last person in the family she cared for left everything to her, creating quite a stir in the White community. Not long afterward, a distant relative of the Lankesters sued Celia for the property and she lost five hundred of the original one thousand acres in the lawsuit settlement. Even so, with the remaining five hundred acres of farmland, farm equipment, buggies, money in the bank, and a thirteen-room house filled with antiques, she was well off. After she came into her inheritance, Aunt Celia, who had waited on White people all her life, hired others to cook and clean.

As a child, I didn't understand the price Aunt Celia had paid for her wealth, living twelve years as a slave and many more continually at a White family's beck and call. I didn't think much about her past or that she was rich. I only knew she had a big farm where we went in the summer to play in the fields and gather vegetables and fruit to take home.

Growing up, I never thought much about our being poor. Because of Pop's hard work, we always seemed to have what we needed. My biggest worry as a child was the fear that I would die before anything really important happened to me. As my early childhood passed, I became more preoccupied wondering what I would do and how my life would turn out. I wanted to control my own destiny, but I never seemed to move forward except in response to some outward crisis.

My parents thought I would grow up, get married, and have children. Period. But when they conveyed their image of my future to me, I felt infuriated. I knew there had to be more. I didn't want to wait for my real life to begin. I wanted to get on with it; but what that "it" was or how and where to search, remained a mystery.

Looking back, I can see that my youth seemed to lurch restlessly forward between intervals of apparent calm. I reacted strongly only when in adverse circumstances.

Even my coming to Louisville was precipitated by a dramatic event, a tornado that hit Jimtown. One afternoon, my brother Jay (our family nickname for Joseph) and I were taking a nap on my bed. Suddenly, a whirling funnel of wind whipped through our house, flipping the bed upside down and blowing my mother and father outside. It was March 18, 1925, and we were directly in the path of the storm—one of twelve that tore through Missouri, Illinois, Indiana, Tennessee, and Kentucky that year. They caused record death and destruction, 740 people dead, more than 2,000 injured, and twenty million dollars worth of property damaged.

Jay and I huddled together under the bed, safe in the midst of the destruction around us. I was only seventeen months old and already in the eye of a storm, a forewarning of the tumultuous life that lay ahead of me.

My parents had never expected to leave their rural home in Springfield, but with our house gone, we had to go somewhere. My mother's oldest sister, Mary Kaufman, lived in Louisville, fifty-seven miles away. She urged us to move there. Aunt Mary found us a small house on West Oak Street in the Limerick area and we moved in.

At that time, Louisville, like the rest of Kentucky, was totally segregated. Poor Blacks lived in an area known as "little Africa," whose unpaved streets extended south from Virginia Avenue and west from Thirty-sixth Street. These slums circled the downtown area. It was only steps from the business district to the surrounding alleys where Blacks built their homes, raised chickens, and kept hogs in pens. The houses, made mostly of concrete block or wood, were crudely built by the people who lived in them. Professional Blacks lived on more affluent West Chestnut Street and Grand Avenue. North of Broadway, the west end was all White.

As soon as our family was settled, Pop began searching for a job. He went first to the American Radiator and Standard Sanitary Company where a crowd of men gathered each morning, desperately hoping for employment. He wasn't among the few hired that day, but he was doubly determined the next. Each morning, from then on, he stopped at the site on his rounds. After two weeks, Pop was hired and began the first day of what would become forty-two years of hard labor, years during which he worked enameling bathtubs in the foundry. He pulled the heavy tubs in and out of the forge, working in heat that would rise to 212 degrees.

Despite our living in a Black area, most people were confused by my father's skin color. "Is your daddy White?" kids at school would ask.

"I don't know," I'd shake my head. To me he was just Pop, good to us and good to Mom. I loved him with all my heart, and I didn't think about his color. People in my family were all different shades. Pop was the lightest. Mom and two of my brothers, Jay and Phil, were darker. My own complexion was somewhere in between the two. At home we never talked about color. I can only remember one time as a child when it was mentioned. My brothers were talking about a new friend they had made.

"He's lighter than John Albert," one of them said. We all laughed.

"If he's lighter than John Albert, he must be White!" another brother said, and we laughed again.

However, not everyone viewed color the same way. Once, a trip we all took downtown in the car caused an ugly stir at Pop's work. One of his co-workers at American Standard saw him with us and went to work and reported that Ben Montgomery had a Black family. The workers created a furor, talking angrily among themselves. Pop knew something was wrong, but he didn't know what. Finally the president of the company, who had heard the gossip, called all the workers together.

"I understand some of you don't want to work with Ben Montgomery any longer," he said. "Those who don't want to work with Ben stand on the left and the others on the right. Those who go to the left can pick up their checks and keep on going."

The men went back to work and, at the time, no more was said. What happened that day illustrated to me the importance of leadership. When a leader takes a stand for justice, whether he or she is the head of a company or an elected official, people will usually follow. It was a lesson I never forgot.

Some of the workers continued to call our neighbors and ask, "Is Ben Montgomery White or Black?" When the neighbors, in turn, asked Mom, she would answer, "You'll have to ask him." Of course, they didn't have the nerve to do that.

Did it make any difference if my daddy was White? In my childish innocence, I didn't believe it did. But looking back now, I know differently. By the time I was ten, I remember wondering why he didn't take us places. I thought he might be ashamed to be seen with us. Where did that idea come from? How had racism slipped into my young head, and from where, to hint to me that a man who looked White would be ashamed of his wife and children who looked Black?

We didn't go many places as a family. Later I understood that Pop was trying to protect us from racist treatment, but it was also because when I was a small child we didn't have extra money for entertainment. I never ate in a restaurant until Pop took us to the World's Fair in 1939. On that trip my eyes were wide with excitement because of all the wondrous sights. We stopped at a small cafe on the South side of Chicago for dinner. After everyone finished eating, my parents sat talking. Anxious to get on to the next thing, I jumped up, cleared off the table, and started carrying the dirty dishes into the kitchen.

Pop looked up amazed. "Georgia," he called out to me. "Won't you please sit down?"

My brothers still tease me about that meal.

While my father labored at the plant, my mother worked equally as hard, or harder, at home. Mom was an immaculate housekeeper and a talented cook. She could never rest for more than ten minutes at a time; she always found something else that needed to be done. People tell me now that I look like her. Her skin was darker than mine, warmer, almost the shade of rich, brown gravy. She was good looking, tall and graceful, with soft, shoulder length brown hair which she curled at the bottom. Her voluptuous figure was still attractive even after she put on weight from carrying children.

She provided for all our physical needs, and I always knew I could depend on her, but we never spoke of the intimate things that I, as a young girl, pondered. Neither was she a demonstrative person. Mom showed her love by working day and night to take care of us—not with hugs, kisses, or even words. As she lay dying, I said, "I love you Mom."

"I love you too," she softly replied. That was the only time those words ever passed between us.

Though neither Mom nor Pop had much formal education, he had finished third and she eighth, both read and wrote well. The eighth grade was about as far as a Black child could go in Washington County. In 1904 the Kentucky legislature had passed The Day Law (named for Carl Day, the bill's sponsor) which made it illegal for Blacks and Whites to attend school together. Consequently, there were far fewer places for Black children to continue their education. In George Wright's *History of Blacks In Kentucky*, he cites a 1924 survey of public education that reported only eight fully accredited Black high schools in the state.

My parents were determined that their children would go to school, but if they were bitter about the educational opportunities denied to them because of their race, they didn't talk about it, at least not in my presence. They were too busy earning a living—trying to survive—to complain about the past. Despite the fact that they had little education and no wealth, my parents were able to leave me a rich legacy—a tradition of hard work and determination.

Within the closeness and warmth of our family life, I was sheltered from some of the painful realities of growing up Black in Louisville. Since we seldom ventured far from the familiar and safe environment of our family, I, as a young girl, never directly had to confront the antagonism toward Blacks or our lack of opportunity compared to Whites. I felt secure within my family, attending Virginia Avenue Elementary School and playing with my older brother, Jay.

Religion played a large part in our lives, as it did in the lives of many of our neighbors. Faced everyday with hard work and oppression, religion offered the thing most despaired of—hope. Never mind that relief would be in a life beyond this one—it was still something to cling to, a beautiful promise to await. Religion also brought drama and diversion into, what for most Blacks, was an otherwise hard and dull existence.

Of course, Jay and I didn't understand the oppression of Blacks and how religion helped them endure. We only knew that going to church was fun. Looking at everyone dressed up, listening to the infectious shouting and singing, watching the drama as people proclaimed themselves "Saved," it was a thrill to bear witness to the excitement. We'd stare wide-eyed, until finally we'd grow too tired to keep up with what was going on around us. Then we'd curl up under Pop's big, brown, flannel coat and go to sleep.

For five years we attended a Holiness Church, Triumph the Church and Kingdom of God in Christ. Our congregation was composed only of Blacks and the building itself was a stripped "shotgun" house. The term "shotgun" meant that the rooms were built one directly behind the other on the theory that if someone were chasing you, you could run right through and out the back.

It was Vernice Hunter, a tall, plump member of my church, with smooth, pretty brown skin and a commanding presence, who first demonstrated to me the power of social action. After failing repeatedly to convince city officials to put a traffic light at the corner near her house, a busy inter-section where one child had been killed and several more had been hurt, she hobbled into the street on her crutches. She stood there, absolutely still, stopping traffic and refusing to move until the officials agreed to put in a traffic light. Hers was an act of courage which has remained with me ever since.

Vernice attributed her courage to faith. My aunt Mary Kaufman also possessed a deep faith. Petite and vocal, with a shock of graying hair and a young-looking face, she was an activist herself. She was, in fact, a preacher. However, her church was the street corner, her congregation anyone who passed by. Each Saturday, she would take her place on the corner, shaking her tambourine and singing a hymn. After a crowd gathered, she would begin her sermon.

"Come to Jesus, *come* to Jesus," she implored. As children, we had no doubt that Aunt Mary was a woman of God. When we had any aches or pains, we went to her. She laid hands on us and prayed for our recovery. When she finished, we would run off to play, convinced we'd been healed.

Church services at Triumph were held on Friday night and all day Sunday. They would start with a member of the congregation who, in a deep, emotionally charged voice, would sing hymns like "Glory, Glory, Hallelujah, Since I Laid My Burdens Down," or "Come By Here, Lord, Come By Here." The pianist would hit several keys until she found the right one, the drummer would beat his drum, and all the others would clap their hands or shake tambourines. Then the real singing, shouting, and praying would begin. Another church member would read the scripture. Accompanied by the spirited affirmations of the congregation, the preacher would pray a simple but profound prayer, such as "The Country Preacher's Folk Prayer," written by former Kentucky State University Professor Leonard A. Slade, Jr.:

Eternal God,
We come this mornin'
With bowed heads and humble hearts.
Uh hum.
We thank you for sparing us another day
by letting your angels watch over our
bedside while we slumbered and slept.
Uh hum.
We come to you without any form or fashion:
just as we are without one plea.
Uh hum.
You blessed us when we didn't deserve it.
When we traveled down the road of sin,
You snatched us and made us taste of the
blood of Thy Lamb.
Yes, Lord!
This mornin', touch every human heart.
Transform tears into Heavenly showers
for the salvation of sinful souls.
Yassir.
Remember the sick, the afflicted,
the heavy laden.
Open the windows of Thy Heavenly home.
Let perpetual light shine on them in the
midnight hour.
Yes, Lord.
When we have done all that we can do down here,
take us into Thy Kingdom, where the sun never sets,
where there's no more bigotry, hypocrisy, backbiting;
no more weeping and wailing, before Thy throne, where
You will wipe away our tears, where we can see our
mothers;
Ma ma!
where, in that city, where the streets are paved with gold
and adorned with every jewel,
where we can see Jesus, sitting on the throne
of glory.

Ummmm mmmmmm a hummmmmmm
When we get home, when we get home,
when we get home,
We'll rest in Thy bosom
and praise You forever.
Amen.

Though the complex meaning religion held for my parents and other Blacks in the South couldn't be fathomed by a child, going to church became as natural to me as getting up in the morning and going to school. The emotion and feeling reflected in the singing, shouting, and praying became a part of me. Though there have been periods of my life when I didn't go to church, those early experiences of going to services, hearing my parents read the Bible and pray for and with us, instilled in me a strong belief in God and the values expressed in the Bible—a belief that has had a strong influence on the rest of my life.

2

STORMY
WEATHER

After four years on Oak Street, during which my parents carefully saved every extra penny earned, they bought a house on Grand Avenue. It was May of 1929, and our new block was in transition from White to Black—only four White families remained. These four families were considered to be poor, but the Blacks moving in were thought of as middle-class.

Like most of the things for which my parents silently sacrificed, to them our new house represented a better life for their children. The wood frame house had four rooms, a bath, and porches in both the front and rear. When we moved in, Pop, who, in fact, was colorblind, chose to paint the house his favorite color—canary yellow. He also added on two more bedrooms.

Our family was growing rapidly. My brothers Robert

and John Albert, named for the Apostle, had both been born on Oak Street. More children would be born in the new house on Grand Avenue. Each time Mom became pregnant, I fervently hoped it would be a girl. But our next baby was Phillip, then James. I was giving up hope. However, when Mom was about to give birth again, a strange event seemed to foretell that my wishes for a sister were about to become a reality.

In August of that year, a neighborhood boy threw a brick during a fight. Instead of hitting its intended victim, the brick hit me. At that time, Pop's cousin Laura Frances Anderson, from Bloomfield, was living with us. (She had first come to Louisville to work for Joseph Ray, a neighbor whose wife was seriously ill. After working for the Rays, she moved in with us and helped Mom.) She and Mom had already bathed the cut with alcohol and bandaged it up by the time the boy's mother came over to apologize. The woman also gave Mom ten dollars to take me to the doctor.

Since I was all right, Mom and Cousin Frances took us all to the State Fair instead of going to the doctor. With that ten dollars we rode the Ferris wheel, ate cotton candy, and looked at the animals. Mom and Frances were having as much fun as we were.

As we walked the midway, a wily fortuneteller with a captivating manner lured us to her tent, saying in a deep, throaty voice, "I can predict the baby's sex."

"Let's go in," Frances urged. "Maybe we can find out if Georgia's going to get the little sister she wants." Though Mom laughed, she told me to wait outside while they went in.

The dark tent was lit by glowing candles. The fortuneteller, seated at a low table, motioned to Frances and Mom to sit down.

"You have a girl there," the fortuneteller assured Mom.

Though usually skeptical and levelheaded, for some reason, Mom and Frances became so excited they went out and bought a pink bassinet and all pink baby clothes. On September 24, Mom gave birth to my brother Lawrence. I cried and cried for the little sister I was never to have. I refused to go in and see him. Of course, when I finally did, I immediately fell in love with him, as I had all my other baby brothers.

Mom gave birth to most of her children at home. During her next pregnancy, however, because she had gained a lot of weight and developed high blood pressure, her doctor felt she ought to have the baby at City Hospital. Of course, it was another boy. When I visited Mom, she said she was going to name the new baby Walker Montgomery.

"Mom, you can't do that," I said. "He'll have two last names!"

Although we were not allowed to question our parents once a decision had been made, I spoke up and gave my opinion that day—as I had in many other situations. Mom had chosen Walker because it had been her maiden name. I suggested the name of a boy I knew, Randolph. We compromised and named the baby Rudolph Walker Montgomery.

That this name was partially my choice assuaged my disappointment at the baby's sex, but I missed not having the sister and confidant I wanted so badly. Perhaps that is one important reason why, growing up among so many males and without really close female friends, I kept my intimate questions, thoughts, and dreams to myself.

Not long afterward, in the autumn of 1937, my family and I watched with astonishment as rain pelted Kentucky for days. Our neighbors congregated to stare at the water gushing from manholes and pooling in the streets. No one thought the water would get so high, but one day, as the bad weather continued, our street became covered with water from curb to curb. The Ohio River was flooding Louisville.

Pop began building small bridges by stacking bricks with planks laid across them, enabling people to get from one side to another. As the water continued getting higher, he decided to go to Ross's Market a few miles away to stock up on groceries. Though he was gone only a short time, the waters rose so quickly that we had to evacuate. The Red Cross people came in boats and used megaphones to blare the news that we were in danger and had to leave.

We were one of the last ones to go, since Mom insisted on waiting for Pop to return. Finally, though, even she relented. We stepped from our porch into two of the rowboats manned by the Red Cross workers. These boats were traveling down our street, picking up stranded people.

"Bring nothing with you," one worker shouted, but I managed to slip in an extra clean dress anyway. On that occasion, as on so many others, I was determined—some would say headstrong.

Just as the boat started to push away, I realized that our dog Rex had been left behind. "Let me go back!" I insisted, but no one listened.

The boats took us to Thirtieth and Kentucky Streets where we were loaded onto trucks to take us three further blocks, where we'd be out of the water's reach. Getting out, we looked around anxiously; we were worried about my father, praying he'd be safe.

"There's Pop!" someone shouted. And there he was, sitting in his car, the seats piled high with groceries, trying to get back home to us. He swooped us all up, loaded us in, and headed for Bardstown. First, he dropped Mom and three of my brothers at Aunt Celia's. He took two other brothers to Grandma's house, left one brother and me at Aunt Emma's, then, always concerned that others might not be as fortunate as he, headed back to Louisville to help repair boats at the flood headquarters at Eighteenth and Broadway.

To us kids, it was like going on a vacation. We were children and we weren't worried about the four feet of water in our family's house or all the ruined furniture and other lost possessions. The only serious concern I had was for our dog, Rex, but he, like his owner, was a survivor. When my parents returned home to begin cleaning out the debris, Rex greeted them at the door. His muddy footprints were all over a mattress on which he'd floated during the flood to survive. It wasn't until two months after the flood that we were able to return home to live again.

Long after the excitement had faded from our memories, the water marks remained on houses and trees—sober reminders of the ability of the river to leave its banks and wreak havoc, of the power of nature and the helplessness of its victims to stop the destruction.

Despite such fateful events as tornadoes and floods, most of my memories of those childhood days are happy ones. Ours was a house neighbors came to often. Pop was interested in what was going and liked to keep up with world events, especially elections. He was also a big fan of country music; it was no surprise, then, that ours was the first radio on the block. In addition to listening to the serious stuff, like news and elections, friends gathered on our front porch or in our living room to be entertained by the antics of Amos and Andy or to be enthralled by the adventures of "The Shadow."

We were all huddled around the radio, adult and child alike, when Orson Welles's "War of the Worlds" aired. All the children grabbed each other and started crying. We ran and hid in the corner until Mom calmed us. "It's just a program," she said. "It's not real," but I think even she and the other adults were fooled at first.

Not only did Pop keep up with current news, especially elections, but he also kept abreast of modern innovations. We were the first family on Grand Avenue to own a washing machine. Pop bought a Standard, a forerunner of the Maytag washer. It had a huge tub with roller wringers. He built a wash house in the back yard and ran water out there. The neighbors brought their clothes, washed them, and left a quarter to pay for the water. That may have been the first coin laundry in Louisville.

Because we were a large family, there was never enough time to do everything in those days. I had to help my mother, of course, and it seemed to me like I was always on call to do something. Mom put an apron on me and taught me to cook. I cleaned right along with her and helped her wash and iron our clothes. The only jobs I liked at all were the washing and ironing. I hated to cook and clean. But most of all, I didn't like having to jump up and do something any time Mom assigned me some chore. I knew even then that "A woman's work is never done" would not be the motto for my life. I wanted to do what was necessary and then be done with it. So I made a deal with Mom. Since she didn't like to iron, I would do the ironing and she would do the rest. I developed a system that allowed me to finish in one day. The night before ironing day, I would sprinkle the clothes with water, roll them tightly, and put them in a tin tub. The next day, the clothes would be damp all the way through and ready for ironing. I feel similarly compelled to exercise control over what I do and when I do it to this very day.

Though I did what my mother asked as quickly as I could, such tasks still took time—in my opinion, too much time—and gave me a lifelong perception of the hard role women had, staying home, having babies, and cleaning up after other people.

At the same time, I was accumulating other perceptions as well. Many of them came from getting to know all of our neighbors on Grand Avenue. Little did I know how fortunate I was to be growing up among such nice people. They were my extended family.

There was the soft-spoken Miss Brown, whose first name I never knew. I sat on the steps of the sidewalk every day, waiting for her to get off the bus. A school cafeteria worker, she carried a brown bag with sandwiches left over from the day's lunch and gave them to the waiting children. The tasty sandwiches were either tuna fish or Waldorf salad mix on white bread. To this day, I think they were the best sandwiches I have ever eaten.

Six-foot-two Joseph Ray Sr., usually dressed in a black suit and stylish hat with the brim turned down, was another of my favorite neighbors. He was a gentleman and tipped his hat to me when he passed. It made me feel like a real lady. No wonder Mr. Ray was always one of my role models on the block. He was president of a Black-owned bank, First Standard Bank of Kentucky, until it closed during the Stock Market Crash of 1929. After that, he went into real estate.

Mr. Ray and his wife, Ella, had one son; Joseph Jr. spent more time at our house than he did his own. His mother was sick, but I didn't know what was wrong with her. The neighbors would just say, "Mrs. Ray is not well." In those days, people didn't openly discuss their impairments, especially with children nearby. Many years later, I learned that Ella Ray had undergone a bilateral mastectomy.

One year, Joe Ray got a white bicycle for Christmas. I thought it was beautiful and asked, "Joe, can I ride your new bike?"

"Not till it gets old," he said, and raced off. Bicycles were just the beginning for Joe. He graduated to motorcycles and later became famous as an accomplished race car driver, one of the first Black drivers for the United States Auto Club. He bought a Henry J. stock car, and my brothers Jay and Phillip were his mechanics. They traveled with Joe to the races, and sometimes I was allowed to go along and watch.

Teachers, doctors, educators, coaches, politicians, and athletes—Grand Avenue had them all. Nearly every field open to middle-class Blacks at that time was represented on Grand Avenue, my childhood community. Many who left Louisville found recognition both regionally and nationally. Herbert Ralston became chief of staff at Chicago Hospital, Wade Houston became head basketball coach at the University of Tennessee, and the inimitable Muhammad Ali became famous as the heavyweight boxing champion of the world. He lived with his parents, Cassius and Odessa Clay, four doors away from us.

I'm sure my desire to "be somebody" came partly from observing the people around me as I grew up. I was blessed to have lived among people who had such high standards and values. They wanted to do something meaningful with their lives. There was only one problem. I was a wise child and quickly figured out that all those I wanted to emulate were men. To me, they were the ones out in the world doing interesting things.

First among the men I idolized was my father, who many people thought resembled the movie star Clark Gable. I saw him as a powerful figure, both in his towering physical stature and in his air of authority; to me, if he said it, it was true.

Once, two police officers came to our house to question my brother Robert about some tire slashing in the neighborhood. At that time, White policemen routinely entered the homes of Black people without knocking. That day, one went to the back door and another to the front.

Without knocking, they strode into our house, grabbed Robert, and took him to the Jefferson County Children's Center.

My father wasn't home, but when he heard what had happened, he was furious, insulted that they had crashed in and frightened my mother that way. He hired attorney Leon Shaikun to get Robert released from the Children's Center and to challenge the officers' behavior. Within a short time, Robert was released into my father's custody, and later the two policemen were fired. I felt so proud of Pop. After that, I thought he could right any wrong.

Money was not my biggest worry as a child. I always thought my father had lots of it. Of course he didn't, but he made good money for the time, more than some of the professional people on our street. He bought new cars, Fords, while many people owned second-hand cars or none at all. If my father didn't have it, he could always get money for whatever I needed.

I felt close to my father. As long as he was there, I felt I was safe. He was not demonstrative with Mom or us children, but he was a good and loving man. During the Depression, Pop was not only good to us, he was good to everyone. He was literally his brother's keeper—a true, practicing Christian. Through the Depression, he worked three days a week making fourteen dollars a day. When neighbors with children had their water or electricity turned off, Pop paid to have it turned back on. Once a month we went to Nelson County to Aunt Celia's farm to get food for the neighbors and us. We would bring back smoked meats—ribs, backbones, sausages, and hams. Pop would load the car with a hundred pounds of potatoes, canned fruits and vegetables, jellies and jams, bags of pears from the orchard, and other foodstuff. Back in Louisville, he'd divide the food and send it around to the families with children.

I'm sure other members of my family would say he was partial to me. He was quick to stand up for me whenever I needed his support, and he made sure that my brothers never hit me. He whipped them with peach tree switches for their frequent misdeeds, but he gave me only one small spanking, though I probably deserved more, during my entire childhood.

3

GROWING
PAINS

Who doesn't remember being thirteen?—that in-between time when you're neither child nor adult. Overnight I seemed to stop being a child, yet I wasn't a woman either. Confusion and restlessness reigned. Along with wondering what I would do when I grew up, I was now trying to cope with puberty. No one told me anything about the changes that were occurring in my body. Even with all those babies born in our home, I didn't understand the reproductive process. I just knew that having babies caused my mother to get terribly out of shape, with swollen ankles and a swaybacked walk. Why do girls have to have babies, I wondered. Why not boys? It wasn't just having them, either—it was all the work afterward. I felt that it all fell on Mom.

Boys had all the advantages. My brothers had to work in the garage and learn to be mechanics as soon as they were old enough. They probably thought I was the one who had it easy, but I wanted to work in the garage with them. I begged my father, but he refused to let me.

"What are they doing in there that I can't do?" I protested.

"Now, now," my family placated me.

Like her sister Mary Kaufman, Mom was also religious. She continually told us to be good and to avoid sin. On any appropriate occasion, and on some occasions that I considered inappropriate, she would quote the Bible. One of her favorite exhortations was "What doth it profit a man if he gain the world and lose his soul?" I'm sure setting her children's thoughts on higher matters was ultimately very beneficial. However, during the years I went through puberty, it became painfully apparent that it was my body, not just my soul, about which I needed more information.

My breasts started to develop and my brothers teased me, pointing to them and laughing. One morning I woke up in a pool of blood. I screamed. Mom and Cousin Frances came running. Two years earlier, Frances had asked me to go to the store to get her a box of Kotex.

"What's Kotex?" I had asked.

"Never mind," she had said, "You'll find out soon enough." I found out that morning.

Frances lent me an elastic Kotex belt and pad, then Mom sent me to the bathroom to wash and put it on. "You'll have to wear this until your menstruation stops. Change the napkin often, wash often, but don't get in the tub," she admonished.

That's all she said! Nothing about pregnancy or sex, just that I would bleed for three or four days every month. How disgusting, I thought. I know people can smell the odor. I don't like this.

I Shared the Dream

I didn't understand about sex, and certainly not love, except I knew it made people miserable sometimes. About that time, Cousin Frances—my beautiful Cousin Frances with the café-au-lait complexion and impish freckles—had fallen in love with a married man who had broken her heart.

When I was fifteen, I learned about sex the cruelest way a girl can. A man, who was ten years older than I, lived down the street with his mother. He had a thin build, curly black hair, and walked with a limp because one of his legs was shorter than the other. He was always nice to me, giving me candy and other treats when I visited his mother.

One afternoon he saw me on the sidewalk and said, "Georgia, let's go to my house and make some candy." It sounded like fun and I loved candy, so I went.

Once there, he said, "Come out back to get some coal for the stove." When we got inside the shed, he grabbed me. He forced me down onto the dirt floor, pulled open his pants, and stuck his penis into me. It hurt badly. I yelled, kicked, and tried to push him off.

"Let me up, you dirty dog!" I screamed, but he kept on moving inside me. Though I fought with all my might, he was much too strong. Finally, he let me up. Blood streamed down my leg. Sobbing, I ran straight home, went to the bathroom, and began to wash. I didn't understand what had happened and I didn't feel close enough to anyone to talk about it. I kept the awful secret to myself, but I suffered over it for a very long time. Now, as I reveal what happened for the first time, I feel relieved to finally break my silence. If I'd had a daughter, I pray to God I would have built enough trust and love between us so she could tell me if anyone had violated her body.

In a way, though, I was luckier than many women who have been raped; I've never been tortured by the idea that it was my fault or that there was something I could have done to prevent it. I did not tell anyone because I felt dirty. I felt that I had been tarnished by losing my virginity, but I always knew whose fault it was. The rapist had abused me and I hated him for his crime, but I did not hate myself.

After the rape, the man stopped coming to my house and I didn't visit his mother again as long as he lived there. So, I was surprised when, months later, I came home from school and met him coming out my front door. I looked away and said nothing, just passing by him and going straight inside.

Later I learned that the man had come to ask my parents if he could marry me after I graduated from high school. As I entered the house, I heard Pop saying angrily, "If he ever touches my daughter, I'll cut off his head and throw it out in the snow!"

I just stood there, afraid to say anything. I had never heard my father speak with such anger. It made me uneasy, so I just kept quiet. I thought to myself, sadly, You're too late, Daddy, he already has.

Because of the rape, I was slow to acknowledge my burgeoning sexuality. Boys, however, had begun to notice me. Joe Ray Jr., who had always been a close friend to my brothers and me, now wanted to spend time alone with me. Often, he would come and sit with me on the porch of wherever I was baby-sitting.

Eventually, though, my traumatized feelings calmed down and I began to look at boys in a new light. I fantasized about Carroll Mason, a good-looking boy I met at a party in Bloomfield, where I had been visiting my cousin Josephine Bishop. I wondered if I would ever fall in love and get married.

Then I met Duke, the first boy for whom I felt a real passion. I was a senior at Central High, the Black high school, when he transferred from Crispus Attucks, the Black high school in Indianapolis. I met him at Coach Willie Kean's house on Grand Avenue, but I had already noticed him in my trigonometry class. George Duke Beasley. He wore suits custom-tailored by his brother in Indianapolis and was the star of Central's basketball team. We became lovers.

Duke kept a room with an older couple, but his meals were not furnished; he was always hungry. My love for him was such that I gave him my lunch money. I thought this an important indication of the depth of my affection. Because the Kean's were one of the families I cleaned for, I had a key to their house. We would meet there when we knew they were going out. One night, though, they caught us.

"What's that?" whispered Duke. "It sounds like the back door opened."

"Quick!" I said. "Get under the bed!"

Straightening my clothes, I went out to meet the Keans and nervously explained that I had come over to do some cleaning. I went home and laid down on the couch, worrying about Duke under the bed at the Kean's. About two hours later, I saw him coming up our sidewalk and I rushed outside.

"What happened?"

"After you left, they came into the bedroom and Coach called, 'All right, Duke, you can come out now.' He lectured me for an hour about how I could have gotten you pregnant."

After Duke left, I tossed and turned all night. When morning came, I told Mom I was too sick to go to school. Around noon I told her I was feeling better and was going over to the Kean's to clean. Because it was the middle of the day, I was alone in the house. By the time Coach and his wife Helen came home, the place was spotless. I had cleaned like I'd never cleaned before.

I apologized to Mrs. Kean. She said, "Georgia, you know what you did was wrong, and you know I'm going to have to tell your parents."

I was frantic. I couldn't let her tell my parents. I ran down to the basement where Coach Kean was working.

"Mrs. Kean says she's going to tell my parents what happened last night. I know it was wrong and I apologize, but you can't let her tell. If you do, I'll have to tell her how you pat me on the behind when she's not looking."

"I'll see what I can do," he promised.

My stomach was in knots for the next few days. As time passed and nothing happened, however, I decided I was out of the woods and relaxed. I had intuitively negotiated from a position of strength and won. It was a lesson not lost on me.

I had always hoped to go to college, but I really didn't know how I would do it. I had no money for tuition and books and there was no way Pop or Mom could help me. My teachers knew I wanted to go, so Helen Kean and her sister Naomi Lattimore persuaded Alpha Kappa Alpha Sorority to give me a two-year scholarship to Louisville Municipal College. Duke received a basketball scholarship to the same school.

Duke and I graduated high school together in the spring of 1940. We celebrated by going to one of the few restaurants in the area where Blacks could eat inside. It was a roadhouse on River Road owned by Mrs. Gertrude Ake, a friendly Black widow. Her specialties were tasty country fried chicken and liver and onions with sweet potatoes.

After graduation, Duke went to Indianapolis for the summer and I went to work in Louisville at Grant's Five and Ten Cent Store on Fourth Street. We hated to part, but we knew it was only for summer vacation.

At Grant's I worked as a counter girl, serving hot dogs and root beer. "Georgia," my supervisor admonished on my first day, "you can serve colored people, but don't let them eat at the counter."

I said nothing, but I knew I could never tell anyone that they couldn't stand at the counter and eat. In my third week on the job, my physics teacher, Victor Perry, came in. He saw me and walked up to the counter, where I stood. "Mr Perry, would you like a hot dog and a root beer?" I asked.

"I believe I would," he answered.

I'm sure he assumed it was all right for me to serve him or I wouldn't have offered. He stood at the counter eating and as we talked, I could see my supervisor watching. I knew what was coming. When Mr. Perry left, she strode over to me. "Georgia, go to the office at the end of the day," she said sternly. I didn't wait until the end of the day, though. I knew she meant to fire me and I didn't want to give her the satisfaction. I quit then and there.

Mom's last child, my brother Carl, was born that summer. I was sixteen and embarrassed that Mom was pregnant again. When Carl was born, I loved him dearly, but I wouldn't take him outside of the house because I didn't want anyone to think that I'd had a baby. Inside our home, though, I held and cuddled him all the time. I may have been compensating for my resentment of Mom's pregnancy, or I may have had a premonition that our time with Carl would be short.

Both Duke and I did above-average work our freshman year. We had no money and few new clothes—but we had each other. We were happily planning our future together when I learned that he had left Indianapolis because a girl had been pregnant with his son. He had not wanted to marry her, but after his son was born, he supported him. Duke didn't tell me about the baby. I found out by reading a letter he had written to his mother. I cried for three days and refused to tell my parents what was wrong. When I finally did tell them, Pop, who had always been wary of Duke, said, "I knew there was something about him I didn't like."

At the end of the school year, Duke went back to work in Indianapolis. Heartbroken over what I had found out about him, I looked for a summer job in Louisville. I went to work for the Tuckers, a well-off family who lived on Cherokee Road, an upper-class neighborhood. Every morning, Mr. Tucker would get the *Courier-Journal* to "see what the stock market is doing." This was my first contact with people who had unearned income; everyone else I knew labored for a living. While Mr. Tucker was studying the stock market, I was working every day of the week, from seven in the morning until it was nearly dark, keeping his house clean. I made seven dollars a week.

I'm sure that the Tuckers weren't any worse than other people who hired domestic help and that they were probably paying the going rate. It was my early experience at this job and others like it that gave me a deep conviction that poor, working people don't "get their share of the pie" in our country. My experience with this type of unfairness made me determined to do something about it.

Before school began again, my brother Jay, who had a good job, gave me a special present. I didn't have many clothes, mostly what I could make myself. One day Jay said, "Georgia, I want you to have a new coat when you go back to school. I have an account at Levy Brothers. Go and get what you want and charge it to me."

In fact, he let me buy two coats—a fitted, black dress coat with jeweled buttons down the front and a medium blue, plaid wraparound coat. I felt like a million dollars in those coats.

That fall, when I returned to Municipal for my second year, I made a discouraging discovery. I found out for the first time about the discrimination within the Black race based on shades of skin color. If you were light, you were invited into the Alpha Kappa Alpha Sorority; if you were brown, then Delta Sigma Theta accepted you; and if you were dark, you pledged Zeta Phi Beta. I was in the Ivy League Club, a precursor to belonging to Alpha Kappa Alpha. My family was composed of people with a wide range of skin tones, but I despised these distinctions. Disgusted, I dropped out of the Ivy League Club and refused to pledge a sorority.

For his second year of college, Duke went to A and T College in North Carolina. When school ended in the spring, he came to see me on his way home to Indianapolis. We went out to dinner at Betty's Grill on Tenth Street. Duke knew he had hurt me, but he didn't know how badly.

"Georgia, I'm sorry I hurt you. I love you. I want us to get married." He pulled a package out of his pocket and handed me an engagement ring.

I knew what I had to say. "I love you too, Duke, but I can't marry you."

"Why, Georgia?"

"I don't think I could ever accept that you had a family and kept it a secret from me. You betrayed my trust by doing that. If you couldn't tell me something that important, I can't marry you, no matter how much I love you."

It was hard for me to say, and when he cried, I cried too. We parted, two very sad young people. We did not meet again until twenty-five years later, when he came to Louisville as part of his work as regional director of the National Equal Employment Opportunity Office.

II

THE UNSETTLED
YEARS

4

DREAMS
DEFERRED

At the age of eighteen, I knew precisely what I did not want to do with my life—clean other peoples' houses—and I also knew what I did want to do. I wanted to become a medical doctor, a surgeon. I had cherished that dream for a long time. I was not afraid of blood and never had been squeamish about dealing with family medical crises such as broken bones or fainting. Word got around among the girls in town that I could pierce ears, and many asked me to do so. As the reputation of my medical services grew, a girl showed me a wart on her finger. It was big and ugly and she wanted it off.

"I'll remove it for you," I offered. Taking a sharp razor blade, I cut into the wart. It bled profusely, but I just kept on cutting until it was all gone. Then I poured on alcohol and bandaged the finger. Now, I shudder to think what a disaster it could have been. In those days, just as later when I turned my attention to other difficult pursuits, I had supreme confidence in my abilities. I simply assumed that if it could be done, I could do it.

Despite my talents, my mother's friend and our neighbor, Edna Leavelle, who had a college degree, once said to me, "Georgia, you're gonna be just like your mother—get married and have a houseful of children."

Biting my lip, I didn't say anything. But at that moment, I hated her. As I walked away, I mumbled to myself, "How do you know what I'm going to do when I don't even know yet myself? I *do* know I'm not gonna be just a housewife with a house full of kids, though!"

By then, I knew I had to do something better, but I had admitted to myself that I had no chance of becoming a doctor. Looking back, I think I could have done it if I had had some guidance and financial help. However, I had neither. To my parents, finishing high school was an accomplishment, since neither of them had. As for my college scholarship, it had been an unbelievable stroke of luck in the first place. Despite my grand ambition, a Black woman went to Municipal College to become a teacher or to find a husband. There was no counseling program to help ambitious students like me, and after my scholarship ran out, I didn't even have the money to stay in school.

I felt angry, and once again, impatient. At the time, I was going out with a nice, but to me, boring young man. Robert Jones, with curly black hair and a ready smile, had had a job in a woodworking plant since high school and my parents liked him.

Robert asked me to marry him. I refused, at first, because I didn't love him. He pressured me to say yes and so did my parents; I guess they thought it was time I settled down with a man who had a steady job.

However, all that mattered to me was that the fall term at Municipal was approaching and I had no money to enroll. All I could think about was getting back into school. At that point, I did something foolish. I told Robert I would marry him if he paid my tuition. He agreed. When I realized a short time later that my education would cost too high a price, I told Robert I had changed my mind. He went to my father and Pop told me that I must go through with the wedding. "A promise is a promise," he said.

My father's decisions had always been the law; so I thought I had to do it. I was angry and felt betrayed. "You can make me marry him, but you can't make me stay with him!" I shouted at my father.

Juliette Williams, a girl who was almost twenty, had moved in with her brother and sister a few houses down from us. She was getting married that August. We had a double wedding at her pastor's office. Afterwards, the four of us went out to dinner. Then Robert and I went to the room he had rented for us at the home of Mrs. Ida Tilford. She was a local seamstress who immediately took a liking to me, and she persuaded me to have a reception to celebrate the marriage. She had sewn a long, beige satin dress with high, puffed sleeves and a fitted waist for a customer who had failed to pick it up. Generously, she offered to alter the dress for me to wear.

The reception was lovely, but I soon found out that I had celebrated for nothing. When the time to enroll for college approached, I asked Robert for the tuition money.

"You're a married woman now. You don't need to go to school," he said.

"You're going back on your word!" I cried angrily. "That was our bargain. If you're not going to live up to your end, I'm not living up to mine. I won't stay with you!"

He wouldn't relent, and although I didn't leave him immediately, I became more and more bitter about his reneging on our deal. That, however, was not our only problem.

Robert's idea of sex was to satisfy himself without giving any thought to me. There was no tenderness in our lovemaking—I felt as though I were constantly being raped. We fought a lot. One night I refused to have sex with him. Trying to end the discussion, I jumped up from the bed and went to the closet. I was reaching for my robe when Robert, furious, shoved me inside and locked the door.

Soon after that terrible night, Robert, who by this time was in the Signal Corps of the Armed Services, was sent to Lexington, and from there to Fort Monmouth, New Jersey. As soon as he left, I filed for divorce and moved back to my parents' home. When Robert received the divorce papers, he called and said he was getting an emergency leave to come home. "I can't believe you're doing this," he pleaded.

"Believe it," I said. "And there's no use coming home. I won't be changing my mind."

Robert got his leave and came home anyway. I did not want to see him, but because he had come such a long way, I finally agreed to meet him at his parents house to talk. However, as I had told him on the phone, my mind was made up. After our meeting, I went back home. What now? I wondered. I can't go to school and I can't be married, at least not to a man like Robert. My life is going nowhere.

In that dejected frame of mind, I met Esther Jones, a pretty, sophisticated girl from Buffalo, New York. Esther was staying with her grandmother, who lived on Grand Avenue. Although I still kept my serious thoughts largely to myself, she and I began to spend time together chatting, as young women do, mostly about young men. She took me to a USO dance at the YMCA where soldiers from Fort Knox were brought in by bus. I was ready to have some fun, but I felt inexperienced. I didn't dance, smoke, or drink.

I SHARED THE DREAM

At that first USO dance I stood apart from the crowd like a wallflower, but one well-built fellow with classic features and shapely lips did ask me to dance. He showed me how to do the box step and stayed with me for the rest of the evening. His name was Norman F. Davis and he was from Brooklyn, New York. Nicky, as I called him, was handsome and sophisticated. He took me out for several weeks, taught me to dance, and I had my first drink, a whiskey sour, with him.

He was different from the other young men I had known. For one thing, his family was well-off financially; his father worked on Wall Street. Nicky played tennis and attended plays and concerts—activities to which I'd had no exposure. He showed me pictures of himself as a child dressed like a little rich kid, with fur on the collars of his coats and miniature Eton suits.

When Nicky was transferred to Fort Hood, Texas, I decided to go to Buffalo with Esther. She told me her brother went to the University of Buffalo and I thought I could save money and go there, too.

First, though, I had to get the money. Since it was Derby time in Louisville, I was able to get a job rather quickly as a waitress in the English Grill at the Brown Hotel. The first time a customer ordered a beer, I put ice in a pilsner glass and poured the beer over it. My customer was kind.

"Is this your first night here?" he asked.

I nodded yes. He pulled my face down to his and whispered, "Beer is not served with ice."

I felt stupid, but I made $127 that week and soon had the money for my trip.

In Buffalo, Esther and I stayed with her parents. I paid five dollars a week to share her room at the back of their house, which was also a funeral home. Within a week I had two job offers—one with the Buffalo Telephone Company, and the other at the Curtiss-Wright Defense Plant. Since the defense job paid more, I took it.

On the job I wore blue denim overalls. Just like the famous Rosie, I was a riveter. I worked at the Curtiss-Wright plant, which produced C-26 cargo planes. We worked in pairs: one person would drill the hole in the metal and place the rivet in it while the other held a bucking bar behind the rivet and flattened it as the riveting gun pressed on the rivet head. My partner was a red-haired girl from Erie, Pennsylvania. Her name was Virginia Wright and she became my first true, close female friend.

Even making what to me, at the time, was the enormous sum of forty-five dollars a week, it was soon clear that I couldn't save enough money to go to the University. By the time I paid rent, bought food and clothes, and sent some money home, there wasn't much left. My parents hadn't asked me for money, but I knew they needed it for my siblings still at home; I sent some every week.

I was still writing to Nicky, and it was clear from his letters that he was getting serious. I knew he was going to propose, but I didn't know what I was going to say. I wasn't head over heels in love with him, but I liked him a lot. Maybe you only feel that strongly about your first love, I thought, remembering Duke.

Not very long afterward, Nicky proposed and I accepted. Nicky was still in Texas, and so, boarding a Greyhound bus, I headed there. After a brief stopover in Louisville to see my parents, I took another bus to Temple, Texas. Walking down the aisle, I chose an empty window seat in the middle of the bus. A Black soldier sat down next to me. Late that night, in Dixon, Tennessee, the driver stopped the bus, came back to us and said, "You niggers move on back to the back seat."

Trying to be brave, I replied, "I'm as far back as I'm going to go."

"Let's move on back," said the soldier. "We don't need this kind of trouble."

Turning from him, I stared out the window at the darkness and lost my courage. I could easily end up a corpse, I thought.

"Either move back or get off the bus," the driver ordered. I wasn't as courageous as Rosa Parks would later prove to be. We moved back. But I never forgot the incident or the outrage I felt.

Nicky met me at the station. In his uniform, with his cap "broken down" like General MacArthur's and his spit-polished shoes, Nicky was even more handsome than I remembered. He took me to a house where he had rented a room. The next day, we were married. He gave me a white gold wedding band with five small diamonds. After the wedding, we stopped at Western Union and Nicky sent his mother a wire. "Dear Mom. Everything is swell. Happily married. Love Norman and Georgia." That night, his love-making was gentle. I am happy, I thought. I've made the right decision.

After two weeks, when Nicky's leave ended, I went back to Buffalo and my job at Curtiss-Wright. A few days later, my brother John Albert called and asked if it would be all right for him to come to Buffalo. At seventeen, he had been working in Louisville washing buses at the Greyhound garage. When his White supervisor had called him a "nigger," Albert hit him over the head with the metal pole he had been using to wash a bus. He needed to get out of Louisville.

I told him he was welcome and moved from Esther's room into two rooms over the funeral home in the same building. John Albert moved in and I helped him get a job at Curtiss-Wright.

With only my brother for company and Nicky still in Texas, there was little to do but work. Ed, Esther's husband, was a musician at a nightclub called The Moonglow. When visiting bands came to the club, Ed would have a party for them at a hotel after they performed. One night, when Louis Jordan and his Tympani Five were playing, Ed arranged a party and invited me. When I arrived, the band members were sitting in a semi-circle, smoking marijuana. They invited me to join them. I had barely even heard of pot. When I refused to join in, they "invited" me to leave. I left and didn't give it another thought. I have always done pretty much what I wanted to do, and I do not enjoy being pressured.

Three months after I started working at Curtiss-Wright, I was promoted from riveter to expediter. I went from one department to another, looking for missing parts. I now wore dress slacks instead of the work pants I had worn as a riveter. After that, I had more than thirty jobs ranging from airplane riveter to data processor. With many men away during World War II, women who wanted to work could easily find jobs that would not have been available during peace time.

I would take a job and learn all I could about my duties and those of others working around me. Then, if I did not get promoted, I would become restless. Three months was about as long as I would stay at a job if I didn't get a promotion. It wasn't always that I disliked the job or the people I worked with; it was just that if I wasn't going to move up, I thought I might as well move on.

Sometimes my thoughts turned to my almost forgotten dreams of finishing college. It was something that meant a lot to me, but there seemed to be no way to make my heart's wish come true. Still, I did not forget; I told myself that my dreams weren't lost, only deferred.

Soon after my promotion at Curtiss-Wright, Nicky's parents sent me a telegram to come to New York. They didn't give a reason, but I later learned that they had somehow received word that Nicky would be passing through there on his way to the European war theater. I had to wire them back that I was unable to get time off from work. It was too soon after the wedding to ask for another leave.

Sadly, Nicky left for battle without my seeing him. He was in the 761st Black Panther Battalion, America's first all-Black tank battalion. During the next six months, they battled their way across Belgium and Germany, spearheading the Allied drive and inflicting thousands of casualties on the Nazi army. In its record 183 straight days in combat, including the Battle of the Bulge, the unit suffered a heavy casualty rate. A total of 36 men were killed and 260 were wounded; 71 tanks were lost.

During Nicky's tour of duty, flying shrapnel pierced his leg and hand. He was shipped back to Lake Placid for thirty days of recovery. Leaving Buffalo and my brother, I went to New York City to be with Nicky and his parents until he recovered and we could make some plans. His father, J. Frederic Davis, a high-spirited, slightly built man who smoked cigars continuously, met me at the airport and took me to his family's small apartment in Brooklyn. At the apartment, Nicky's mother, Helen, was waiting to meet me for the first time.

"Now I can die happy," were her first words to me. "Nicky is happy."

The Davises had adopted Nicky when he was nine months old. His natural mother was a wealthy, White woman from upstate New York. His father was the family chauffeur. Nicky's natural grandparents forced his biological mother to take him to Spence's Foundling Home; from there he was adopted by the Davises.

My in-laws, who doted on Nicky, accepted me graciously and I stayed in New York after Nicky returned to duty. My father-in-law explained, apologetically, that he had lost money during the Depression and wouldn't be able to help us financially very much. Although I appreciated his thoughtfulness, I never counted on getting assistance from my in-laws.

I knew I would have to work, and took the first position I was offered. The job was at the home of an Englewood, New Jersey family who needed someone to care for their infant grandchild. The room they gave me was small and dirty. When I arrived, the grandmother just handed me the baby and left. I had never had full responsibility for a baby before. I did the best I could, but the child cried all the time. Feeling lonely, I made friends with the family's laundress, Della Powell, a stocky, mahogany-complected woman from Athens, Georgia. Della was good-humored and she let me sit in the basement with her, while the baby napped, as she ironed and talked nonstop.

On Sunday, after I had been there a week, Della invited me to church. I asked my employer for my pay and then took a cab. As I sat through the service, tears rolled down my cheeks. I'm sure the other worshippers thought the preacher must be delivering a powerful sermon to touch me so. The truth is, I was so discouraged by the situation I was in, I couldn't help crying.

After the service, Della invited me home for dinner. She made fried chicken, greens, mashed potatoes, sliced tomatoes, apple cobbler, hot rolls, and iced tea. I hadn't tasted food like that since I had left home! We visited for the rest of the afternoon. When I started to leave, she could see how sad I was.

"Georgia, you don't have to go back there. You can stay here with me." Quitting my job, I accepted her offer, staying with her until I got another job in a sewing factory.

On that job I learned to use the serger, a machine that over-stitched the edges of the seams on women's blouses and pajamas to keep them from raveling. After working my usual three months, I began searching for something that paid better. I heard that Wright Aeronautical Corporation in Paterson, New Jersey was hiring and I got a job there checking defense items as they were sent down the conveyor belt. They paid me a decent wage and I stayed until the war ended and Nicky came home.

Nicky and I were excited about being together again, but we found that we had become strangers after so much time apart. He drank more than I remembered and kept a gun by our bed; his war experiences seemed to be preying on his mind, but I didn't know how to assess his behavior. After all, we had only spent two weeks together as husband and wife. We both worked patiently at getting to know one another again.

Nicky's father got him a job as a messenger on Wall Street and I became a counter clerk with Chock Full O'Nuts, working at whichever of their twenty-three stores in the New York area needed me.

As a native New Yorker, Nicky knew lots of exciting places in the City; he wanted to show me all of them. To my delight, we began spending our weekends in Manhattan. We would go to the Savoy Ballroom where big-name musicians like Erskine Hawkins would play. We would jitterbug all night every Friday, stay over, and go to the Paramount Theatre on Saturdays, where they always had a good stage show. We'd often go to the Dickie Wells club for a quiet evening of drinking and dancing. Like many young people at the time, we were enjoying ourselves without giving much thought to the future. After a while working at dead-end jobs, though, our thoughts turned to more serious things.

We decided it was time to start a family. After months of trying to conceive, and still not becoming pregnant, I went with Nicky to see a doctor. He tested us both, then said that we would probably never have children. The news was a blow. Even though I hadn't wanted a large family, I had hoped to have at least one or two children. Nicky consoled me in his gentle way. "We still have each other," he said. Nevertheless, for many years afterward I'd felt an overwhelming sadness whenever I picked up some other woman's baby.

Nicky was an easy-going person who enjoyed simple pleasures and liked to dress in nice clothes. At home he would wear a velvet smoking jacket or silk pajamas. When we made love, however, it was only pleasant, not passionate. More often than not, our lovemaking was at my initiation. At first, because of the rape I had suffered as a teenager and the sexual assaults of my first husband, I appreciated Nicky's lack of interest in sex. However, as I matured and my own sexuality developed, I knew there was something lacking. Looking back, I can see that we were not sexually compatible and that this was a major factor in the failure of our marriage.

In our family, it had always been understood that we would help each other. When my brother Phillip called to ask if he could come to Englewood and live with us after he graduated high school, I said, "Sure, come on." Phillip got a job in a bakery, starting work at 4 A.M. and sometimes walked the twenty miles to Hackensack where the bakery was located.

For a while, things seemed to be going smoothly, but then Nicky began to drink more, and his once even disposition began to change. He was unhappy with his job as a messenger on Wall Street and decided to open a small, storefront restaurant in Harlem with a friend of his who cooked. It was a bad time to go into the restaurant business; meat was hard to get and sugar was rationed. I supported his efforts as best I could. Phillip and I helped out, but after a few months, the restaurant flopped.

I Shared the Dream

Later that year, Mom and Pop came to visit us in Englewood. They stayed for a week and it was a very happy time for me. We took in all the sights and went to dinner at Nicky's parents' house in Brooklyn. I wanted to give them their first subway ride, but I was so excited that I got us lost two or three times before we got to the 168th Street Bridge where we could catch the bus over to Jersey. Having them with us, I realized how much I had missed Mom and Pop. After they left I started talking to Nicky about moving back to Kentucky. I thought I was homesick. Looking back now, I know the longing I felt was not for home, but instead for some direction in our lives, for some goals to work toward. Homesickness is a longing for what you once had and left; I was longing for something I had not yet found.

Nicky didn't like Kentucky, but he saw how much I had my heart set on the move, so he agreed. My brother Phillip was married by this time; he and his wife, Rose Marie, decided to go back to Louisville with us. I sold all our furniture, except a new mattress set, to our landlady for twenty-five dollars. We tied the mattresses to the top of Nicky's Ford, put the luggage in the trunk, and the four of us, with our two cats, piled into the car and left for Louisville. After traveling for five full days, we pulled up in front of our parents house, looking like a bunch of vagabonds. They welcomed us.

Nicky went to work for International Harvester. However, the employees went on strike twice during the first year he was there. Nicky became so discouraged, he reenlisted in the Army. He was sent to Fort Knox, thirty miles from Louisville. During this period, I was hired by Enro Shirt Company as a power machine operator, setting the collars on men's shirts. In the plant, the restrooms were segregated, as were the steps to the second floor on which I worked. The workers couldn't even walk up the stairs together. I resented this deeply. I promised myself I would only stay there until I found something else. After three months, I found a job at Robinson Realty Company working as a secretary. I had been taking a business course at Central High's night school, but my typing and shorthand were not very good. I explained this to Mr. Robinson and he gave me the job on a trial basis. A week after beginning my new job, I received a call from James Rosenbloom, the president of the Enro Company.

"I was considering making you a supervisor," he said in a deep, authoritarian voice. "Will you come back if I give you a promotion?"

"I quit," I told him, "because I detested the separate restrooms and stairs." I paused, and when he said nothing, I continued. "I had made friends with some of the White girls and we couldn't go to lunch together. We couldn't even go up the same set of steps!"

"Georgia, I'd really like to have you back. I think you'd make a good supervisor." That was all Rosenbloom said. It was like he hadn't even heard me. He didn't offer to do anything about the conditions that caused me to quit in the first place, so I didn't go back.

5

THE PHILADELPHIA LAWYER

Nicky had been sent to Germany from Fort Knox and I was living with my parents while looking for a place of my own. When I mentioned my search to Mr. Robinson, he said, "Mrs. Robinson and I have plenty of room in our two-story house on Chestnut Street, and we'd be glad to have you there."

The Robinsons and I got along well. Soon I was driving us both to work in Mr. Robinson's new Buick. As we drove in one day, I noticed a tall, Black man with charismatic eyes standing, waiting for a bus. He was handsome, dressed in a gray, stylish suit, and was carrying a newspaper under his arm. In his tapered fingers he twirled a long cigar. Slowing the car I thought, he looks just like a Philadelphia lawyer. I watched him for a long moment, then continued on my way.

With my husband in Germany and little to do after work, I had a lot of free time. One evening I went to the Grand Bar for a drink and began talking with the shapely, bronze-skinned waitress who served me. Her name was Inez Gillings and she came from Costa Rica. High spirited and attractive, she played poker with some of the fellows who frequented the Grand and invited me to go with her to the sessions, even though I didn't play. At one of the poker parties, I met the man I had seen on the street corner—the Philadelphia lawyer. His name was Jim Powers. He and I talked that night and he told me he was born in Canton, Ohio. He also mentioned that his wife, Gloria, was in Waverly Hills Sanatorium, a tuberculosis hospital where he visited her every day. "On Wednesdays," he said quietly, "I cook food and take it to her and others in the hospital." He had come to Louisville to work at Churchill Downs for the racing season, but hadn't intended to stay. He had planned to go on to New Orleans for the season there, when his wife contracted TB. He put her in the hospital and found work nearby. They had a small daughter and there was another child on the way. As we talked, I could feel his concern for his wife and thought that he must be a very caring person.

The next time I saw Jim was at a Christmas Eve party at Inez's house. Like that first evening, he was alone. I felt pretty that night. My hair was newly cut stylishly short and I was wearing a long-sleeve, white silk blouse, a black skirt and black suede shoes with ankle straps. I could feel him watching me. Although nothing was said, I think we both felt the attraction between us.

Jim didn't have a car, so when I left he asked if I could take him to the Brown Derby. Since I was already giving another guest a ride, I agreed. When I pulled up at the Brown Derby, Jim tried to persuade me to go in for a drink, but I refused.

I Shared the Dream

In the spring, Nicky returned to the States and was discharged from the Army. He found a job on the night shift at the Brown-Forman Distillery. I was still working at Robinson Realty Company. Robinson had a building listed for sale on Sixteenth Street in the "California area." It was a long, brick building that once had five small businesses in the front and living quarters in the back. As always, I was searching for some ways to make extra money. I bought the building, paying six hundred dollars for it. Nicky and I spent most of our days renovating it into two two-room apartments and two three-room apartments. We added one inside bathroom accessible to each apartment. Once the renovations were finished, I quit Robinson Realty. I was busy working hard to make a home for us, and we had extra income from the rentals. I should have been content.

However, Jim Powers was still on my mind. Nothing had actually happened between us, but every time I saw Inez, she told me Jim was asking about me. By this time, I had also gone back to work at the Jeffersonville Quartermaster Depot as an inspector of Army uniforms. Nine months passed and Inez continued to bring me messages.

"Jimmy wants to see you."

"I don't want to see Jim Powers," I insisted to her, but I couldn't lie to myself.

True, Nicky and I were congenial and pleasant to each other, but by then I knew something important was missing in our marriage. I did want to see Jim Powers even though I didn't want to admit it to myself.

Finally, one night I agreed to go with Inez to the Top Hat. Jim and Inez's boyfriend were there. Jim had asked her to arrange the evening in order to bring us together. That night I finally came to terms with the truth about my feelings for him. When he asked me to meet him the following night, I said, "Yes," almost without thinking.

"Let's meet at the Orchid Bar," he went on. I, who rarely found myself speechless, merely nodded.

Almost from the moment I arrived at the meeting place and sat down at the table where he waited, I knew we would be together later. As we sat sipping our drinks he leaned toward me, saying, "I've rented a room."

That night began an affair that was to continue on and off for many years. I was ecstatically happy when we were together, totally miserable when we were apart, and often tortured by the guilt of cheating on my husband.

I gradually learned everything about Jim, including the fact that what he had first told me about his place of birth was untrue. He had made up that story because he hated the South and the segregated life there and was ashamed of his place of birth. "I left Alabama as a teenager," he told me, "went to Knoxville, Tennessee and worked as a waiter in a railroad dining car. Then I left Knoxville and went to Chicago, continuing to work on the railroad, until I landed a job as a waiter in the Palmer House."

The snob in me was bothered a little by the fact that he was a waiter. He was far too distinguished-looking for what I considered such a menial job. He was a very good waiter, though, and was working at the Old House, one of Louisville's best restaurants.

Gloria, Jim's wife, was now out of the hospital and doing well. One evening at Joe's Palm Room, I saw her for the first time. A tall, almond-skinned woman with black, wavy hair, she was from Jamaica. She spoke with a Spanish accent and was very intelligent. That evening she completely ignored Jim and talked animatedly with Dr. Maurice Rabb, a local physician, and some other professional people. She paid little attention to the others gathered there. Jim had told me that she preferred the company of the well-off and this seemed true, since she spoke to no one else.

I Shared the Dream

Though there appeared to be no good solution for our relationship, Jim and I continued to see each other until fate intervened.

I got a call from a friend, Nellie Taylor, whom I had met in Lexington when my husband, Robert, was stationed there. Her mother had died. I drove there immediately to be with her and went to her home where the body was placed for viewing. Walking in, I could not help but notice a white woman with striking silver-white hair and electric blue eyes standing by the casket, weeping. A little Black boy was holding her hand and a young White girl was standing beside her. All three soon left together and I asked Nellie about them.

"The lady and her husband owned a farm outside of Lexington," she said. "When the little boy was born the doctors told his mother, Eva Marie, that she had given birth to a Black child, even though he looked as pale-skinned as any of the other White babies. They tried to convince her to leave the baby at the hospital to let him be adopted, but she refused. Eva Marie thought she could pass him off for White and she wanted to keep him. She named him William and called him Billy. Of course, as Billy grew older, his Blackness began to show; he had curly hair and his skin began to darken.

"When the woman's husband became suspicious, he confronted her; she admitted that a farmhand had fathered Billy. Her husband ranted and raved but then agreed that she could keep the boy, not as their child, just as a farmhand. This arrangement continued during Billy's preschool years. He was fed and turned out into the fields alone to talk to the animals and the trees. However, word spread around Lexington that his mother had had a Black child. It was considered a scandal and when visitors came to the house, Billy was locked in his room.

"When Billy was six, his mother had to find a school for him. Kentucky schools were segregated and Billy couldn't go to the neighborhood school with his older sister. Eva Marie sent him to live in Lexington where he could go to a Black school during the week and come home on weekends.

"My mother," Nellie continued, "had been keeping Billy in Lexington and sending him to school, but now other arrangements will have to be made for him."

Soon after I returned home from the funeral, Nellie called me.

"Would you be interested in adopting Billy?" she asked.

I was taken by surprise. Even though I knew I couldn't have children, Nicky and I had not considered adopting a child.

"I'll have to think about it and talk to my husband," I replied.

Nicky and I talked about it for a week. The more we talked, the more we felt we wanted Billy. I had always wanted a child, and even though we had been married eleven years and had become accustomed to thinking only of ourselves, we believed we could adjust and become good parents. We went to Lexington to talk to Billy's mother. Eva Marie told us the story of Billy's conception and birth, crying the whole time. She said she had become close to Billy's father because her husband was away a lot. She came to depend on him.

"He was always there when I needed anything. After a while, he was so good to me that I came to love him."

She had agonized over her decision to give Billy up, trying to find any other solution.

"I've tried to find an integrated boarding school I could afford and I've also considered leaving my husband and going to New York. I've had to reject both of these plans because I don't have any money of my own."

"We really want Billy," Nicky and I told her and we arranged to pick him up at Nellie's. That morning, he carried a little suitcase in which, besides his clothes, he had several cans of tuna fish, his favorite food, and a picture of his mother.

We enrolled Billy in Phyllis Wheatley Elementary School in the fall. When Christmas came, we spent as much as we could afford to make it a happy one for him, buying him winter clothes and nice toys.

In the beginning, he seemed to enjoy being with us, but after a while he became withdrawn. He lost his appetite and would sit at the table picking at his food. One day, tired of waiting for him to finish, I got up and started washing the dishes. I turned around and saw him holding his plate below the table where our collie, Shep, was. I hid my smile.

"Good, Billy. You've eaten all your food, I see." I didn't let on that I had seen him feeding it to his constant companion, Shep.

Nicky and I grew to love Billy. He called us "Mom" and "Dad" as we asked him to, but we couldn't seem to get as close to him as we wanted. He was reserved, quiet, and spent a lot of time looking out the window in the front room. It wasn't until much later I found out that Billy had not been told the truth about where he was going and why. His mother had told him he was going to Louisville on a vacation after which she would come and get him. To save herself the pain of telling him the truth, she had set him up for the incredible disappointment and lifelong pain of wondering why his mother never came. Billy was in high school before he gave up hope that his real mother and dad would come back and get him. He, of course, believed that his mother's husband was his biological father. I wanted so much to be a good mother to Billy and I couldn't understand why it was impossible to bridge the distance between us in those early years. I understand it now.

It is one of the regrets of my life that I didn't seek counseling for Billy to get to the root of the problem while he was still a young child. However, professional counseling was not a part of ordinary peoples' thinking in those days; even if we had known about it, we wouldn't have had the money to pay.

With my new home and Billy to take care of, my life seemed settled. Inwardly, however, I was in turmoil. I knew I had to do something about Jim Powers. Our affair had gone on for three years. Even though I had stopped seeing Jim at that point, I knew I would start again and it was just a matter of time before Nicky found out. Not long before, Nicky had met Jim at a party and talked about how much he liked him. This made me even more nervous. Moreover, Jim was making our relationship increasingly difficult and dangerous for me. He told me he'd never give me up. He was drinking heavily because he felt trapped in his marriage and in his job as a waiter.

Once, in the middle of the night when Nicky and I were asleep in bed together, the phone rang. I answered it.

"I just had to hear your voice before I went in," I heard Jim say.

"You must have the wrong number," I said, and hung up quickly.

The next time we spoke, I begged him not to ever call my house again, but if he was drinking, he did. Even to me, my excuses to Nicky began to sound like lies.

Questions ran through my head all day, every day. What am I going to do? Jim is not going to leave his wife and their three children. We're never going to be together legally. I have to get him out of my system, I decided. The only way I could foresee ending the relationship was to put miles between us. Nicky and I would have to leave Louisville and make a life somewhere else.

I decided that we would go to California, where my cousin Frances lived. It was not hard to convince Nicky to leave since he didn't like Louisville. I called Frances in Los Angeles, put our building on the market, and made plans to move to California. I didn't dare tell Jim about my plans. He was still saying, "I will not give you up."

I decided I'd write him after I got to California. We sold our building for three thousand dollars. Afterward, Nicky, Billy, and I left for California in a 1949 Ford convertible with only our clothes, a little cash, the check for three thousand dollars, and Shep the dog. It took us four days to drive there.

There was no such thing as electronic banking at that time, but it had not occurred to us that we wouldn't be able to cash our check right away. We couldn't, of course, and it took ten days for the check to clear. Meanwhile, we ran out of money and lived on the fruit basket hotel management had placed in our room. Finally, we had to tell Cousin Frances about our situation and borrow some money from her. In addition to the money, she generously gave us a large box of home-cooked food—a roast, green beans, mashed potatoes, and homemade rolls. As we gratefully accepted it, I couldn't help thinking that home-cooked food is a bond between poor people, Black and White, a special pleasure that the rich cannot fully appreciate.

As soon as we got some money, we rented a three-room apartment and bought just enough furniture to get by. I went to Cheli Air Force Base in Maywood and applied for a job as a data processing trainee. They were only hiring six trainees and I had to take a comprehensive test in all kinds of academic subjects. The test lasted for four hours and it was difficult. I was skeptical about my chances of being selected, but a few days after the test I was called and told to report to work. My test score had been a ninety-four, the highest actual score made. Another trainee had gotten a score of ninety-six, but she had had five points added on because she was a veteran.

During the next few weeks, I learned how to operate IBM data processing machines and how to do minor repairs when the IBM cards were torn and got tangled in the machines. I liked the work and they seemed to appreciate the seriousness with which I approached it. In three months, I was promoted to supervisor at Cheli and taught others how to operate the machines.

On Sundays, I attended the St. Mary's Baptist Church with Cousin Frances. It was a far cry from the "shotgun" house church I had gone to as a young child. St. Mary's was a huge, beautiful, pink stucco structure which had cost more than a million dollars to build. Sunday services were broadcast live on the radio every week.

Robert Harmon, the tall and stylish pastor, was in his late thirties. He had a smooth, mocha-cream complexion and a voice to match. The man was an actor in the pulpit. Each Sunday after his sermon, he would leave the podium while the choir sang a couple of songs. Ten minutes later, Harmon would re-enter wearing a complete change of clothes and "open the doors of the church" to new members. After a few Sundays, I responded to the call to be *saved*.

The church clerk asked "Do you believe Christ died for your sins and rose again?"

"Yes," I answered.

"Will you come by letter or baptism?"

"By baptism," I said.

I had never been baptized by immersion in water. Two Sundays later, the day of the baptismal service, the clerk called out the names of those to be baptized. My name was not called. Thinking it was just an oversight, I went down anyway and was baptized. As I was leaving the church that day, the pastor asked me to come back to the church at six o'clock that evening. "I want to talk to you about church doctrine," he said sternly.

I did as was requested. When I went to his office that evening, he locked the door. It was soon clear what "doctrine" he wanted to discuss.

"Were you wearing a bra when you were baptized this morning?" he asked. When I didn't reply, he went on. "Your name wasn't called because I wanted to personally baptize you this evening."

He put his arms around me and embraced me tightly. I was caught off guard. Even though men had made unwanted advances toward me before, no minister of the Gospel had ever tried to seduce me. He tugged at me, trying to kiss me and pulled at my dress until he tore the seam under one arm. I continued to resist and finally was able to get to the door, unlock it, and run.

I stopped going to church; there was no way I could sit and listen to Harmon after that. Later that same year, the *Los Angeles Sentinel* reported that a girl had charged pastor Harmon with trying to seduce her when she joined the church. As I read her account of what had happened, it was like a tape replaying in my head; he had used the same words with me. Once again, as when I had been raped, I kept the fear and humiliation engendered by the incident to myself, continuing my childhood habit of keeping my own counsel and bearing my sorrows privately.

I was still in California when I read in the newspaper about the Supreme Court decision on school desegregation. The very concept of "separate but equal" schools had been struck down. The Court ruled that segregated "schools were separate, but inherently unequal." The landmark decision caused me to remember the five-year-old, obsolete, hand-me-down books passed from the White schools to students in segregated Black schools. By the time we got them, they had been written in and pages were missing. This had emphasized to us that because we were Black children, we were not first-class citizens.

On December 1, 1955, I first saw Dr. Martin Luther King, Jr. on national television. He was responding to questions from a reporter about the arrest of Mrs. Rosa Parks, an attractive, Black woman whose dark hair softly framed her face. She was a charming and respected member of the local chapter of the NAACP in Montgomery, Alabama who had refused to give up her seat on the bus to a newly-boarded, White, male passenger. I was impressed, surprised, and happy to see Black people confronting the discriminatory bus system. But I was afraid for them, thinking of the danger they would face in the days to come.

The reporter asked Dr. King, "What does the Negro want?"

He responded, "What the Negro wants is absolute and unqualified freedom and equality in this land of his birth, and not in Africa or some imaginary state."

I thought, this man is expressing my thoughts and feelings. This is what I want.

The reporter asked, "A majority of the bus passengers are Black, how will they get around if they don't use the buses?"

King said, "Where there is a will, there is a way. Many will walk, others will use private cars and taxis."

Watching the television intently, I felt my own pride growing. By facing the Whites who opposed their bid for equality without visible fear, Blacks were dispelling the image of being scared and slovenly people with low self-esteem. For the first time, I was seeing Black people as a race rise up against their oppressors and I knew eventually Black people would get justice in this country. I wanted to be there.

By then, Nicky was working at the California Gas Company as a laborer. With two salaries coming in we were able to move to a better apartment building called "Cadillac Square." The circular design of the building enclosed a large swimming pool. On Christmas Day 1955, nearly a year after we had arrived, we spent the holiday California-style, swimming in the pool.

A few months later, Nicky and I bought a two-bedroom house in a suburb of Los Angeles. We were working hard, but we still found time for family outings. We enjoyed going to the beach in Santa Monica and went there almost every weekend. Nicky would put Billy on his shoulders and wade out into the surf. While they played in the water, I sunned on the beach and watched them.

Although I told myself that I should be happy with our new home, a good job, and our young son, I still thought about Jim Powers. Soon after we got to California, I had written to him explaining that I had to get away to try to make a life for myself—but distance did not erase my feelings.

That August I made one of my usual Sunday calls to my family in Kentucky. When I asked about everybody, there was silence on the line. "We're all well except Carl," Mom finally said. "He's been lying around all day and he's got a temperature. I'm taking him to see a doctor tomorrow."

The next day, when I called I found out that a Dr. Rosenbaum had examined Carl and done some medical tests. On Thursday, he sent for my parents and broke the shocking news that Carl had acute leukemia and had only three months, at the most, to live.

When my brother Phillip called to tell me, I couldn't believe it. Though I knew older people who had died, no one in my family had. I couldn't believe such a thing could befall my youngest brother. Still in a daze, I went to work the next morning and arranged to be off for two weeks. I left Billy, who was nine, with Nicky and took the Super Chief train home.

Seeing my brother and knowing his fate was one of the most difficult things I'd ever done. Carl had grown since I left, he was six feet tall now. He had lost weight. He didn't know he had a terminal illness and he was proud of the weight loss. He wanted to stay in shape and play sports. My parents made up excuses why they wouldn't let him. He talked of going to Central High School and practiced his saxophone, so he could be in the school band. The rest of us watched him with tears in our eyes. My heart ached for him. It was so hard to keep up a good front, but I did my best.

Though I told myself not to, I called Jim Powers while I was home. "When can I see you?" he asked. We spent the next day together and saw each other a lot after that.

Because of my guilty conscience, I called Nicky often. He always assured me that he and Billy were doing just fine and said that I should stay as long as I needed to. I called work and asked to have my leave extended for another two weeks.

Carl entered high school in early September and joined the band. He still hadn't been told the truth about his illness. One night we were watching television together. The program was about a person with leukemia. The narrator said the woman's body was creating an overabundance of white corpuscles. At one point, Carl quietly said, "That's what I have." We all sat there motionless. Every heart in the room was breaking.

It was almost impossible to leave Carl when my four weeks were up. I knew I would not see him alive again. Back in California, I went to work every day, but my mind was still in Louisville. I called home as often as I could. The news was always bad. He received more and more transfusions, felt progressively weaker, and was in and out of the hospital. Finally, Carl's condition became critical and he entered the hospital for the last time. The family stayed with him around the clock and prayed for his soul to be saved. Weeks before he died, Carl accepted Christ as his Lord and Savior.

"I'm not worried about Carl now," Mom said. "He'll go home to live with Jesus."

I didn't intend to make the trip back home when Carl died. I had said all I could to reassure him of my love while he was alive. In addition, I now knew I couldn't stay away from Jim Powers if we were in the same town.

When I told Nicky the news about Carl's death, I said, "I don't think I'll go to the funeral since I was just there."

"Georgia, your family needs you. You'll never forgive yourself if you don't go," Nicky responded.

I have to try to be truthful with this man, I thought to myself. "Nicky, if I go, I won't be back," I said. If Nicky had said he wanted to stay in California, our marriage would have ended then. He didn't and he didn't question me.

"If that's what you want, we'll all go back," he answered.

We were just getting settled in our new home. Both of us were working; we each had our own car and we had just paid off the debt for our four rooms of furniture. We were much better off financially than we had ever been. None of that mattered to me. I told myself I was going home to be with my family and say a final good-bye to Carl, but in my heart I knew it was Jim who was drawing me back to Louisville. Even though the relationship caused me so much misery, I couldn't give it up.

Grieving for Carl was hard on all of us, but Pop's grief overwhelmed him. My mother seemed to be able to block it out somewhat by keeping busy, but Pop couldn't. He had prayed so hard for Carl to live. My father actually believed that he could pray Carl back to health and so he felt betrayed by God when Carl finally died. For six months, Pop went to work, ate, and when he was home, laid on the living room couch staring at the ceiling, not speaking to any of us.

We faced death again as a family in 1962 when my brother Rudolph was killed in an automobile accident in California. He had just finished Bellarmine College, where he had been a basketball star, and was serving in the Air Force in Ft. Ord, California. Driving on a rainy night, he lost control of his car in a curve and was impaled on a railing. He was killed instantly. Even though our grief over losing Rudolph was great, it was not as terrible as watching Carl slowly die.

Carl was buried on December 6, 1956. I called Nicky and asked him to send Billy by train so I could be with him for Christmas. Nicky stayed in California to sell the house, the furniture, and my car. In March, he joined us in Louisville. We rented a small four-room house near my parents. Nicky got a job as a laborer at DuPont and I went to work in the data processing department of the Louisville Medical Depot, a federal installation. After living in the "doll house," as we called it, for nine months, Nicky and I had saved enough money to buy something bigger.

Looking for a house to buy, I learned that the one thing that had not changed in Louisville was housing discrimination. Blacks were still relegated to living in certain areas in the city: the periphery of the downtown business district; a section in the west end called Parkland, where we lived; a small area in the east end of downtown called Smoketown; and the semi-rural area in the city called Little Africa. Blacks in Little Africa still raised chickens and hogs within the city limits, just as they had when I was a child. The financial institutions limited property loans to Blacks at 80 percent of market value of the property, if you could get approved. Blacks had to have exemplary credit and paid higher interest rates. The insurance companies redlined targeted properties in the Black areas, blocking out and refusing Blacks from acquiring insurance.

We bought a duplex with my brother Jimmie and his wife. It was an ugly, brown, two-story wooden frame house with a porch across the front. There were just no duplexes in good condition for us to chose from. Marie and Jimmie had three large rooms and a bath on the first floor and we had the second floor with two bedrooms, a large living room and kitchen combined, and a bath. Nicky built a food bar to separate the two rooms and put a fireplace in the living room.

Marie and I spent many days and nights sitting on the porch, talking about world news and what was going on in the country. Marie was born and raised in West Medford, Massachusetts. She had not experienced the blatant discrimination that Blacks faced in the South. Jimmie had met her while he was in the Air Force in Texas. Nicky and I were trying to make a home, but I was haunted by my feelings for Jim Powers. Eventually I gave in and saw him again. Before long, our relationship picked up where it left off.

Nicky and I didn't argue, but we didn't communicate either. He was unhappy with Kentucky, but I didn't want to live in the Northeast again. The pace was too fast. While living in New Jersey and working in New York, I found myself talking and walking faster, trying to keep up with the Easterners. I was not accustomed to not knowing who lived next door to me or to not offering a guest a drink or some food, as is the custom in the South. I vowed that if I ever made it back home, I would never move from Kentucky again. As time passed, my consciousness of the inequalities faced by Blacks and by the poor grew as my life took dramatic turns and I faced new experiences.

In 1958, I learned firsthand how poor people were treated in public institutions. I was having severe pains in my abdomen; my monthly periods were erratic and I bled profusely during them. I had never had any real health problems before and I didn't know what was happening to my body. Nicky and I were only able to meet our financial obligations monthly and I did not have the money to get a private physician. My alternative, therefore, was to go to the general hospital where indigent people were treated.

I walked into the huge lobby of the yellow brick building on Chestnut Street. The place looked dirty inside. Sick people, Black and White, were slouched on benches, waiting. Empty food wrappers and cigarettes littered the floor. I signed in at the registration desk. An arrogant, elderly, White woman looked over her glasses at me and said, in a loud, demeaning voice, "What are you doing here? You don't look like you belong; you're too well-dressed." Before I could answer, she said, "Have a seat until your name is called."

I sat down next to a Black woman who said, "I have been sitting here over an hour. I am so sick, but they don't care." I turned to look at her more closely. Her mouth was wet, her bottom lip protruded and saliva drooled from her mouth due to the medication she had to take. She said she came to the hospital on a regular basis to get treated.

I said, "This is my first time here."

She answered, "I can tell that. If you want help here, you have to look poor or they think you can afford a private doctor."

I didn't think I was overdressed as I had made the wine-colored, crepe, sarong-type skirt that I was wearing. With it I had on a simple white blouse and black patent leather sandals. My hair was neat and I was clean. But as I looked around, I saw that many of the people there were disheveled, unclean, and unkempt.

After waiting for an hour my name was barked loudly on the loudspeaker. I went to the caller; she gave me a slip of paper and directed me to go to the gynecology clinic. I took the elevator to the second floor. The sign read "Gyn Clinic;" a clerk was seated at a desk in the hallway and there were chairs lined up next to the wall. I handed her the slip and was once again told to sit until my name was called. As I waited for another hour, I was thinking about the public servants' condescending attitude toward indigent people. Because these people are indigent, the officials think they have nothing but time—nowhere to be or nowhere to go.

Eventually, I was handed a short, pale blue, wrinkled gown that opened in the back, and told to go into the examining room, undress, put the gown on backward, and wait for a doctor to come in. Two doctors came in; both looked like young interns. One was White, the other Asian. They took my medical history. The Asian one said in a monotone, "Sit on the table." It was padded with a white sheet covering it.

Without another word, he took my temperature, looked in my eyes and ears with a light, thumped my knees for reflexes, and pushed the little, round, cold, metal end of a stethoscope on my chest and back. Then he said, "Lie back on the table and scoot your buttocks to the end with your feet in the stirrups." A nurse assisted him. She put a cloth across my knees, and I felt better that I was not as exposed. The doctor sat on a wheeled stool and rolled right up to the table facing my genital area. He said, "Open your legs as wide as possible." He pushed the cloth up, so he could view my bottom.

I was thirty-five years old and had never known this type of embarrassment. He put some cream in my vagina and inserted a cold, metal speculum into me. I wanted to fade away or faint, so I wouldn't know what was happening. Since I had never given birth, I didn't know what to expect. The doctor had one hand pressing on my abdomen and the fingers on the other hand inserted into me, probing. After the examination the two doctors consulted with each other. Then they told me to get dressed and they would talk to me.

I dressed and went into the hall to sit until they called me. I hated to face the doctor who had done the internal examination again. He came out and sat down in the chair next to me.

"Georgia," he said brusquely, "you have a fibroid tumor in your uterus the size of a grapefruit. They are usually benign, but we think you need a partial hysterectomy to alleviate the problem with your menstruation."

"What's a partial hysterectomy?" I asked.

He quickly explained, "The uterus is surgically removed, but your ovaries will be left intact. They are not affected and will continue to produce estrogen. This hormone is needed to keep your bones strong."

They didn't ask me if I wanted to have the operation or not. Neither was I given an opportunity to voice any additional questions I might have had.

Looking down at his watch, the doctor said, "Go to the scheduling clerk to make a date for the surgery. It should be done as soon as possible." Then he left.

In two weeks, I was in the hospital having my organs, including my appendix, surgically removed. I remained in the hospital on an open ward for four days, then moved into a semi-private room for the remainder of the week. I was so weak when Nicky picked me up at the hospital and took me home that he had to carry me from the car to the second floor apartment.

During my three months of recovery, Nicky was kind and considerate. He took the first week off from his new job at the post office to take care of me. He did the cooking, washing, cleaning, and waited on me, but we had little to say to each other. I spent most of my time relaxing in a recliner and watching television as I healed.

I had no regrets about the surgery. My mother and other older women talked about the problems they had "going through the change,"—the nervousness, the sweats, the anxiety. I was relieved that I wouldn't have to go through those things. I had always hated menstruation and no longer had dreams of having a child—I had Billy. I returned to the hospital two weeks after the surgery to have the sutures removed and I experienced no problems after that.

I believe that everything happens for a reason. Sometimes we don't realize it at the moment, but we learn later. The insensitivity and lack of compassion shown toward me in this experience made me more sensitive to the needs of poor and disadvantaged people. I personally felt the disrespect of those paid to serve the public. It remains in my consciousness.

Jim Powers and I were briefly seeing each other again. Once again, I was painfully reminded that there was no possible future for Jim and I. He wouldn't, and I felt he shouldn't, desert his family. It was time for me to abandon my obsession with him and concentrate on my own life.

I had been laid off from the Medical Depot but was soon hired by the United States Census Bureau in the data processing unit as an IBM tabulating operator. After three months, I was promoted to supervisor and had seventy-five employees assigned to me.

Meanwhile, I was saving money for a down payment on a house. One Sunday, I saw one listed on Cecil Avenue. Nicky and I looked at the house together and fell in love with it. The white stucco walls and large porch reminded me of the California-style ranch homes. On the first floor was a living room, a dining room, two bedrooms, a bath, and a kitchen. The second floor had three rooms. There was a concrete basement under three-fourths of the house. We bought the house for ten thousand dollars—a thousand down and an FHA mortgage of nine thousand dollars. We moved in and, except for one brief period, I have lived there ever since.

I stopped meeting Jim. Nicky and I now had our lovely new home and I really was trying to make our marriage work. For two years we were busy renovating the house. We took out the partition between the living room and the dining room, carpeted the whole house, tiled the kitchen walls, and painted all the woodwork in colors to match the walls. We also put in a new gas furnace. I joined the New Covenant Presbyterian Church; Nicky and Billy also became members. Nicky wanted Billy to be a Boy Scout, so he organized a troop sponsored by the church.

When Jim called me one day, I said, "Leave me alone. I'm a mother and an active Christian now. I can't see you ever again."

III

THE CIVIL RIGHTS
YEARS

6

FATEFUL
CHOICES

By the spring of 1962, that same vague, undeniable restlessness which had always preceded change in my life was again stirring within me. Since Nicky and I were renovating our house, I took a leave of absence from the ten-hour days and seven-day weeks of the Census Bureau. At the time, we were also devoting some of our energy to the activities of our church. One Sunday after services, I was approached by Verna Smith, a gracious Black lady with an infectious enthusiasm. She was locally active with the Democratic Party.

"I'm supporting Wilson Wyatt for the United States Senate," she said, smiling. She also contributed financially to the Democrats. "We need someone to work in his headquarters and I thought of you."

At that moment, immersed as I was in my personal life and tired from two long years of overtime, her idea did not seem that attractive. I answered her politely, "To be perfectly honest with you, Mrs. Smith, I have never been involved much with politics except to vote."

In fact, I had never given politics much thought. I was a registered Democrat, primarily because my parents had been Franklin D. Roosevelt Democrats. My mother had registered in 1932, so she could vote for Roosevelt, and my father, the only person in our family with a keen interest in politics, had changed his registration from Republican to Democrat so that he too, could vote for Roosevelt.

That morning in church, after much talking and cajoling, Verna Smith succeeded in piquing my curiosity. She persuaded me to go down to Wyatt's headquarters to talk to his campaign manager, Ed Farris.

Wyatt, a prominent attorney in Louisville, was a well-known political figure in Kentucky. He had been mayor of Louisville, had managed the unsuccessful presidential campaign of Adlai Stevenson in 1952, and had played a central role in Stevenson's 1956 presidential campaign. In 1959, Wyatt announced his candidacy for governor of Kentucky. He withdrew before the primary, endorsed Bert Combs's candidacy, and ran for lieutenant governor on the winning ticket with Combs. This year, Wyatt had won the Democratic nomination to challenge the Republican incumbent, Senator Thurston B. Morton.

That week, I went to the Seelbach Hotel, the most prestigious accommodation in Louisville, to see Farris. The building was impressive and though I had never been inside, I had passed the entrance many times. Blacks were not allowed to register as guests. Purposely, I avoided using the side entrance, since I did not want to be mistaken for hired help. Instead, I walked in the front doors, through the hallway and toward the gift shop. Standing there for a moment to get my bearings, I surveyed the lobby. Facing me was the information and registration desk. It looked to me like an oversized headboard made of dark, carved oak. The imported tiles on the floor were partially covered in one area by a jewel-toned Oriental rug on which sat a Victorian sofa and several stylishly upholstered chairs. Facing the desk in the rear was a wide, marble stairway leading to the mezzanine and also a bank of elevators. I walked toward them, impressed but saddened that I had been denied access to this accommodation for so long merely because of the color of my skin. I took the elevator to the second floor. Suite 743 had a sign on it: "Wyatt for United States Senate."

I went in and said to the receptionist, "My name is Georgia Davis. I'm here to see Mr. Farris."

"He's expecting you, have a seat," she replied

In no time, Ed Farris came out to see me. His first question to me, "Can you type and take shorthand?" was off-putting. Although I could do neither well, he offered me the job. I thought his hiring me was strange since I didn't possess the skills he was looking for, but I agreed because the pay was ninety dollars a week. This was more than my base pay at the Census Bureau. As I looked around the office, however, it did not take me long to figure out why I had been hired. I was to be the token Black.

I said to him, "Ed, I will work for you for one week. If I like it, I'll be back. If not, I won't and you won't have to pay me."

"Oh, we'd have to pay you," he stammered, startled by the straightforwardness of my statement.

A tall, blond woman in her late thirties entered the room. She had a big smile, a firm handshake, and introduced herself as June Taylor.

"Georgia, how soon can you start?" she asked.

It was Thursday. "I'll start on Monday," I said. I left the headquarters, not knowing that I had just been presented with the opportunity I had been looking for all my life.

I believe the choices we make, large and small, follow us throughout our lives. I had always been searching for empowerment, and this job, although I didn't know it then, was going to be the beginning of my journey toward that goal. Since I could have easily blown my opportunity that day, I can't help feeling that some greater power than myself had placed it before me and helped me make the right decision. Perhaps Verna Smith, to whom I've always been grateful, was part of that unknown plan.

However, my first two days at the office seemed pretty meaningless. I helped at the reception desk, mimeographed political material, and stuffed, sealed, and stamped hundreds of envelopes.

The volunteers I worked with were almost all White women from the east end—the affluent area of Louisville. Some with whom I worked closely were Deborah Isenberg, Elizabeth Cherry, and Lucretia "Lukey" Ward. One of the few Black volunteers was Hortense Young, a physician's wife, who came by often to pick up material to be distributed in the Black community.

The Democrats were looking for a big vote from the Black community in the general election. They didn't encourage Blacks to help select the nominee, but the party came looking for them when it was time to vote for the candidate the Whites had selected in the primary. Later, when I urged Blacks to vote in the all-important first election, many would say, "I don't vote in this election, I just vote in the big one."

Although I didn't like the discriminatory tactics or the mundane duties, I plunged in with my usual fervor. On my third day, June came to me and said, "Georgia, Fred Tucker, the chairman of the volunteers, was in an automobile accident last night and will not be able to return to the campaign. Ed and I want you to take over his position."

I mulled it over, "What would my duties be?"

"We are setting up a room for volunteers to come and address envelopes," she said. "They have to stuff and stamp them so they can then be mailed all over the state. You'd be in charge."

Having supervised so many people at the Census Bureau, I knew I could handle the job, so I accepted the position. This was in the days before computers, of course; so we first had to run the material off on an antiquated mimeograph machine. I felt like I was back in the time when I had been assigned dreaded household tasks by my mother. Once again, though, I made a schedule; I organized the duties and the volunteers, equipment, and supplies I needed for each. At least the humdrum tasks would proceed as quickly and efficiently as possible.

After working for a week, I found out that the other employees were receiving a hundred and ten dollars a week for their time. I immediately confronted June, saying, "I know others in the campaign who are making more than I am and I want what they are getting."

She said, "Georgia, I will talk to Ed and see what we can do." They knew my job at the Census Bureau was still waiting for me. The following morning, June came to my office and said, "Georgia, we will pay you the same."

June had taught me how to forge Wyatt's signature and sign his name in green ink, but I still had not met the man. He finally came into the office during my second week. June buzzed me, "Come into my office and meet the candidate."

When I walked in she smiled and introduced me: "Georgia Davis, this is Wilson Wyatt."

He reached out his hand and I shook it. He said, "I'm glad to meet you and we're glad to have you aboard."

I replied, "I am happy to have this experience and I hope you win."

My first impressions of the tallish, stocky, ruddy-skinned man with a double chin were positive. He had a hearty laugh and seemed affable. He spoke distinctly and had perfect diction. I learned later that he had debated in college and was well known for his mastery of the English language and his oratory.

The campaign work seemed endless. We mimeographed most of the campaign material; brochures had to be folded, never-ending envelopes addressed and stamped. We had extensive lists of voters from all over the state and kept a series of mailings going out.

For lunch each day, I went out to get a sandwich anywhere I could in downtown Louisville. Some of the White-owned restaurants had reluctantly opened their doors to Blacks, but I went to Black-owned establishments. After a while, I began to notice that the other campaign staff workers ordered their lunch from room service and simply signed the bill. There had been no mention of any such arrangement to me; I continued to go out alone. One day, I took a very long break. When I returned, June came over to me and said that volunteers had been there, but no one had known what to tell them to do. I had planned it that way; I wanted to be missed, in order to negotiate a better lunch arrangement.

June asked me politely, "Would you mind taking lunch in the hotel, so you'll be available if we need you?"

I met her eyes. "June, I'll stay here if I can order my lunch from the hotel restaurant and sign the check like everyone else. I'd also like to invite a volunteer to eat with me. I don't like eating alone every day." I should not have had to point out the obvious disparity in treatment to her, but when I did, she agreed to my terms.

During the next few weeks, President John F. Kennedy came to Louisville to help Wyatt's campaign. I was surprised that he was even more handsome in person than in his photographs. His rugged complexion and tousled hair made him look athletic and like a movie star. I stood in the receiving line with other campaign workers during the reception at the Seelbach Hotel. I was breathless as I struggled to say, "Good evening, Mr. President," in a calm voice. I couldn't believe I was actually shaking hands with him.

Watching the election momentum grow, and thinking about the opportunities for change it implied, I began to be intrigued by politics. The seeds had been planted.

Nevertheless, when it became evident on election night that Wilson Wyatt had lost, mine were the only dry eyes in the suite. I didn't have the emotional investment in this campaign that my other co-workers did. I hadn't known Wyatt before I went to work for him as many of them had. Also, my experience of having been hired as the "token Black" and having to remind the staff of the inequities in the pay and lunch arrangements had taken some of the enjoyment out of my work on the campaign.

Though I didn't know it then, my earlier desires for direction and meaning were germinating. They would eventually burst forth, empowering me to bring about personal, political, and social changes.

Immediately after Wyatt's defeat, I was recruited to work in another political campaign. Edward T. "Ned" Breathitt was running in the Democratic primary for governor in 1963. June Taylor managed his campaign headquarters and she asked me to work for him.

Breathitt, a lawyer from Hopkinsville, had served three terms in the Kentucky House of Representatives and later served as Personnel Commissioner under Governor Bert Combs. He had also been a member of the state's Public Service Commission.

Breathitt's major opponent in the Democratic primary was Governor Albert "Happy" Chandler. Chandler was seeking his third term. Previously, he had served two four-year terms as governor (1935-39 and 1955-59), had been baseball's second commissioner (1945-1951) and had served one term in the United States Senate (1939-45).

Our candidate won the primary and I was asked to begin working for him again in preparation for the general election right after Labor Day. By that time I had given up my job at the Census Bureau.

"I'll do it," I agreed, "but I have to have a job for the summer months." Party officials arranged for me to work in the Louisville offices of the Department for Human Resources.

In the fall, Breathitt won the gubernatorial election. Most of the office employees went to the state capitol with him, but no one even mentioned the possibility of my going to Frankfort. The only commendation I received was a letter from the new governor:

Dear Georgia:

I want to take this opportunity to commend you for your dedicated and effective efforts during our many months of campaigning. As a member of our headquarters staff, you can take justifiable pride in knowing that our victory was due in large measure to your devotion and hard work. I can repay my obligations only by justifying the confidence you have placed in me. With kindest regards and deepest appreciation.

Sincerely,
Ned.

He could also have repaid me with a job, but he didn't. Despite this, I soon had another offer, and, ironically, that job put me in the position of opposing the newly elected governor.

7

A
MEETING

Only two months had passed since the vibrant, young president who had shaken my hand had been assassinated, and the fight for the civil rights of Black people was still being fiercely waged in the South. In January 1964, Frank Stanley Jr., the editor of the *Louisville Defender*, a Black newspaper, organized a group to visit Governor Breathitt to discuss his position on civil rights in Kentucky. A bill outlawing discrimination in public accommodations and employment was pending in the legislature. Stanley had mobilized a group of Black and White Louisville leaders to meet with the governor and ascertain his position on the legislation. After leaving the meeting dissatisfied with Breathitt's response, they immediately organized the Allied Organization for Civil Rights. The AOCR was a coalition of groups whose sole purpose was to pass a law fighting discrimination in places of public accommodation.

Many civil rights leaders in Louisville, both Black and White, joined forces in AOCR. Frank Stanley Jr. and Dr. Olof Anderson, the White pastor of Central Presbyterian Church, were the co-chairmen. Eric Tachau, the White owner of an insurance agency and a community activist, served as treasurer. While it had been formed as a local organization, there was a network of people throughout the state who acted in support of AOCR. Lukey Ward, one of the volunteers I had worked with in the Wilson Wyatt campaign, was one of the group's leaders, and she recommended that I be hired to run the office.

Lukey had come to Louisville from Scarsdale, New York, with her husband Jasper, an architect. She had deeply tanned skin and wore her black hair in a short, straight cut with bangs. Years of sunning made her appear older than she was, but even after having five children, including a set of twins, she had still kept her attractive figure. When I met her during the Wyatt campaign, I had thought she was an affluent woman from the east end, but I found out later that her family often struggled financially. Still, I never knew her to have a paying job. In order to keep up the image of affluence, she had "hired help" answer the telephone when creditors would call the office. She was the second White woman with whom I would share a friendship and only the third member of my sex with whom I would break my childhood habit of keeping my private thoughts to myself.

Frank Stanley Jr. secured free space for the AOCR downtown in the Eli H. Brown building. It was on the corner of Third and Main Streets, one block south of the Ohio River. We were allotted two large rooms; one housed the office and the other served as a conference room.

The organization started with very little money and the National Office of the NAACP provided funds to partially equip and staff the office. To generate capitol, the

AOCR implemented a novel plan to issue and market stock in "The Interest of Human Dignity." Shares sold for a dollar each and became prized acquisitions of social, church, and school groups. Additionally, thanks to the diverse board of directors, other donations were obtained from many sources.

Such support was encouraging, but the group also faced interracial opposition. Congressman M. Gene Snyder spoke against AOCR. He labeled Roy Wilkins of the NAACP an "outside agitator" after Wilkins spoke at a mass rally held by the organization. Bishop C. Ewbank Tucker, respected seventy-year-old attorney, civil rights leader, bishop in the African Methodist Episcopal Church, and also pastor of the AME Zion Church, instructed his ministers and congregations to refrain from joining or supporting the group. The aging Tucker seemed to feel his leadership in the community waning, and, I believe, was embittered by not being included in the inception of the AOCR; he therefore spoke against it.

Bishop Tucker was a leader of the local Congress on Racial Equality (CORE). In his role as attorney, he had defended, with other lawyers, a local White couple. Carl and Anne Braden were charged with sedition for buying a house in a White neighborhood for a Black couple, Charlotte and Andrew Wade. Andrew, a licensed electrician, had been my classmate at Central High School and Charlotte was the sister-in-law of my brother Jay. The house the Bradens bought for the Wades was deliberately burned to the ground. Instead of going after the arsonists, the Commonwealth Attorney prosecuted Anne and Carl under a state sedition law. They were convicted and Carl served time in prison. He was later freed after all such laws were declared unconstitutional in a Pennsylvania case.

Frank Stanley Jr. was small in stature, but very aggressive. An attractive man in his twenties, he possessed a tireless energy. He had been the catalyst for ending segregation in most of the downtown businesses in 1961. In January of 1964, while Frank, Lukey, and I were planning the march on Frankfort, he suggested, that we contact the young, dynamic preacher and president of the Southern Christian Leadership Conference, Dr. Martin Luther King Jr., and Jackie Robinson to be our principal speakers.

Lukey said doubtfully, "It would be great if we could get them both—"

"How can we contact them?" I interrupted.

Frank replied, "My father worked with them both and has their phone numbers in his file. As a matter of fact, I met Dr. King when he was in Louisville in 1956."

A week later Frank walked into the office wearing a grin. "They have agreed to come," he announced proudly.

"Now we really have to get to work spreading the word about the march," Lukey said excitedly.

"I have a list of the NAACP chapters in Kentucky; let's send them a letter urging them to organize for March fifth," Frank said.

I added, "Frank, you'll have to travel to some of these cities to boost their interest. Let them know how important it is to be in Frankfort that day to show support for the Public Accommodations Bill."

Frank tapped the pencil he had been holding on the desk, "You and Lukey can handle the organizing from the office by phone. We must get social clubs, schools, and the churches involved."

I nodded my head in agreement, "Yes! If we can get their interest, we can increase our numbers greatly. There's a lot to do, Frank. We'll also need volunteers to help in the office and one paid secretary to aid in all the work we have ahead of us."

Frank agreed, "You hire a secretary."

I went to see Martha Cochran, a legal secretary I knew. At the time, she was unemployed. When I asked her to work with us, she enthusiastically agreed, but said sadly, "I'm not as energetic as I once was. The doctors have told me I have sickle cell anemia."

This was the first time I had heard of the disease. She explained, "It's genetic and most Negroes have it."

I looked at her closely; she did not show any signs of illness. She was an attractive, thirtyish, maple-skinned woman who wore her soft, dark hair in a pompadour. Despite her illness, she worked hard right along with the rest if us during the six weeks it took to organize the march.

Two weeks before the event, the Ohio River flooded and city officials were unable to locate the flood gates regulating our block. The water soaked into the basement of the Brown building, causing the power to shut off. Undaunted, Frank brought in gas-powered tanks for heat and light, and Lukey and I began organizing once again.

March fifth was now only a week away. Frank, Lukey and I met together to finalize plans for the march.

"I will be in Frankfort to make sure everything is in place, the platform constructed, the loudspeakers working, and the portable toilets in place. I have talked to K. L. Moore and he will be responsible for getting those things done," Frank said, referring to a Black minister. "He is organizing the other ministers in the bluegrass area—Frankfort, Versailles, Georgetown, and Lexington—and coordinating the rest of the incidentals. We can depend on him."

Frank continued, "Galen Martin is working hard, too. He is coordinating his people throughout Kentucky." Martin, the executive director of the Kentucky Commission on Human Rights, was using his board members and field workers to get the word out about the march.

"Lukey, I will need you in Frankfort with me to see that things are going smoothly," Frank went on. "The folk group Peter, Paul and Mary is coming into Frankfort on a private plane and will meet us at the platform. Georgia, we need you to arrange for Dr. King and Jackie Robinson to be picked up from Standiford Field Airport that morning. Bring them to Second Street and Capitol Avenue where the march will start. We'll walk east on Capitol Avenue for four blocks to the steps of the capitol building."

"We'll be there waiting for you," I said. "I'll take care of the transportation and see to it that they are there no later than 11:30 A.M.. I'll talk to my brother Lawrence who works for Hathaway and Clark Funeral Home, and get him to borrow a limousine."

Frank looked pleased, "Okay, did we send invitations to the members of the General Assembly asking them to participate?"

I laughed, "Yes, but they and the governor will probably take a holiday." The legislature had only ten more days in session before adjournment.

Although we had planned carefully, the closer the day came, the more nervous we grew. We badly wanted the march to be a success so that the members of the General Assembly would know that there was solid support for the Public Accommodations Bill from across the entire state and from all races of people. We were hoping for a good showing, somewhere around five thousand people, but with all the rain that had been falling, the weather could have proven to be a deterrent.

The sun was shining on the morning of the march, but it was cold and blustery. With trembling hands I began to get ready, first putting on a light gray wool dress. Over my dress I wore a darker grey cloth coat with a white mink collar and a wool scarf around my neck. My brother was right on time to pick me up.

The airport is five miles from downtown and can be reached in fifteen minutes from any part of Louisville. By 8:30 A.M. we had arrived. Two police escorts were parked there, waiting. They had Lawrence park directly in front of the airline. We went into the building to check on the flight arrivals and were relieved to find that both flights would be landing on time.

Jackie Robinson got there first. Many people recognized him, and they rushed toward him seeking autographs. He didn't seem to mind. I walked up and introduced myself, telling him that I was here to take him and Dr. King to Frankfort and that Dr. King's flight would arrive shortly.

"That's fine," he said. He was better-looking than he seemed to be on television, playing ball with the Brooklyn Dodgers. He was tall and his skin was a warm, mahogany brown. Most of his hair was gray, but it only complemented his skin color. His voice, though high-pitched, was pleasant, and his smile was genuine.

As the arrival time for Dr. King's flight moved closer, I grew ever more nervous and excited. This is the man I have admired for so long, I thought, a man who wants the same equality for all that I want, a man of great strength and courage, and a man who believes in non-violence, even under fire. I'm meeting him and I'll be able to talk with him. I felt so fortunate.

Minutes later, he strolled through the lobby of the airport. My heart quickened as I saw him move toward us. The first thing I noticed was his small stature. I was surprised; somehow, from his image on television or perhaps the one in my own mind, I had envisioned him being taller. His skin was a mahogany-bronze and he wore a thinly trimmed mustache above his full, shapely lips. His dark brown eyes looked straight into those of whomever he was addressing. He greeted Robinson, then turned to me and smiled.

"Dr. King," I said, hoping he wouldn't notice the slight tremble in my voice, "I'm Georgia Davis, a co-planner of the march, and this is my brother Lawrence who'll be driving us to Frankfort."

Lawrence said excitedly, "Is there anything you need before we leave?"

King answered in his long, drawn-out Southern accent, "No, I took care of everything before I deplaned. I believe I can make the trip alright." We all laughed.

We went out to the car; Robinson got in the front seat and King motioned for me to get in the back. One police car drove ahead of us and another picked up the rear.

For a few minutes we rode silently, then to open the conversation I asked, "Well, how was your flight?'

"It was a smooth and pleasant ride," he replied.

I wanted to keep the conversation going. Who knew if I'd ever get another chance to speak with this man I admired so much? I thought I had better make the most of my opportunity. I began, "Dr. King, I don't know how much you know about the Public Accommodations Bill that has been introduced in the Kentucky House of Representatives or what has transpired over the last few weeks. Allow me to inform you. The bill was introduced by Norbert Blume, who is a White business agent for the Teamsters union. The two Negro state representatives, Arthur L. Johnson and J. E. Smith, co-sponsored the bill. Unfortunately, right now there are not enough committed votes for it to pass."

"What else is AOCR doing to drum up support for its passage?" he asked.

"We have been working closely with several groups. The local chapters of the NAACP throughout the state; Galen Martin, the director of the state's Commission on

Human Rights; churches; schools; and social clubs have all been actively supporting us. We have asked all of them to urge their members to write or call their representative, stating their support for the bill and asking their elected officials to vote in favor of it," I replied fully.

He nodded, "That sounds like an effective strategy. Do you think it will work?"

"We are hoping the show of support today will sting them into doing the right thing. The problem is, Negroes are a minority in most of these small towns."

"What's the Negro population in Kentucky?" he asked.

"There are three million people and only seven percent are Negroes," I answered.

"Do most of them live in Louisville?"

"Yes, they make up thirty percent of the population there. The next largest number of Negroes lives in Lexington; the rest are scattered throughout Paducah, Owensboro and Hopkinsville."

King looked thoughtful. "Where does the governor stand on this bill?" he asked.

I grimaced, "Governor Breathitt has not helped. He has agreed to a compromise bill that covers fewer places of accommodation than ours, but we simply cannot accept the watered-down version. He could use his influence to get our bill out of committee if he wanted to, but so far, he hasn't."

He listened attentively as I talked, but I wanted his opinion, "Do you think the demonstrations will help? How long do you think we may have to demonstrate, march, and boycott?"

He replied, "We must illuminate the imperfections of an unjust society such as ours. We must continue marching in the streets of every city and every town to point out the faults in our democracy. This will not only get the 'Nee-gro' off his stool of do-nothingness, but will also awaken the White man's thinking."

As when I had seen him on television, the clarity of his words and thoughts struck a responsive chord within me. "Dr. King, I must congratulate you and the others for the gallantry shown during the Montgomery bus boycott. It was so successful; maybe we need to withdraw our money from other businesses that discriminate."

Again, he nodded, "It was the withdrawal of the money and support from the bus company that brought the demonstrations to a successful conclusion. We must use our bargaining power as consumers. The Negro spends his money and should be discreet in his choice of where he spends it."

I said, "Yes, we spend our money and often get no respect for it. There are department stores in Louisville—Kaufman-Strauss, Stewart's, Selman's, and Byck's—where they will sell quality clothes to Whites and Negroes alike, but until just two years ago, we were not permitted to try garments on before we purchased them, while the Whites were. There are several credit clothing stores like Lewis's and Olshine's where we can try on clothes but will pay more for less quality. Negroes and poor Whites bought clothing for their families there on installment plans."

King, his voice steel-edged, said, "That is just another case of man's inhumanity to man."

A moment or two of silence passed, then I said, "We patterned this march after the 1963 March on Washington."

"Were you there?" he asked.

I shook my head, "No, at that time I was busy working on Breathitt's gubernatorial campaign. I watched it on television. I now regret the choice I made."

His eyes held mine and a slight smile played on his lips, "How ironic, and now you are confronting him."

"I sure am," I said definitively.

As we approached the city limits, the streets were filled with cars. The temperature was dropping and a fine, icy sleet was beginning to fall. The police escort pressed through the heavy traffic for the last mile leading from Second Street onto Capitol Avenue, a wide boulevard with a large strip of grass in the center and two traffic lanes on either side.

Thousands of people, Black and White, lined the avenue. Lawrence stopped the car and got out, opening Robinson's door and then King's. When we got out, Frank Stanley Jr. was standing with Dr. Ralph Abernathy, Reverend Wyatt T. Walker, Dr. Olof Anderson, Reverend K. L. Moore, and Reverend D. E. King, all eagerly awaiting their chance to talk to Dr. King.

After the introductions had been made, it was at last time to start the march. The demonstrators formed behind the leaders and we began on our way. Proudly, nearly ten thousand people, cold and wet but determined, participated. After walking the four blocks, the speakers and special guests were escorted up the capitol steps and onto the platform. The group Peter, Paul and Mary was already there. Lukey and I had seats on the side of the platform since we were not part of the program. I said to her, "Can you believe the number of supporters who've come from all over?"

As we looked over the crowd, as far as our eyes could see there were people, huddled together shoulder to shoulder, trying to keep warm. The news had spread throughout Kentucky and beyond state lines. People were here to be a part of history.

We looked for legislators and the governor. The sponsors of the bill were there, but few other elected officials were present. A newsman leaned towards us, "The governor is in his office but refuses to come out and address the crowd."

Lukey looked puzzled, "What's he doing, then?"

The reporter grinned, "Nervously waiting for all of you to leave and go home." The friendly reporter continued, "In fact, to prepare for today, Governor Breathitt had asked Burke Marshall, the head of the United States Justice Department's Civil Rights Division, to advise him on arrangements for the march. Marshall told Governor Breathitt that President Johnson had invited the leaders of the march to meet with him in Washington immediately afterward. As this was being discussed, the governor asked, 'What was Lyndon going to serve the group?' Of course, the president wasn't going to serve anything, but to think that Breathitt's biggest concern was food when ten thousand people would be demonstrating for equality astonished me."

After the invocation by D. E. King, Frank opened the program, explaining the purpose of the march and what we were hoping to achieve. He exhorted the people to "leave here and continue putting pressure on your representatives by calling and writing, urging them to vote for the bill. They understand numbers and votes counted."

The program proceeded. Jackie Robinson spoke next, passionately telling of the discrimination he faced as the first Black major league baseball player. Afterward, Peter, Paul and Mary performed, their voices ringing out with freedom songs; asking the question, "How many years can some people exist before they're allowed to be free?"

Dr. King then warmed the crowd with his speech, eloquently verbalizing the innate injustice of being denied a hotel room or a decent meal because of the color of one's skin.

As he was speaking, I looked, listened and wondered, sure that the man I was watching lived under the inspiration, guidance, and protection of God. I responded strongly to the words he spoke and recalled the powerful speech he made at the March on Washington seven months before. I had been glued to the television while he spoke. When he reached the crescendo, repeating "I have a dream . . . ," I felt sure that my heart would burst with joy and pride. At the Frankfort march, I felt the same emotions, only more intensely because I was actually in the presence of this powerful man while he was speaking.

When the program ended, Dr. King went to the governor's office with eight of us; Frank Stanley Jr., Lukey Ward, Abernathy, Robinson, Walker, Moore, Anderson, and myself. As we walked through the reception room, June Taylor, now working for the governor, greeted us coolly. This saddened me; she and I had had a very good working relationship during our two campaigns together. She became office manager for Wilson Wyatt as United States senator and for Breathitt as governor. As she ushered the others through the door into the governor's office she said to me, "Georgia, I never thought you'd do something like this to Governor Breathitt."

"June," I replied, "when I was working for his campaign, I never thought he would refuse to offer me a job because of the color of my skin, or be afraid to support strong civil rights legislation."

"We can certainly find something for you if you're willing to commute or move to Frankfort," she hissed, obviously not having understood the meaning of my words.

"June, I'm working for AOCR now," I said, disgusted, and joined the others with the governor. Frank had introduced the guests to him by the time I caught up with the group. Breathitt was standing with them, shaking hands. When I went in, he looked up at me for moment and then simply nodded.

As was hoped, King led the discussion, "Governor, there are reportedly over ten thousand people on the capitol grounds today in support of public accommodations, Negroes and Whites, old and young, Democrats and

Republicans. We need your help. Lend the strength of your office to get the bill out of committee," he implored, looking Breathitt straight in the eye.

Breathitt turned his face away and evaded the request. "There are not enough votes to get the bill out," he said. King continued to press the governor, but to no avail. After thirty minutes, we left, disappointed and discouraged by the governor's remoteness and seeming lack of concern.

As we walked out of the office, Dr. King said, "That old governor is hard core. Did you see how he wiggled and squirmed around our questions and kept smiling?"

I said, "Yes, and you can bet that smile was to conceal his discomfort at our meeting on his doorstep and barging into his office without an appointment. He's not used to our kind walking in on him with our heads held high, looking him straight in the eye." We all laughed, but the sound did not soothe our bruised spirits. Leaving Frankfort, we returned to Louisville. There was not much conversation; we were tired from the busy day and the letdown we met at the hands of the governor.

King asked, "What are the plans for the AOCR now; what do you think will happen?"

I answered, "While we are battling to pass a Kentucky public accommodations law, other advocates are also urging Kentucky's congressmen to pass a national civil rights law. An interracial delegation of Kentucky leaders will be traveling to Washington, DC to express support for the proposed Federal Civil Rights Act. I don't believe our bill has the necessary support to pass this session of the General Assembly, but we will continue to drum up support for it in the 1966 legislature. Today's setback just means that we'll get a head start on our next challenge."

When we reached the airport, King and Robinson each had a half an hour wait for their flights. King politely said to me, "It isn't necessary for you to come into the airport, you've had a trying day. Thank you for what you have done and are continuing to do in the struggle for justice. Good-bye." He shook my hand.

Jackie Robinson also shook my hand, "Thank you for all you have done and for including me today. I bid you God's speed. Good-bye."

Lawrence walked with Robinson and King into the lobby of the airline. I waited outside, curled up in the car, trying to keep warm on the cold March afternoon.

Even after all our hard work, the bill still failed to get out of committee and was thus "dead" for the session. Immediately after the General Assembly adjourned, civil rights leaders began planning their strategy for the next legislative session; workshops were held throughout the state. The AOCR office closed.

IV

THE POLITICAL
YEARS

8

SMALL STEPS, BIG CHOICES

By late April 1964, I had established a reputation as an effective campaign organizer; so Norbert Blume, a state representative, asked me to be co-chairman of his campaign for the Third Congressional District seat. Blume was a handsome man, six feet two, about one hundred eighty pounds with a kind of Southern aristocratic bearing. His gray hair looked distinctive against the tan he always had, and he was always well-dressed. We liked each other as friends. There were whispers in some circles that we were more than that, but we were not. Since I was a novice politician, he taught me about both the clean and dirty sides of politics, impending dangers, and what to watch for.

The contest pitted Blume against Charles P. Farnsley, a Southern gentleman, whose black string tie was his trademark. He was a former mayor of Louisville, who was supported by the local Democratic organization while Blume was a trade unionist (as business agent for the dairy workers local of the Teamsters Union). Farnsley was a strong, effective legislator.

However, Farnsley was also a traditional politician. As mayor of Louisville from 1948 to 1953, he had supported the arts and pioneered the use of an occupational tax to fund local projects. He is credited with putting the city on a sound financial basis.

Blume challenged the party "regulars" who were rumored to be controlled by Lennie W. McLaughlin, the paid party secretary who had devoted her life to her job. "Miss Lennie," as she was called by most party regulars—I refused to address her as "Miss"—had a coldly calculating attitude and a way of talking down to people which I disliked intensely. Many said she was the "Boss." Although Lennie never held public office herself, she had much power in deciding who would be a candidate. She had begun working for the Democratic Party in the early 1920s as a grass-roots organizer. As a result of a power struggle with the faction headed by Mayor Joseph Scholtz, she was ousted as party secretary in 1939. In 1947, she was again elected Democratic Party secretary and wielded political power until she retired.

Lennie managed to have under her control a few Blacks in each precinct who worked for the city. Blume's headquarters were set up in the local Democratic headquarters. One day when I accidentally picked up the telephone on the line she was using I heard her say, "We can win the election this fall if we can get the niggers out to vote."

Upset and angry, I went to Tommy Carroll, the county chairman of the Democratic Party. "Tommy," I said emotionally, "you are going to have to do something about that old woman. I will not sit here and be insulted by her."

"Georgia," Tommy replied, "I promise I will speak to her and if it happens again I will take her before the Executive

Committee." This incident and Lennie's hateful attitude towards so many people caused me to dislike her. Rage swells up in my chest whenever I am discriminated against. Sometimes it takes years for me to find a resolution, but I never forget it.

The campaign between Blume and Farnsley turned nasty when Farnsley charged that Blume worked for Jimmy Hoffa, the national head of the Teamsters Union accused of having mob connections. Norbert, of course, had no ties to Jimmy Hoffa, other than working for a local of the Teamsters, a fact which his constituents were well aware of when they elected and reelected him as their state representative. I had evidence the Farnsley campaign resorted to dirty tricks, such as having one of their workers, Sam Jones, take the certified election papers of the captain of my precinct, because she supported Blume. She had been certified by the election commission, and I reported Jones's action to them.

My contacts with local and state Democrats continued. As co-chairman of the Blume for Congress campaign, I was involved in making strategy plans. Blume, who had been active in the Teamsters Union for years, knew many national figures. We invited Senator Robert F. Kennedy, the brother of the slain president, to speak. He was already being spoken of as a future presidential candidate, and we felt his appearance in Louisville would boost the lagging campaign. Because of his own hectic schedule, Kennedy could only fly into town for a short visit, so we decided to have a reception at the airport. The meeting place was a hangar in a small airport next to Standiford Field. Kennedy would be landing there in a private aircraft. We built a platform, decorated the stage with red, white, and blue banners and streamers, and had Blume's posters in the background. To prepare for Kennedy's visit we mailed a thousand invitations to Blume supporters; then we set up a phone bank to follow up on the invitations. More than five hundred people attended.

Meeting the flight, we formed a receiving line; Blume introduced each of us to Kennedy. When it was my turn he said, "Senator Kennedy, meet my co-chairman, Georgia Davis." I nervously added, "Senator Kennedy, I am pleased to meet you. Thank you for coming." We led him to a private room to brief him on Blume's accomplishments and his stand on national issues, but Kennedy had received Blume's biography in the mail and he'd already familiarized himself with it. Finding this out, we took him to the platform to speak to the crowd. He spoke for twenty-five minutes, then departed.

I was surprised, but pleased, when I later received a letter from him.

Dear Mrs. Davis,

It was good of you to assist in the preparations for my trip to Louisville this fall. I meant to write to you sooner. I thoroughly enjoyed my visit and thought the day was a wonderful success, due in no small part, I am sure, to your efforts. Thank you for everything. With best wishes.

Sincerely,
Robert F. Kennedy.

While my foothold in politics was becoming firmer, it was causing trouble at home. Nicky, basically an introverted person who was content to live a quiet personal life with his family, resented my political activities. They brought public exposure and were taking more and more of my time.

Nicky was drinking too much and staying away from home more and more. I was trying to make my marriage work, but Nicky felt threatened. When he had attended the reception for President John F. Kennedy with me, Nicky had felt so out of place that he said, "It's the last such function I'll ever go to." In the spring of 1964 Nicky bought a small house on Wilson Avenue and moved out.

In the primary election, Blume lost his bid to represent the Democratic Party for the Third Congressional seat, but his campaign served as a catalyst. After the primary election, a committee was formed to launch a grass-roots reorganization of the party. Members of this steering committee were Phillip Ardery, Kathleen Carroll, William Friedlander, Howard Haynes, J. Benjamin Horton, Thomas Mooney, Paul Sweitzer, Eric Tachau, Lukey Ward, Edgar Zingman, and I.

But I was lonely and so was Nicky. On Labor Day that year, Billy and I were home alone. Loneliness will lead you to do many things that you wouldn't do if you listened to your common sense. As I sat there that day on my porch, I decided to call Nicky. He invited me to dinner and I went. During the evening we talked about our marriage and our desire to give Billy a home with two parents in it. We agreed to try living together again. I rented my house on Cecil Avenue and Billy and I moved in with him.

A life in politics had become my goal. I decided to run for district chairman, wanting to have a seat on the Democratic Executive Committee. It would be a position of power, and offer a way for me to bring about changes to benefit Blacks and the poor of every race. I went door to door gathering support from committeemen and committee-women in the Fortieth District.

The Irvin Whitehouse Paint Company was located directly across the street from Nicky's house on Wilson Avenue, and we had become friends with its president, Robert "Bob" Whitehouse. Bob's was the largest contract painting business in Kentucky. His company painted bridges all over the country. After making my decision, I walked across the street to Bob Whitehouse's office and said, "Bob, I plan to run for the Democratic chairman of the Fortieth Legislative District and I need your help." I explained to him that the district was comprised of twenty-two precincts, and what I had to do.

He looked intently at me. "Well, Georgia, I've never been involved in politics, but what can I do to help?"

I said, "The first thing I need to do is send a letter to some key Democrats who are consistent voters. They will be the ones who will show up."

Bob said, "Explain to me just how these elections work."

"As you know," I replied, "I have been working in campaigns for the last two years and I have met many Democrats, plus I have the list which includes the name, address, and when they voted last. This is called a sidewalk election."

Bob leaned toward me, obviously intrigued. "I've never heard of them, but—"

"On the Saturday following the President's election every four years," I interrupted, "Democrats meet at two in the afternoon to vote for one committeewoman and one committeeman from each precinct. The following Saturday, the elected committee members go to a place designated by headquarters and meet at two o'clock to vote for the chairman. By virtue of this office, you become a member of the Jefferson County Democratic Executive Committee. This committee sets the policy for the party."

Bob rubbed his thinning blond hair and said, "Yes, let's do it."

When the Democratic headquarters officials learned that I was organizing the district, they put up a Black man who was rumored to be under their control as a candidate. His name was Tom Jackson. Jackson was a city sanitation employee and it was also rumored that Lennie had great influence over him. Since I was running in a predominantly Black district, Democratic officials knew they had to have another Black oppose me. They would not risk supporting me, because they didn't know me and didn't have any leverage to exercise control over me.

At that time, there were two opposing factions in the party. One was headed by Oldham Clarke, an attorney; the other was led by Mary Helen Byck, a businesswoman who was a national Democratic committeewoman, and Norbert Blume.

Byck and Blume's faction opposed the regular Democratic organization, because they believed the party needed a broader base. Eleven candidates, including another Black man, J.E. Smith, were running for district chairmanship as doubly slated candidates—meaning they were endorsed by both factions. I was the only candidate targeted for defeat by the party regulars led by Lennie McLaughlin. On the day of the election, she sent one of her "big guns," attorney Sam Stallings, to my district.

Sam Stallings was a ruddy-complexioned man in his fifties and was dressed in typical "lawyer clothes"—a white shirt, striped tie, and a well-worn suit with wing-tipped black shoes. His brown eyes held a look of surprise when he saw me and we first spoke. In order to hear us, sixty people crowded into the hall with no chairs. The half-hour meeting was much longer than prior meetings, when the outcome had been set before the vote by those at Democratic headquarters. This time was different, because there was opposition to the party regulars.

I went to the election armed with a copy of *Robert's Rules of Order* in case I ran into parliamentary trouble. That precaution proved a pivotal one. After the temporary chairman, James Mulligan, opened the meeting, I made a motion and moved towards the chairman, waving the little red book.

"Mr. Chairman, I move that all votes taken today be taken by secret ballot." The motion was seconded by one of my supporters. I knew I had to have a secret ballot, because the party regulars who wanted to support me would not dare do so openly for fear of retribution from "Miss Lennie."

Stallings, one of Lennie's followers, spoke up. "No, we can't do that."

"Mr. Chairman, we have a motion on the floor," I called out. I raised my *Robert's Rules of Order*, turned to a random page, and said in a strong, firm voice, "Mr. Chairman, it states right here in this book that this is a proper motion."

He had no choice but to put the motion to a vote saying, "All in favor of voting a secret ballot, raise your right hand. Now, only elected committee people can vote." After the vote, the chairman appointed counters from each side to count the ballots as the candidates looked on.

Before we went into the building, I met a young, blond-haired couple. I introduced myself to them and asked them to vote for me. The man said, "I'm Clarke Fenimore and this is my wife, Pat. This is our first time participating in this kind of election." They did not make a commitment then, but as the vote was being taken and I handed them each a blank ballot, our eyes met and they blinked their eyes a certain way to let me know they would vote for me. Their vote turned out to be key.

My motion carried, and I passed out the sheets of paper I had brought. There were forty-two votes, and I won by two. However, the Oldham Clarke faction claimed eleven of the seventeen slots for committee persons. The party regulars who had opposed me ignored my election. Immediately following the election, the new Jefferson County Democratic Executive Committee met to select a chairman and a secretary. Thomas C. Carroll, a local attorney, won the chairmanship, and Lennie McLaughlin was elected secretary again.

The Democratic Executive Committee now had two Blacks—J.E. Smith and me. Chairman Carroll said, "This is the headquarters of *all* Democrats in Jefferson County." He paid his respects to several "outside groups." The outside groups were Negroes, labor groups, young Democrats, and citizen committees who had campaigned for candidates without regular party endorsement.

Carroll went on to proclaim, "The Democratic Party should tackle the specific problems which face our Negro citizens and our responsibility should be that there be acceptance of the rights now guaranteed to them by law." Carroll proposed, and the Executive Committee created, sixteen subcommittees for the purpose of broadening the base of the party. I was appointed chairman of the Women's Committee. My responsibilities were to recruit women for volunteer work on the precinct level during elections, and to act as liaison between the regular organization and Democratic clubs. A Black person was appointed to every subcommittee.

The Community Relations Committee dealt almost exclusively with improving the relationship between Blacks and the Democratic Party. In the 1930s, President Franklin D. Roosevelt and the Democratic Party had wooed many area Blacks from the Republican Party, the party of Lincoln. However, growing numbers of Blacks were now voting Republican because of what they considered a conservative local Democratic organization.

This disillusionment with the Democratic Party had reached a peak in 1961 when black voters cast large blocks of votes for Republican candidates for local office. The Democratic nominee for mayor, William S. Milburn, a high school principal and president of the Board of Aldermen, was quoted as saying, "I don't need the Black vote to win." The Republican candidate for mayor, William Cowger, subsequently won. Republican Marlow Cook won the county judge's office. Many attributed the Democratic loss to the failure of Democrats to support a proposed ordinance to prohibit discrimination in public accommodations, and to Milburn's arrogant statement.

To help gain Black voters, I went to Tommy Carroll and told him, "You ought to hire a Black person for the headquarters office. The only Black here is a janitor." After a few more well-chosen words, Carroll agreed and asked me to recommend someone.

"What about Maxine Caldwell?" I asked, naming a woman I had met who worked with the Allied Organization for Civil Rights. Maxine was about thirty-five and always fashionably dressed. She kept her wavy hair shoulder length and curled. She and her husband had moved to Louisville from Danville, Kentucky, a small town. I knew she wasn't a good typist, but most of the work required cataloguing registered voters and giving information over the telephone, which I felt Maxine could handle.

Carroll interviewed her, and quickly turned her down because she couldn't take shorthand. When I heard about it I asked, "Tommy, why did you reject Maxine Caldwell for the job? I think she is the ideal person for it."

He said, "Now Georgia, I interviewed the young lady, but she can't type or take shorthand."

Rage swelled up in my chest again. I shot back, "You know as well as I that Kate Smith has been here umpteen years and she has never taken shorthand nor typed." I was getting louder and more emphatic. "The job doesn't call for those skills anyway. It is mostly answering the phone, giving voter precinct information and filing registration cards. Now Tommy, what is the *real* problem?"

He could see I was upset and said quietly, "Have her come in again and I will reconsider her."

When she went back, he hired her. I lived to regret my

action, however. In my opinion, Maxine picked up Lennie's hateful manner and was rude and arrogant with voters. She fought me in every election in which I was involved.

I was eager to serve on the Jefferson County Democratic Executive Committee. Jefferson County had a population of more than 610,000 people, including those who lived in the only first-class city in Kentucky. Louisville and ninety-four small cities encompass Jefferson County. The Ohio River flows from Cincinnati southwestward and curves around Louisville on both the north and south sides. Louisville's population was more than 390,000. The Black population was 18 percent of the city and 13 percent in the county. Kentucky has been called the "gateway to the South" and the "backdoor to the North." It is also referred to as a Border State, neither South nor North. Kentuckians fit that image. They are not as swift as Northerners, yet not as slow as Southerners. Some call them laid back.

In that climate, I felt I could make a difference. My great-grandmothers weren't even allowed to vote, and here I was serving in a leadership position in the Democratic Party. I owed it to my ancestors to work for changes to improve the lives of Blacks and make what I considered positive suggestions to the Executive Committee.

To continue developing my political connections, I supported Marlin Volz, a law professor at the University of Louisville, for mayor. He had won the primary election in May and the general election in November was fast approaching. Kenneth Schmied, Volz's opponent, was a Republican running for a second term. Volz was a quiet, retiring man with dark blond hair trimmed high above his ears and glasses. He looked like a typical professor and didn't seem like the type to make a good politician.

Since I was elected chairman of the Fortieth Legislative District, it was important for him to have my support. I determined who the precinct captains and workers were at the polls. In August I gave a coffee klatch for him in my back yard in August. Thirty-five people came. This was the year the Democrats were placing emphasis on neighborhoods to convince voters the Democrats, not the Republicans, were interested in their welfare.

Volz had been to a plant in the morning, shaking hands with workers. He looked out of place and unlike a working man. Despite this, I introduced him as "Our next Mayor of the City of Louisville," not really believing it myself and wondering how the Democrats had selected him.

As we stood under a hundred-year-old silver maple tree, Volz said, "President Johnson wants to build a great society, and great societies are built on great cities. This was a lower-middle-class neighborhood. We have been walking the streets of this neighborhood, and talked to many of the residents, to develop a tailor-made plan for neighborhood improvement."

After his speech I announced, "There are plenty of doughnuts and coffee. Please help yourself."

Volz drifted about shaking hands. He said to an older White man, "Wasn't this a nice meeting?" I overheard the man respond, "There's three things I don't like—a Communist, a Ku Klux, and a Republican."

Later, I escorted Volz around the neighborhood to greet people and shake hands. Passing out bumper stickers to those who wanted them, we stood in front of a neighborhood shopping district where there was some pedestrian traffic. Walking over to Volz I said, "There's a lady over here who wants two bumper stickers. She's a *double* Democrat."

"Ah," he said, "one in the front and one in the back."

"No, she's got two cars", I replied.

"Oh, a two-car Democrat, that's fine."

In November, despite my support for Volz, Kenneth Schmied won his second term as mayor of Louisville.

The Democratic Executive Committee was holding monthly meetings, which I attended, at its headquarters. I was the only woman on the committee. Each meeting I would offer suggestions for change. "Mr. Chairman," I said one day, "you have asked this committee for suggestions to improve the image of the Democratic Party since the first loss of the mayor's office to the Republicans three years ago. Democrats outnumber registered Republicans by a two-to-one margin in this county. There have never been more than two Blacks out of twelve on the Board of Aldermen." Lennie McLaughlin flashed me a mean look. I continued, "Mr. Chairman, we need a better system to nominate aldermen. We could get the law changed to nominate aldermen by ward in the primary election and elect them citywide in the general election in November. There are four wards with sixty-five percent Black voters and a fifth with more than fifty percent." I looked at J.E. Smith, the only other Black on the committee, to support me, but he sat there like the other fifteen White men, most of whom were in their sixties. There were ten lawyers; one district judge; one medical doctor; one bank vice-president; one owner of an insurance agency; and Smith, who was an officer in the Black-owned Domestic Life Insurance Company.

Carroll said, "Georgia, we will take this suggestion under advisement."

That was the last time it was brought up. The party did not encourage Blacks to vote in the May primary. The Black city employees and city workers were urged to vote for the party-supported candidate. They would tell Black voters, "You want to vote in the *big* election in November."

Even though I felt discouraged, I didn't give up making suggestions.

9

SELMA

Martin Luther King had announced on January 2, 1965, that a new and more militant phase of the civil rights movement would be initiated in Selma, Alabama. "We are not asking, we are demanding the ballot," he said decisively.

His brother, Reverend A. D. Williams King, had been called to Louisville to pastor Zion Baptist Church in November, 1964. A.D. was pudgy, medium-brown-skinned, with a full face, and was about 5'8" tall. He was one of the more liberal Baptist ministers in Louisville. He allowed non-preachers and women to speak from the podium of his church—unlike most of the Black Baptist ministers, whose guests had to speak from a side lectern. A.D. and I once talked about this issue. I reasoned it was an ego thing with the other preachers: This is my pulpit and I will not let an outsider invade it. I asked him if a minister's pulpit was holy ground. He said, "Only if the one standing there is holy."

We laughed, and I responded, "Well in that case a lot of them shouldn't be there!"

A.D. loved his brother, Martin Luther, whom he called M.L. He helped him in whatever he was asked to do. A.D. once told me that he did not want to be a preacher, but wanted to be a mortician. He said being a minister was forced upon him by his strong-willed father and domineering mother. I liked A.D. and respected his abilities. However, I always felt he had an inferiority complex about being in the shadow of his brother. This, I also believe, had a lot to do with his drinking problem.

Now, in a demonstration of solidarity with his brother, A.D. invited some Louisville leaders to his church to discuss the Selma March. Most of the fifteen people who attended were prominent ministers: Reverends G. K. Offutt, F. G. Sampson, Charles Kirby, Charles Elliott, Jeffrey Joseph, B. J. Miller, William Summers III, and others were there. Lukey and I were the female exceptions. Reverend King said, "My brother M.L. called and asked me to organize a contingency of Kentuckians to participate in the fifty-mile march from Selma, Alabama to Montgomery. I want to know how you feel about it, and if we should get involved."

William Summers III stood up and said, "It is my personal opinion that we should do whatever we can do to assist in the struggle. Do you have any suggestions?"

King replied, "There are several things we can do. We can raise money to help, or we can physically help by participating with our bodies. How do the rest of you feel about it? The March began on Sunday, March seventh, when my brother gave his approval for Reverend Hosea Williams to lead several hundred demonstrators to the Pettus Bridge in Selma. You have seen the news and the blood bath that took place there."

Almost in unison they replied, "Yes, we want to do something." We quickly organized a committee. Summers was unanimously elected to chair what we called "Operation Selma."

King said, "We need someone to take notes. Lukey, will you accept being secretary of the group?"

She answered, "Yes, if no one asks to read the notes."

We laughed. A.D. said, "The church has the little house next door that we use for a nursery, but we can clear the front room out for an office."

Later that day I smiled when I saw it; it was a three-room shot-gun house. A hall led from the back door of the house into the church. A.D. looked at me and said, "Will you manage the office for us?"

I shook my head affirmatively, "Yes, I will."

King, thinking of how to transport the marchers to Alabama, had already checked out the availability of the Purdue University football plane. He told us, "The plane will cost thirty-two hundred dollars to lease. It will be available March twenty-fourth. We have little more than a week to raise the money."

Someone asked, "How will we do it?"

Several suggestions were made. The final plan was to hold a rally and take up donations. The ministers said they would take up special collections at their churches.

Lukey had assumed her familiar stance, standing with her bare, shapely legs set wide apart in her high heels. I saw some of the ministers looking at her with lustful eyes, and bit my lip thoughtfully.

King said, "Although M.L. will be at the march, he won't be able to be at the rally, but I can get Ralph Abernathy to come."

Lukey said, "There are a lot of rich White folk who ought to donate to the cost of the plane. Georgia and I can get on the phone and solicit money if some of you can pick it up." Elliott, Joseph, and Kirby volunteered.

I turned to her, "I don't know any rich White people."

She laughed, "I'll make up a list. We have one weekend to get them."

"Okay," I said. "I'll make the calls."

King, who'd been listening, added, "I have two phones in my office that you can use."

Lukey nodded, "We can start Friday."

"That will be fine," King replied.

Lukey and I spent Friday and Saturday soliciting money on the phones. As soon as we got the agreement from a person to donate, we sent one of the ministers to pick up the money. We wanted to be sure there was no time lag where someone could change his or her mind. In two days we collected more than three thousand dollars.

On Sunday, the ministers announced from their pulpits that there would be an "Operation Selma" rally on Tuesday night. They urged their congregations to attend. Zion Church was filled to capacity. It was estimated there were more than five hundred people. Abernathy spoke. He said, "In Selma we are dealing with Sheriff James Clark, an avid, shrewd segregationist. It was just a little more than a month ago that Reverend James Bevel was beaten unmercifully and Jimmie Lee Jackson was murdered. You have seen on national television how the demonstrators, Black and White, led by Reverend Hosea Williams on the Edmund Pettus Bridge, were brutally beaten." Anger and rage showed on the faces of the people as Abernathy told of the inhumanity of the state law enforcement officers. He continued, "Governor George Wallace has a ban on marches, but we are going to defy his unjust law for a higher moral law." Cries of, "Amen!" often interrupted him.

The rally was effective, but we wanted participants at

the march from other cities, too. A.D. contacted several ministers he knew from Lexington and had them announce the trip to Selma from their pulpits. Several people called and wanted to go. Pauline Gould Gay came from Lexington with a male friend, and two people came from Winchester, Kentucky.

At 8:15 A.M. on Wednesday, March 24, 1965, forty-six people boarded the Purdue University plane. There were ten White people, including Maxine Buchman, a teacher at Manual High School; Beth Bogue; Lukey Ward; Ruby Ezelle, wife of the executive director of the Kentucky AFL-CIO; and others. Lukey and I sat together.

We landed at the Atlanta Airport to pick up Dr. Martin Luther King Jr., Ralph Abernathy, and several staff persons. They boarded the plane. As they walked down the aisle, Dr. King stopped near my seat, bent down, and said, "Hello. It's good to see you again. I'm glad you are here." Then he straightened up and walked on to the rear of the plane. A. D., Sampson, Summers, and other preachers were already seated. At the Montgomery Airport, we deplaned. It was dusk.

We walked out to Highway 80 where the marchers were waiting for us. They had marched forty-five miles from Selma. Dr. King walked up to Harry Belafonte, who stood at the head of the line. They talked a few minutes as we started lining up to continue the march to the St. Jude Church complex, where a program filled with nationally known entertainers was to be performed that night on a makeshift stage. A.D. came to Lukey and me and said, "We're going to a lady's home to spend the night." We nodded and he continued, "Sampson is going with us."

The lady whom A.D. had mentioned drove us to a small one-story frame house with two bedrooms. She gave her room to Lukey and me. Sampson and A.D. stayed in the other bedroom.

The march reassembled the next morning on Highway 80 outside St. Jude's. The weather was much warmer and I had on ankle-high fur-lined boots. They were the wrong type shoes for marching, and made my feet too warm on the unusually hot asphalt. I took out a pair of soft, leather, flat shoes from my case and switched from one pair to the other. The downpour of rain during the night made the air steamy. As we marched the last leg of the fifty miles, the highway filled with spectators, including some White people who waved Confederate flags and yelled racial epithets. Many Blacks, some who were elderly, some even in wheelchairs, lined the highway. A.D., Lukey, Sampson, and I kept together. We had started out in the fourth line of marchers but drifted further back as we soldiered on. Now we were marching in front of the flag bearer.

As we walked, I saw Dr. King's humbleness. I saw his concern for the downtrodden. Many times he went to the side of the road to shake hands with an old person in tatters, say a kind word to a drunk, and rub the head of a child. He talked to them personally, and he listened. Meanwhile, as the march continued, others fell right in line and joined us. When we arrived in downtown Montgomery, thousands cheered us.

We came to Dexter Avenue, where Dr. King had once pastored the Dexter Avenue Baptist Church. There we stopped for a few minutes. Lukey and I went into the church to freshen up before the program. A.D. walked over to us. "Meet me in front of the church afterward," he said.

We started marching again, soon reaching the Alabama capitol. Lukey and I stood in the crowd listening intently as Dr. King began to speak. First he referred to the past week's struggles in Selma.

"They told us we wouldn't get here, and there were those who said we would get here over their dead bodies, but all the world today knows that we are here . . ."

Then, slowly, his voice increased in loudness and power as he asked and began answering the question:

"How long will it take?"

He gave the final reply:

"Not long, 'cause my eyes have seen the glory of the coming of the Lord, trampling out the vintage where the grapes of wrath are stored. He hath loosed the fateful lightening of his terrible swift sword. His truth is marching on."

The crowd stood up, almost in unison. The people roared their approval, stomping their feet and applauding.

At approximately the same time, Joseph Lowery, an Southern Christian Leadership Conference board member, led a delegation into the capitol attempting to deliver a petition for redress of grievances to Governor George Wallace. They were met by resistance from the guards and his assistants. The delegation persisted in seeing the Governor, but were told he had left for the day.

Meanwhile, in Selma, the crowd began to thin out; Lukey and I waited in front of the church. A.D. King and Sampson walked up to us. A.D. said, "Follow us to the parking lot." King had arranged to use someone's car. Lukey sat in the front seat with A.D. The sun was going down and darkness was falling. We drove on Highway 80 towards the airport. The traffic was heavy and moving slowly, bumper to bumper.

When we reached the airport we heard tragic news: Viola Liuzzo, one of our volunteers, had been shot and killed while transporting Negro passengers back to Selma.

As we wearily trudged towards our plane, we saw a small group of people surrounding a man lying on the concrete floor. To our surprise, it was A. Phillip Randolph, a Black man who had organized the Brotherhood of Sleeping Car Porters. He had apparently passed out from exhaustion.

Boarding the plane, we checked the list as the passengers entered. We returned to Louisville, minus one volunteer, after an exhausting but memorable experience.

Days passed uneventfully. Nights quietly.

Then, one morning I awoke startled from a dream I'd been having. Dr. Martin Luther King Jr. and I had been together in a hotel room. He was nude, and we were about to make love. I was frightened, as I had no conscious sensual attraction towards him. I didn't know what to make of this vision, whether it was a premonition, a subconscious wish, or whether I should just shrug it off for what it was—a dream.

I tried to analyze my past meetings with Dr. King. The brief time we had spent together riding to Frankfort and back, and the brief moment we'd spoken while on the plane to Selma were the only times I had ever met him.

Badly jarred, I telephoned Lukey. She'd been in analysis for years, and had spoken to me about the meanings of dreams. I thought she might know something about the mystic powers of the mind that I didn't know. "It sounds like it may be a Freudian dream," Lukey said pensively.

"But why would I dream such a dream when I have no sexual thoughts of Dr. King whatsoever?" I asked agitatedly. She continued to try to explain different theories to me that she didn't completely understand, and I didn't believe.

There was no resolution. I finally said, "I'll just get a dream book, Lukey, and check it out for myself. I've seen them in the drug stores." I could hear her half-stifled laugh.

10

MOVING
AHEAD

After two years of trying to be effective on the Executive Committee, my discouragement turned into complete depression. I went to a meeting with my letter of resignation in my hands. I said, "Mr. Chairman, I have served on the Jefferson County Democratic Committee for two years and not one of my proposals has been discussed. I hereby tender my resignation." No one objected.

In January 1966, Norbert Blume got me a job in the Kentucky House of Representatives during the legislative session. I worked in the "bill room." Each day of the session, I put the bills which had been filed onto the representatives' desks. This gave me an opportunity to be on the floor of the House and to get to know the members. During that session, I had the chance to see government functioning firsthand; ambition grew within me.

A career in politics, I now felt, was the divining rod by which I could tap into my inner reservoirs. This focus, this centering for which I'd always searched, unleashed a deep but hidden well of strength within me—to fight for those things I knew to be right and just.

Kentucky civil rights groups made plans to lobby for passage of an anti-discrimination law in this session. It had been expanded to include the arena of employment. Neither Governor Breathitt, the legislators, nor the civil rights leaders wanted another split like the one which occurred in 1964. They all backed a broad bill which was taken from the model act of a national group.

Representative Lloyd Clapp, a newly elected thirty-nine-year-old Democrat from Wingo, was seated at his desk one day. As I handed out the bills, he announced, "I see no reason to change things from the way they are. If I voted for that bill, the people in my district would never send me back here again." I didn't say what I was thinking, which was that they probably shouldn't. I had been told he was against the bill, so his poor attitude was no surprise. Sensing I was about to question his position, he hurriedly got up from his desk, smoking a cigarette, and rushed out of the chamber. Inside I felt hurt again, because I knew I was being judged by the color of my skin.

When he returned to his seat, I made a prophetic statement to him: "What I need is my own seat in here. I will vote right and do what is fair for all people." He said nothing.

Blume had several co-sponsors on the bill, including Jesse Warders, the only Black member of the legislature. Warders, a forty-nine-year-old Republican, was a real estate and insurance broker from Louisville.

The proposed anti-discrimination law prohibited racial discrimination by employers of eight or more people. It provided that all places of public accommodation—except barbers, beauty shops, and rooming houses—be open to all races. The enforcement provisions were among the most comprehensive and complete in the country. The bill gave the Kentucky Commission on Human Rights the enforcement power it needed to ensure that individuals and groups within the state complied with the law.

Several House leaders spoke eloquently for the passage of the bill. Warders was dynamic. He said:

> It is altogether wrong that I should have to . . . speak on the issue of the civil rights bill. It is not wrong that I should do so but wrong that I *have* to do so.
>
> It is wrong, but nevertheless true, that in 1966 Negroes are turned away from places of public accommodations in Kentucky because of the color of their skin.
>
> It is wrong, but true, that in our state, qualified Negroes are denied equal access to job opportunities.
>
> It is wrong, but true, that each year Kentucky loses the cream of the crop of Negro college graduates . . . because they are unable to find meaningful work.

Warders was applauded. The civil rights leaders had done their homework well. The 1966 Civil Rights Act passed the House of Representatives, seventy-six votes to twelve. The act passed the Senate thirty-six to one. On January 27, at the base of the statue of Abraham Lincoln in the capitol rotunda, Governor Breathitt signed the historic act. Attending the signing were Reverend A.D. Williams King and Robert Estill, chairman of the Kentucky Commission on Human Rights.

At this point Billy and I were still living in Nicky's house. It was very small and I didn't like the neighborhood. I heard that our old house on Cecil Avenue was being vacated, and I wanted to move there in order to transfer my voting registration. That way I'd be in position to run for office. I convinced Nicky to move back, but I didn't tell him any of my political reasons. I knew without a discussion that it wouldn't make him happy, and I was unwilling to give up my plans.

During this period I continued to nurture my political contacts. Henry Ward, the state highway commissioner, announced he would run for governor in 1967. Attorney General Robert Matthews was being urged to challenge him in the primary, and I backed Matthews. On the Republican side, Jefferson County Judge Marlow W. Cook and Louie Nunn, an attorney from the city of Glasgow, were running against each other in the primary election.

One morning I picked up the *Courier-Journal* and saw that state Senator Bernard Bonn, who represented west Louisville's Thirty-third District, had announced he was moving out of the district and into the east end of town. My opportunity had arrived. I knew I had to seize it. Senator Bonn had been in the Kentucky Senate for fifteen years. I researched his record, however, and could not find a single bill he'd introduced in all that time. He was a party regular, and it was said he had always consulted with Miss Lennie before voting. I knew I could represent my district better than he had.

No longer could I keep my plans secret. I talked to Nicky about running for Bonn's seat. "If that's what you want to do, it's okay with me," he said quietly. But he didn't mean those words. My senatorial campaign was the final blow to our marriage.

Politics, for me, had not been a life-long ambition. Once I got a taste of it, however, I knew I had found my place. I went from volunteer to committeewoman to member of the Executive Committee of the Jefferson County Democratic Party, and finally, to running for office. Once I knew what I wanted, I pursued my political career with all my abilities—those I had acquired from family genes and upbringing, and those gained from my life experiences.

I approached politics with the philosophy I have held most of my life: Be open to new opportunities and reach out to people, but watch out for those who would take advantage of you. Once it is determined that someone is working against your best interests, bide your time and use your brain to figure out how to come out on top.

To win the Senate race, I knew I had to do two things— raise money and organize. I believed I could do both. I didn't ask local Democratic officials for their permission to run. It was not that I was defying them; I was just too new to the political game to know that I was expected to get their approval.

Instead I made my own plans, asking Addie Thomas, a soft spoken older lady who was president of the Charity Pity Club, to be one of the two Democratic signers of my official papers. Addie was an active church worker at Zion Baptist Church where A.D. King was pastor. The other person I asked to sign my papers was Verna Smith, who was also a member of the Club and the woman whose persistent urging had gotten me involved in politics through Wilson Wyatt's campaign.

The members of the Charity Pity Club were older women who belonged to different churches and visited the sick, provided food baskets for the needy on holidays, and did other good works. Addie and Verna met me at the Courthouse the next day with fifteen club members. She and Verna signed my filing papers, and I attached the other needed signatures to the papers on a separate sheet.

In January 1967, I filed as a candidate for the Kentucky Senate from Louisville's Thirty-third District. This was a big surprise to Democratic headquarters. Democratic officials had already selected a candidate to run for the seat, Dr. Charles Riggs, a chiropractor. He was White, Catholic, a disabled Navy veteran, and a Democratic regular. In addition to these obvious advantages, he was endorsed by Senator Bonn, who was relinquishing the seat.

At the time, the Thirty-third District was 65 percent White. Most of the residents were Catholic and lived in Portland—the oldest section of Louisville, an early settlement built on the Ohio River. To be effective in getting mixed support, I needed the endorsement of Representative Norbert Blume, who also lived in the Portland area. I went after it.

Blume and I met at the Jim Porter restaurant, located in the Seelbach Hotel, for lunch. I asked, "Norb, what do you think my chances are?"

He replied, tongue firmly in cheek, "You stand a good chance to win—if you keep your cards close to your chest." We both laughed. My full chest had caused remarks from men before.

I said, "I need your support and also the endorsement from the Teamsters."

He nodded, "I'll support you, *and* I'll get you the union endorsement."

Norbert was in a difficult position, however, because he and Riggs belonged to the same church. Later he publicly announced, "I have nothing against my neighbor and friend, Charles Riggs, but I am giving my support to Georgia Davis." I think he was influenced by the fact that the district was in transition from White to Black. He also remembered that two years prior, when the Democratic Party regulars wouldn't support him for Congress, I was his co-chairman.

There were other Black candidates from Louisville, including Mae Street Kidd and Hughes McGill. They were both running for representative and were both endorsed by the Democratic Party. To add to the confusion, there was also a second potential Black candidate for senator.

Coincidentally, Verna Smith—who had first brought me into politics and had signed my papers—was McGill's mother-in-law. Since Verna and her husband had been active Democrats and financial supporters of the party, McGill received party endorsement. Mae Street Kidd had been recruited by the party to run as the representative of the Forty-first District. She was an attractive woman—tall, stately, and fair with blond hair—and prominent in the Black community.

Not only was I running without the endorsement of the Democratic Party, I also was actively opposed by a Black faction within the party which was expected to "control the colored voters." Maude Benboe, chairman of the Forty-first Legislative District—which made up one-third of the Thirty-third Senatorial District—was the leader of this opposition. Maude's husband, Claude, owned several bars on Walnut Street in the Black business district. It was rumored he made large contributions to the Democratic Party in order to get the police to look the other way while he carried on his undercover operations.

Woodford Porter Sr., a prominent funeral parlor director and owner, was another Black who opposed me. Not only was he involved in low-level politics in the Democratic Party, but he contributed to the party financially and was designated to secure other Blacks as precinct captains and poll workers. He tried to influence his sister, Clara, and her husband, Dr. A.B. Harris, to be against my candidacy, but was unsuccessful. A.B. was a Democratic nominee for alderman of the Twelfth Ward, and Alexander "Ace" Brown was Democratic nominee for alderman of the Eleventh Ward. They were both endorsed by the party. It was clear that the party supported other Blacks, but was deliberately refusing to help me. This only made me more determined to win.

I was able to secure backing from the Executive Committee of the AFL-CIO and most of the Black professionals, including Dr. Grace James. An outspoken pediatrician who was trying to bring new and innovative health care to the Black community, she became my treasurer. Others who endorsed me were: Attorney Darryl T. Owens, who later was the first and only Black to be elected as Commissioner of Jefferson County Fiscal Court; Attorney David Turner; and William H. Smith, an accountant, who served later as Jefferson County Treasurer. Many of the Black ministers also supported my candidacy, including A.D. King, W. J. Hodge, Leo Lesser Jr., J.V. Bottoms, G. K. Offutt, and others.

I didn't feel hostile toward those Black Democratic regulars who didn't support me. After all, they were just doing what they were expected to do—dance to whatever tune the local party officials played. But I was bitter for a long time because of three Black ministers who called me "Sister" while asking for money in exchange for their support.

It had been suggested that a community meeting of influential Blacks be held to decide which Black candidate should be allowed to run for senator. With two Blacks dividing votes in the race and one prominent White, Dr. Charles Riggs, the White Democratic candidate would win.

Attorney Darryl Owens organized the meeting. I agreed to come, but made no promise to get out of the race. Fifteen people attended. I just listened, making almost no comment. No conclusion was reached about who should run. A few days later, the ministers came to me and said my Black opponent wouldn't file if I made a donation of one thousand dollars. I was upset, but kept my cool and said I would think about it and get back to them. Their demand posed a real threat to my running for office, as I'm sure they knew it would. I didn't have one thousand dollars.

Nevertheless, I knew I couldn't win if the other Black candidate ran too, and I had come too far to let a thousand dollars stand in my way.

In the end, the Beneficial Loan Company loaned me the money. Before I handed it over, however, I asked for a written letter in return, which I have kept ever since.

It took me three years to pay back the loan from Beneficial. I thought of those three extortionists every time I made a payment and whenever I was in their company. However, as all good politicians must do, I rose above my bitterness and later worked with all three men on projects of mutual interest. A successful politician cannot afford to hold a grudge.

To get financial contributions, I had to have endorsements from influential organizations. I worked on that next. Meeting with the officers of the Greater Louisville Labor Council, I sought their endorsement. I received help from W. C. Young, a member of the Council's executive board who had worked with me on Governor Breathitt's campaign, and was now Special Assistant to Breathitt handling the problems of Black constituents. Not only did the Labor Council endorse me, but they also gave me financial help and did most of the printing for my campaign in their office. I was also endorsed by the Kentucky Education Association, the Kentucky Medical Association, the NAACP, and the Louisville Chapter of the Urban League. In addition, many independent unions endorsed me.

The next items on my agenda were to set up a headquarters and hire a campaign manager. I found a vacant building at 3800 West Broadway and invited the three representatives running for reelection from my district to share it with me. It became the headquarters of the "Davis for Senator" campaign, as well as the "Blume, Kidd, and McGill for Representatives" campaigns.

Ironically, the building I leased was owned by Sam Stallings, the lawyer who had been sent to the legislative election by Miss Lennie to unsuccessfully try to defeat me. The building was located only a few blocks from where I lived. It had been a residence, but the partitions were removed, so that it could be remodeled into office space. It cost us one hundred dollars a month for the eight months leading up to the general election.

Next we hired Raoul Cunningham and William Gatewood as co-managers of our combined campaigns. Raoul Cunningham, a tall man who wore a small Afro, had just returned to Louisville from Washington, DC, where he had been a student at Howard University. He was active in the National Young Democrats, and Lukey had recommended him. Our second manager, Bill, was another six-footer. He had a quick, ready laugh and had worked before in local political campaigns. Both men were young, bright, energetic, and enthusiastic. My pretty, black-haired sister-in-law, Marie Montgomery, was hired as secretary.

Raoul was also director of a youth choir at Green Street Baptist Church. He quickly organized the seventy-five young choir members to work in the voter registration drive. They enthusiastically reported to our headquarters, where we had lunch waiting for them every day. Soon the teenagers became very effective in stirring up interest in the campaign and getting people to register.

Though Governor Breathitt and I had had our differences, I decided to see him to ask for his support. He had set up a program at the capitol he called "Citizens Day," a day when people could come to see him without an appointment. On the next Citizens Day I went to see him in his office. Later when he went out to meet the waiting crowd, he announced that he was late because he had been meeting with Georgia Davis, who was seeking the Democratic nomination to represent Louisville's Thirty-third District in the state Senate. He explained, "I feel I should pledge my support to the first candidate who showed up here today. Besides, I think it is a fine thing that a woman is running for the legislature." This was the kind of patronizing comment which demeaned both me and women in general, but I let it pass. There were more pressing matters to attend to.

During that summer, while I campaigned, I became involved in plans to march for open housing. The state Civil Rights Act of 1966 gave communities the power to pass local laws banning housing discrimination. Civil rights advocates were now lobbying to get an ordinance enacted in Louisville.

We worked through the Committee on Open Housing, including: representatives of the NAACP local branch, the Kentucky Christian Leadership Conference (KCLC), the west end Community Council, the Louisville Council on Religion and Race, and the Louisville Area AME Ministers Association. Our pleas to the Board of Aldermen to pass an enforceable open housing ordinance were met with repeated delays by city and county elected officials. County Judge Marlow Cook urged a court study to "determine if such an ordinance would be legal." Mayor Kenneth Schmied, a tall, stocky man with a broad smile, asked his Advisory Committee on Community Development to "study all aspects of an open housing law" and give a report to him.

Meanwhile members of the Open House Committee continued dialogue with the city and county officials. The members of that committee were: A.D. King, KCLC; W.J. Hodge, member and later president of the local NAACP chapter; William Daniels and James C. Maloney, Council on Religion and Race; Hulbert James, director of West End Community Council; Leo Lesser, president of African

Methodist Episcopal Ministerial Alliance; and Dr. Maurice Rabb, acting president of the Louisville NAACP chapter.

Frustrated in our efforts to influence officials, we turned to demonstrations. The first march we planned was to a furniture store owned by the mayor's family. We felt this would show him we were serious. I remembered the store from the era I was growing up on Grand Avenue. Salesmen went door to door in the Black and less affluent neighborhoods taking orders for furniture. They collected on the weekly installment plan.

At the march, in addition to the usual ministers, there were several "Black Power" members marshaling the demonstration. Sam Hawkins, Robert "Kuyu" Simms, Robert Brown, and others. Rev. Randall T. Osborn, one of the Southern Christian Leadership Conference coordinators for Ohio and Alabama, came to Louisville to assist us in marching and strategy.

Before each march there was a service at one of the Black churches, where we would be coached in the techniques of nonviolent resistance. We would go into the south end of Louisville where some of the staunchest segregationists lived. Each time hecklers were there to greet us. At first, we rented buses to take us to our destinations, but so many bus windows were broken by the hecklers, we had to change to a windowless, delivery-type truck.

On our way, we stood tightly packed in the trucks with the sliding door open a foot from the bottom for air. When we reached our destination and climbed out, hecklers, including Klansmen, surrounded us. We could not move, so we began to sing freedom songs and clap our hands. The policemen tried to hold the hecklers back, but nothing could keep them from throwing the rocks, tomatoes, and eggs which splattered all over us. On one of the trips, just as we sat down on the ground, a piece of concrete the size of a large potato hit me in my side. I was amazed that I did not feel any pain.

The demonstration which concerned me most was the one at the intersection of Fourth Street and Broadway. (Fourth was the center of downtown stores in Louisville, and Broadway crossed it.) We organized a half block away on Fourth Street and marched toward Broadway. When we got there we sat down in the middle of the intersection. It was 5 P.M.; traffic had peaked. Then it stopped for blocks in all directions. In order to remove us, two policemen had to pick up each protester and drag or carry him or her to the waiting patrol cars. As they were loading the wagons, Lukey and I, who were sitting on the periphery of the crowd, slipped away and went to the bondsman's office. Claude Benboe went to get the marchers released from jail.

In addition to the marches, Louisville civil rights leaders also participated in mounting a statewide campaign to pass open housing ordinances. Leaders from around the state met with the State Commission on Human Rights, and developed a model local act covering housing discrimination. Everyone thought Louisville and Jefferson County would be the first to pass such a law. As it turned out, we were the last, and we didn't even get an enforceable fair housing ordinance at that point.

11

CROSSING THE LINE

How did it happen? Did we suddenly become so overcome with passion that we fell into each others' arms? Oh no, he was much too cautious for that—and so was I.

The relationship between Martin Luther King Jr. and I began with mutual admiration. I admired him for his conviction, power, and skill in leading the civil rights movement, a long overdue crusade to tear down segregation all over the South. He admired me for rising from being a factory worker to becoming the first Black and the first female elected to the Kentucky Senate, fighting for the rights of the poor and disenfranchised.

This progressed into a deepening friendship in which we shared opinions, confidences, and laughed often. Though few outside his immediate circle knew it, M.L., as I often called him in private, had a wonderful sense of humor and a talent for mimicry. Together we had the ability to enjoy the funny and inane parts of the complex situations, causes, and people—including ourselves—which occupied so much of both our lives.

Gradually, our attachment grew stronger until it passed beyond camaraderie into intimacy. The turning point came one March afternoon when I was volunteering in the office of the KCLC, which was located next to and connected with the church at which A.D. King was the pastor. A.D. telephoned and said, "Come over to my office. I want to see you."

"Okay, I'll be there as soon as I finish running the mimeographing machine," I replied.

About fifteen minutes later, I went to his office and knocked on the half-open door. To my surprise, his brother, who had come to Louisville to attend the national board meeting of the Southern Christian Leadership Conference (SCLC), was there.

"How are you, Dr. King?" I asked. Suddenly feeling somehow disconnected, I ran my fingers through my hair. "I didn't know you were in the building."

Martin smiled boyishly. "It is good to see you again," he said formally, almost shyly, and glanced toward A.D. Like many men since John Alden, Martin chose not to plead his case himself, but to use an emissary.

A.D. cleared his throat, "Georgia," he said, speaking slowly at first and then quickening his pace as if he wanted to get all the right words out, "Martin has been thinking about you since you last met. After the meeting tonight, ride with me to the Rodeway Inn and meet him there."

Surprised—no, shocked—I stared at Martin and stammered, "I . . . I . . ."

"Yes," he said, "I'd like you to come."

Unable to rationally respond, I finally blurted out, "I'll think about it," left, and walked slowly back to my office. A myriad of thoughts rushed through my mind: Why me? What could he want with me when there are so many young, beautiful women available to famous men? I'm middle-aged and not feeling too alluring. Does he feel his secrets are safer with an older woman? Did he have this in mind when we were going to Frankfort?

I had so many questions, but no answers.

By the time I got back to the KCLC office, I was too preoccupied to do anything but stand idly in front of the table on which I'd placed the papers I'd mimeographed. I felt warm all over.

Lukey looked up, "What was that all about?" she asked.

"Has A.D. said anything to you about M.L. and me?"

"Only that he wanted to be with you," she said softly.

Flustered, I snapped, "Well, why didn't you tell me, so I would have been prepared?"

Lukey said, "It's not my decision. It's up to you. What are you going to do?"

I shrugged my shoulders, "I just don't know. I'll have to think more about it."

That evening, hands trembling with excitement despite my efforts to remain calm, I dressed in a flattering, two-piece, red knit dress with black accessories. Lukey and I went to the meeting at Leo Lesser's church, St. James Missionary AME. The rally was a fund-raiser for KCLC to help defray the expenses of the National Board Meeting. During the rally, I was still uncertain about my decision and yet, deep down, I knew what I was going to do.

After the program was over, Lukey and I walked outside the church and stood there. When he left the church, A.D. said quietly, "Ride with Lukey and wait for me in the lobby of the hotel."

We did as he instructed. While we waited in the hotel lobby, Lukey asked once again, "What are you going to do?"

I replied, "It's obvious, isn't it? I'm here."

She looked over at me, "You are so nervous, you need one of my tranquilizers."

"I'll be all right," I said in a throaty voice I hardly recognized. "It is just such a surprise to me, and also a surprise that I'm here." I shook my head nervously. "Lukey, should I feel flattered?"

"You are in shock," she said teasingly. "You thought you had *lost it*, but now you've found it again."

We laughed and I sighed, "What is the answer?"

A.D. strode through the lobby, came over, and said to Lukey, "Wait here for me. I'll be right back." He motioned to me to follow him. He and I took an elevator to the third floor. As we left the elevator I saw that a local policeman, who had been assigned to Dr. King for personal security, was standing there. A.D. went up to him and whispered something. Then he came back and said, "We had to be checked out before going further." The officer, Robert Carter, knew me. Looking into his eyes that night, I first felt the guilt I would carry from then on; yet I had no desire to run. It was as if I were in a trance. I seemed to slip outside my body, watching its movements from a distance. All the while, I was moving through the door. As A.D. was leaving the room, Martin entered it. He said gently, "I know you think it was bold of me to set you up by using my brother to intercede for me. I had no choice."

"Neither of you gave me any hint as to what was going on," I said. "It was quite a surprise." As I stood there asking myself: What am I doing here and how did I get into this situation?, I made a final choice —a choice that lives with me for the rest of my life. I could have left but I didn't. After that first night, I knew there was no turning back. Guilt notwithstanding, I would come whenever he called and go wherever he wanted.

Tornado hits Montgomery home, Springfield, Kentucky, 1925.

(Clockwise from left): Georgia's Aunt, Mary Frances Lewis; Georgia (two years old); Georgia's mother, Frances Montgomery; her brothers, Joseph and Robert.

Georgia Montgomery, sixteen years old.

Frances and Ben Montgomery, 1951.

Left: Georgia and her first husband, Robert T. Jones.

Below Left: Georgia; Georgia and Nicky's adopted son, Billy; Norman "Nicky" Davis, Georgia's second husband.

Below Right: Jim Powers, "The Philadelphia Lawyer," 1949.

March on Frankfort, March 5, 1964. *(First Row):* Dr. Martin Luther King; *(Second Row):* Georgia's brother Lawrence behind M.L.K.; Lukey to his right; G.D.P. to his left with her head turned. (photo: *The Courier-Journal*)

With Lukey Ward.

With Jackie Robinson.

Above: Rev. Martin Luther King Jr, leads 30,000 civil rights marchers into Montgomery, AL, March 25, 1965; G.D.P. to flag bearer's left. (photo: Bettmann Archives)

Right: G.D.P.'s campaign ad for senate, 1967.

5/18/67

VOTE
Tuesday, May 23 – 1967

GEORGIA M. DAVIS
CANDIDATE FOR STATE SENATE—33rd DISTRICT
(Subject to Democratic Primary)

INVOLVED
Civil Rights march on Frankfort, 1964

Mrs. Georgia M. Davis

ACTIVE
With Jackie Robinson at Civil Rights March, 1964

RECOGNIZED

BY PROMINENT LOCAL, STATE WIDE, AND NATIONAL LEADERS.

United States Senate
WASHINGTON D.C.

December 16, 1966

Mrs. Georgia Davis
1755 Wilson Avenue
Louisville, Kentucky

Dear Mrs. Davis:

It was good of you to assist on the preparations for my trip to Louisville this fall. I meant to write to you sooner.

I thoroughly enjoyed my visit and thought the day was a wonderful success, due in no small part, I am sure, to your efforts. Thank you for everything.

With best wishes.

Sincerely,

Robert F. Kennedy

Mrs. Davis Could Be A Senate 'First'

Mrs. Georgia Davis, a member of the City-County Democratic Executive Committee, has announced as a candidate for the Kentucky Senate from the 33rd District.

If elected, Mrs. Davis would be the first Negro woman to serve in the Senate.

Mrs. Davis, of 733 Cecil, is seeking the Democratic nomination in the May primary for the seat being vacated by Democrat B. J Boen.

Mrs. Davis pledged to support legislation in the field of human rights. She called for a state law requiring equal pay for women, and for legislation to permit people to vote in Kentucky after six months residency. The present law requires a year's residency.

Mrs. Davis is the wife of Norman F. Davis, a postal employe. She is a member of the Louisville Urban League, the YWCA, the Kentucky Civil Liberties Union and the National Association for the Advancement of Colored People.

Democratic Campaign Headquarters
743 Sheraton Hotel
Louisville, Kentucky

Mrs. Norman Davis
733 Cecil Avenue
Louisville, Kentucky

December 5, 1963

Dear Georgia:

I want to take this opportunity to commend you for your dedicated and effective efforts during our many months of campaigning.

As a member of our Headquarters staff, you can take justifiable pride in knowing that our victory was due in large measure to your devotion and hard work. I can repay my obligations only by justifying the confidence you have placed in me.

With kindest regards and deep appreciation.

Sincerely,

Ned
Edward T. (Ned) Breathitt

e for GEORGIA DAVIS, who will provide the voice and the leadership y want and need-the VOICE you DESERVE in Frankfort.

Paid for by Laborers International Union of North America, Local Union No. 576, AFL CIO. James E. Stewart, Business Manager.

With Gov. Louie B. Nunn, 2/1/68.

Vice President Hubert H. Humphrey con-
gratulates G.D.P. on Senate election.

Lorraine Motel, Memphis, TN, 4/4/68. The assassination of Dr. King. (photo: Joseph
Louw, *Life Magazine*, © Time Inc.)

G.D.P. *(Third from Right)* leads a group of women supporting St. Petersburg garbage worker's strike, 7/5/68. (photo: Weaver Tripp, *St Petersburg Times*)

(left to right): SCLC Vice-Chairman, Rev. C. K. Steele; G.D.P.; A.D. King; Raoul Cunningham, at sanitation strike, St. Petersburg, Florida, 7/12/68. (photo: *St Petersburg Times*)

Senator, Georgia M. Davis, 1/6/70.

(Left to Right): Lt. Gov. Julian Carroll, Rep. Mae Street Kidd, Sen. Georgia M.Davis, Speaker of the House Norbert Blume, Rep. Charlotte McGill, Gov. Wendell Ford, 1971.

With Benjamin Hooks, former Urban League Director, 1979.

Montgomery 50th wedding anniversary. *(Clockwise from Left):* Frances Walker Montgomery, G.D.P., Robert, James Isaac, John Albert, Joseph Ben, Lawrence Franklin, Phillip, Ben Gore Montgomery. (photo: Nat Brown)

Above: With Rev. Jesse Jackson, upon his receiving the Bellarmine Award, 1979.

Left: With Edward "Ted" Kennedy and Sonny Griffin, 1979.

With Rep. Calvin Smyre, GA (left) and Walter Mondale, 10/23/82.

Retirement/65th birthday dinner. *(Left to Right):* Mary Ray Oaken, Secretary of the Kentucky Tourism Dept.; U.S. Senator Walter D. Huddleston; Jim Powers; G.D.P.; Raoul Cunningham at the podium; Commissioner Darryl Owens; U.S. Senator Wendell Ford.

With Kentucky Lt. Gov. Brereton Jones (left) and G.D.P.'s successor to the senate, Gerald Neal (right), February, 1988.

G.D.P.'s last day in the senate, 12/14/88.

Jim Powers and G.D.P. today.
(photo: John Nation)

Earlier in March 1967, Black leaders had discussed and negotiated with the Board of Aldermen, the mayor, and the county judge, urging them to come out publicly in support of a local open housing ordinance. Still, no enforceable open housing laws were produced from these meetings.

Meanwhile, I was continuously organizing precincts and campaigning for the Senate, though there were other causes I believed in for which I volunteered my time. I was also involved in the local open housing drive, volunteering in KCLC's office and marching daily in the south end. Many advisors told me I should not be marching, because I had to depend on a lot of the White people in the north end of the district to vote for me, and because of my political activism they might see me as a radical. I disagreed. "I have to support what I believe in," I said, and continued marching.

One day Lukey and I entered city hall to attend the meeting of the Board of Aldermen. The bill for open housing was up for a vote. As we walked through the crowded hallway, we passed by a distinguished-looking, mahogany-skinned man with snow white hair. I looked at him and he smiled and said, "Hello!"

"Hello," I answered. He started walking towards me, so I slowed down.

He said, "Georgia, don't you know me?" I looked closer at his face then and realized it was George Duke Beasley, my first love. I had not seen him in twenty-five years. We hugged each other.

He said, "I'm here on EEOC business and will be here for several days."

I asked, "Where will you be later tonight?"

He replied, "I'm staying in a hotel in Indiana. Why don't you meet me for dinner?"

"I'd like that," I replied."

Later that day, in spite of all our efforts to promote the

GEORGIA DAVIS POWERS

open housing ordinance, the Board of Aldermen defeated the measure by a vote of nine to three. One White alderman, Oscar Stoll, joined the two Black aldermen, Eugene Ford Jr. and Louise Reynolds, in favoring the bill. After the bill was defeated, KCLC and other groups who favored open housing vowed the marches would continue until an enforceable local law was passed.

I left city hall and went to the hotel to meet Duke. He met me in the lobby. We strolled to the combination dining room and bar. My neighbor and friend, Joseph Ray Jr., was the bartender. "Come over and meet Duke," I said. He did.

"I remember you, Duke, when you would come to see Georgia on Grand Avenue. I used to envy the tailor-made clothes you wore while I was still wearing store-bought clothes off the rack," Joe chuckled.

Duke and I laughed. We brought each other up to date on what had happened in our lives since we saw each other last. The years had erased the passion I had felt for him in our younger years, but I enjoyed renewing our friendship.

Later that week, after the disappointing results of the Board of Aldermen's meeting, A.D., Lesser, Lukey, and I talked about the problem of apathy. At that time, the civil rights leaders were feeling discouraged, tired, and were looking for a more effective and more drastic action to get people's attention. The Kentucky Derby, run at Churchill Downs racetrack each year on the first Saturday in May, seemed to provide us with an opportunity to do just that.

A.D. said, "It's almost three weeks until the Derby. We need to do something noticeable, yet peaceful."

Lesser asked, "What do you have in mind?"

I broke in, "For one thing, we need to make sure we kick the incumbents at city hall out of office, especially the ones who voted against the ordinance. We can support the ones who favored it."

"What we ought to do is stop the Kentucky Derby," A.D. said agitatedly.

In unison we cried, "*Stop* the Derby?"

Lesser demanded, "Now, just how do we plan to do that?"

Jokingly, I turned to M.L.'s brother. "Yes, sure, A.D. We'll just step out on the track at the third turn when the horses are in full speed and lay our bodies on the track." We all laughed.

Lukey added, "That would be the supreme sacrifice."

I didn't think A.D. was serious, but he was. He continued, "We can start by planning to disrupt the horses, since White folk think more of horses than they do of Negroes."

Lesser said, "We have three weeks, you know."

The more A.D. discussed it, the more excited he got about the idea. He said, "We'll plan a rally on the Thursday before the Derby and bring M.L. in to excite the crowd and keep the interest high in open housing.

"Lukey caught his fervor. "We can notify the Black churches and the few White churches in the west end about the rally. We need to have a big crowd."

A.D. nodded, his voice rising, "We can get a couple of young men to jump the fence and dart across the track as the horses come around the bend going into the stretch."

I said, "Now just who is going to volunteer for that task? And why do they have to be young men?"

A.D. answered, "Well, now, young men's reflexes are better and they can run faster."

I asked, smiling, "Faster than a horse?"

Lesser said, "A.D., you're pretty fleet-footed!"

A.D. laughed and said, "But not fast enough."

"And too fat!" I jokingly added.

The information was leaked to the press and word soon spread that "Negroes" were going to disrupt the Derby.

The closer it got to the first Saturday in May, the more news our plan was making. The question on most people's minds was how it was going to be done. This was a mystery to everyone, however, including me. Still, the rumors got the attention of the city and county officials. They increased security and took added safety precautions.

A.D. reserved rooms for his brother and Reverend Abernathy at a hotel. The two men arrived on Thursday. Before going to the march and then to the mass meeting, A.D. and his wife, Naomi, held a reception for the two men at their house. The Zion Baptist Church parsonage was located on Western Parkway, a wide and beautiful tree-lined street. Ten people were at the reception, mostly Black preachers; Lesser, Sampson, W.J. Hodge, and Summers were among them. Lukey and I were the only exceptions, and once again the only women there other than wives, in this case A.D.'s.

In my opinion, there should be a Black Women's Hall of Fame for the leadership, energy, determination, and sacrifice thousands of women made during the civil rights era. For example, women civil rights protesters led the "Don't buy where you can't work" campaign throughout the country. There were NAACP women such as Ruby Hurley, the youth director who organized branches in Alabama, Florida, Georgia, Mississippi, and Tennessee. She was sent by the NAACP to investigate the death of fourteen-year-old Emmett Till of Chicago, who was killed for allegedly whistling at a White woman. Also, she investigated the death of Reverend George Lee, who was killed for helping Blacks register to vote in Belzoni, Mississippi.

In Little Rock, Arkansas, where one of the most violent anti-integration actions occurred following the 1954 ruling of the Supreme Court on *Brown v. Board of Education*, Daisy Bates, president of the NAACP chapter there, led nine

Black students into Central High School. In imminent danger, she had to decide whether to press on or abandon her cause. She wrote in her autobiography that she made the decision that "it was going to be this generation or never."

In Montgomery, JoAnn Robinson, president of the Women's Political Council (WPC) and professor of English at Alabama State University, sent a letter, dated May 21, 1954 (four days after the Supreme Court Ruling) to Mayor W.A. Gayle. In her letter, Robinson noted that three-fourths of the people who rode buses back then were Blacks and that if they ceased riding, the buses could not operate.

Septima Clark, another unsung heroine of the civil rights movement, was a teacher from South Carolina who believed that most of the Black ministers involved in the movement were selfish chauvinists. Later becoming a leader at the Highlander Folk School, she set up citizenship schools all over the South, recruiting teachers who taught thousands to read, register to vote, and stand up for their rights.

While the boycott was brewing in Montgomery, it was the arrest of Rosa Parks on December 1, 1955 that sparked the civil rights movement into even more serious action. As is well known, she had refused to give up her seat on the bus to a White man and was arrested for her defiance of the segregation laws. Within two hours of her arrest, JoAnn Robinson and members of the WPC blanketed the city with fifty thousand leaflets calling for a bus boycott. Rosa Parks, one of the first women to join the Montgomery NAACP, later became secretary to the branch president.

Black women gained positions in the movement but never any recognition for their deeds. The Black ministers wanted women to participate because they knew that was the only way for the routine work of the movement to be done. They freely used the ideas presented by the women, simply adopting them as their own.

Ella Baker, president of the NAACP of New York, became National Director of Branches and spent much of her time organizing membership drives against de facto segregation in the school system. She later became an SCLC coordinator. As sit-in protests were cropping up around the country, mostly among young people, Ella Baker grasped the importance of what was happening. With more than seventy thousand participants in the sit-ins, she seized the opportunity to coordinate the tremendous potential of the student movement. After successfully persuading the SCLC to contribute eight hundred dollars for a student conference, more than three hundred activists from colleges and communities across the country met at Shaw University in Raleigh, North Carolina.

The preexisting organizations wanted the student movement to become a part of them. However, Ella Baker suggested that they form their own independent group. She said, "Their approach was refreshing, indeed, to those of the older group who bear the scars of battle, the frustrations, and the disillusionment that comes when the prophetic leader turns out to have feet of clay." The young people, with their idealism and zeal, were inclined more toward group-centeredness than toward a leader-centered group plan of organization. Thus the Student Nonviolent Coordinating Committee (SNCC) was born. Ella Baker had a profound impact on two of the most dynamic civil rights organizations, SCLC and SNCC, but like so many other women, she has never received the recognition she deserved.

In 1957, Southern school systems, which were still segregated, became the rallying point of the civil rights movement, with the front lines staffed mostly by Black women. The first Black admitted to a state-supported school, the University of Alabama at Tuscaloosa, was Autherine Lucy. She confronted thousands of angry Whites. Ruby Hurley of the NAACP shared the moment of valor with her.

I Shared the Dream

From my first experience with the Allied Organization for Civil Rights (AOCR), I knew that, since I was a woman, I would have no voice in decision making. Lukey and I had spent ten hours a day, seven days a week organizing the "March on Frankfort." Frank Stanley Jr., the son of the publisher of the *Louisville Defender*, was given all the credit. Lukey and I worked in the office with only lantern light and propane gas heat to get the printed material on the march out to the rest of the state.

My next involvement in the movement was with A.D. King. Again, Lukey Ward and I worked hard, raising enough money to lease Purdue University's football plane in order to take Kentuckians to Selma to join the march. Our part in that march was never even mentioned by the men.

I observed over the years that the Black men in power were not going to relinquish the spotlight and give credit to women for what they were doing, though Black women were the backbone of the civil rights movement. Had it not been for women, there would have been little achieved in the way of organization and demonstrations. As history shows, women's roles were secondary and hidden in the civil rights movement of the 1940s through the 1960s. Although women worked tirelessly behind the scenes to keep the movement moving forward, they hardly ever received any public recognition, and were not included in making policy decisions. In fact, the structure and fiber of the civil rights movement was analogous to that of the Black churches. If women had pulled out of the churches, there would have been no churches; if women had not contributed money to the churches, the doors would have had to close.

The male civil rights workers liked women to be there with them. In private, they sought our advice and our suggestions, but they were the ones who made the public announcements. To them, it boosted the image of Black male power. Realizing that women could not crack that male bastion, I knew I had to find the opportunity to make my own contributions elsewhere. I wanted to be my own woman, to find a place where I would stand out on my own merits.

The ministers who were attending the reception that night belonged to the same General Baptist Association as Dr. King. This was the first time I had seen M.L. since January. We had not talked, but A.D. had conveyed messages to me from him, such as, "M.L. asked about you. How is the campaign going?" Or, "M.L. hopes all goes well with you." Meeting him in public now, I greeted Dr. King as I did the others. My concern for keeping our relationship private was paramount. In the wrong hands, knowledge that Martin and I were seeing each other could have destroyed my political career—and what it would have done to his reputation, I didn't want to speculate.

After we were comfortably seated, Dr. King began talking about how shocked he was to see the level of squalor and deprivation in Chicago. He said, "Segregation and poverty are rampant. There is a difference between the North and the South. In some ways conditions are better up there, but on the other hand, some are worse. We're having to deal with the politics of Chicago's Mayor Richard J. Daley. Black activists are trying to integrate a public school system that Superintendent Benjamin Willis, who is supported by the mayor, declares is not segregated and never has been."

Abernathy chimed in, "Blacks are going to separate schools and sometimes being instructed in trailers, outmoded army barracks, and outbuildings."

Sampson asked, "How did you get involved in Chicago?"

Several of us chuckled and said, "We thought there was enough to do in the South to last for years to come."

King explained, "A group called the Coordinating Council of Community Organizations requested we intervene."

Abernathy went on, "We couldn't have imagined the squalor we witnessed in Chicago. Jesse Jackson, who was in Chicago heading SCLC's Operation Breadbasket, drove us first into the South Side, which is predominantly Negro, and then he took us to the West Side, which was even worse."

When he could discreetly get my attention, A.D. called me aside into the hallway. He whispered, "We're going to have to move M.L. and Ralph from the hotel tomorrow. Because of the Derby, the other hotels are booked to capacity." He paused, then asked, "Can they stay at your house?"

Pondering the request and its possible ramifications, my usual fears arose. I hesitated for a moment, but knew I would agree. "Yes, of course," I replied softly. "They can sleep in the guest room. You can bring them over after the meeting at Fifth Street Baptist Church tomorrow night. I'll just miss the meeting."

The march was set for the late afternoon. After the reception Martin, A.D., Lesser, Hodge, and I headed for the KCLC office to meet the others who were going to participate. Lesser drove my car and I sat between Martin and him. A.D. and Hodge sat in the back seat. When the caravan got to the south end, throngs of angry Whites were waiting for us. I watched as the first rock thrown grazed Martin's face. He neither flinched nor cursed the perpetrators. He sat stoically, unwavering.

The crowd heckled and cursed us as our car tried to get past them. The mass meeting was scheduled for 7:30 P.M. By the time we got through the impass it was too late to lead the march, so we went directly to A.D.'s Zion Baptist Church to regroup and get ready for the night rally.

At St. James AME Church, King used the rock-throwing incident as the topic of his speech, entitling it, "Upon this

Rock." He spoke as always, with deep feeling and eloquence. I never saw him read from a written speech or even refer to notes when speaking. This evening he talked about how an object meant for destruction can also be an instrument for teaching redemptive power. He used the rock to illustrate his points about what the power of love and acceptance can do. "Love is all powerful, although to many, it may seem to take a long time, and results may not be seen within the hour of application. I submit to you, Louisville, that we will build an open city and the gates of injustice will not prevail against us." After the mass meeting, A.D. took Ralph and Dr. King, which is what I called M.L. in public, to the hotel. Lukey and I went with them but didn't stay.

A.D. spent Friday morning with Martin and Ralph at the hotel. Around eleven, A.D. phoned and said, "I am taking them to lunch and will bring them to your house later this afternoon.

"I will be here," I promised. When they arrived at five, Martin looked tired. "We just want to relax before the meeting scheduled for this evening," he said. A.D. went home. Abernathy and M.L. removed their ties, opened up their top shirt buttons, and freshened up. Then Abernathy lay down on a couch in the living room while King made some telephone calls, including one to Stanley Levison in New York. He was Dr. King's legal adviser. I didn't hear all the conversation, but I heard Martin repeat something Levison said to him. After he hung up, he was still repeating this phrase. "Cowardice asks, is it safe? Expediency asks, it is political? Vanity asks, is it popular? But Conscience asks, is it right?"

I asked, "Will you use that in your speeches?"

He smiled, "I will use it when it is appropriate."

I said, "M.L., is anything we do and say original?"

He replied, "Originality comes only from God. Everything else has, is, and will be used by someone else before you." As we talked, I could see he felt comfortable with me and I knew I did with him. Wanting to know more about his early years, I asked, "When you were growing up, were you the precocious child people say you were? I asked A.D. and he said you were normal as far as he knew, just mischievous."

Martin laughed and said, "If I was precocious, it didn't show up in my grades in school. They were average—sometimes not even that! When my older sister, Christine, started school, I went with her and got sent home when the teacher found out my age. She told me to come back in a year."

"You mean you were a deceiver at an early age?" I teased, then became more serious. "From what A.D. says about the strict discipline of your father, you both had to be deceivers."

"Daddy was a very forceful man and we dared not question him, much less buck him. I confronted him more than A.D. did, though. He would say, "Yes, Daddy," and then do what he wanted to do. We had to slip out to play marbles, play cards, and dance. He just didn't allow it," Martin explained.

I asked, "What about your sister?"

"She did what was expected of her. She would never cross Daddy. As the old saying goes, he ruled the roost."

I responded, "A.D. loves your father, but I think he has some underlying resentment of his unbending discipline. Your dad sounds like he was a dictator."

"In our house he was the supreme authority,." M.L. replied.

"Do you think that overpowering force from your dad had a psychological effect on A.D., and caused him to drink excessively?" I asked.

"A.D. would have to undergo extensive analytical psychotherapy to get to the root cause of his problem," he said.

"Did you ever want to be anything other than a preacher?" I asked.

He thought a minute, then slowly answered, "I had several options in mind when I was in school. I thought of medicine, but after remembering how poorly I did in science, I dismissed that from my mind. I gave law some thought, but decided against that."

I interrupted, "You would have made an excellent lawyer."

He said, "I finally realized that with my background and upbringing, rooted and grounded in religious doctrine, I'd already made the decision to become a minister. I didn't always agree with what I learned in my early years in church, though, and I challenged some of the religious theories. Later, the questions in my mind were resolved when I studied the Biblical teachings. Now," he said, changing the subject, "Are you going to listen to the private reading I am going to give you or not?" He pulled two galley proofs of the book he was working on from his bag, and handed one to me.

Opening the book, he walked around the room, reading from it as I followed the text and listened:

The job of arousing manhood within a people that have been taught for so many centuries that they are nobody is not easy. Even the semantical have conspired to make that which is black seem ugly and degrading. In Roget's Thesaurus there are some one hundred twenty synonyms for "blackness" and at least sixty of them offensive—

He stopped to exclaim, "I'm a writer! I really am a writer!"

"Of course you are," I said, smiling. "And when the book is published, I want an autographed copy. By the way, what is a thesaurus?" I asked.

"Every writer has to have one," he said.

"Well, I'm no writer, and I've never heard of a thesaurus, but if you need one, I'll get it," I said.

Around 6:30 P.M., A.D. came to take them to the seven o'clock meeting he had set up with the open housing leaders. While they were gone I put clean sheets on the beds and tidied up the house. At 10:00 P.M., King and Abernathy rang the door bell. Lukey and A.D. were with them. Lukey's eyes were red and swollen, obviously from crying.

"What happened at the meeting?" I asked, looking at Lukey. A.D. did most of the talking, explaining that the others at the meeting had distrusted Lukey and challenged her motives. They did not want to discuss any of the Derby plans while she was there and asked her to sit outside the door. The ministers had accused her of leaking information to the FBI. Abernathy said little, and they all seemed reluctant to talk about the incident.

A.D. had brought some barbecued ribs, baked beans, and slaw with him. Looking at his brother, A.D. changed the subject abruptly. "We're leaving. I'll pick you up at ten o'clock in the morning to go to the airport. We need to leave early because of the Derby traffic." After Lukey and A.D. left, I set the table and we ate.

King said, "They have made their point about stopping the Derby. Now they should concentrate on voter registration and the election."

Abernathy nodded, "The plan was unworkable to start with."

They both seemed tired. "I will show you to your room," I said. They followed me through the hall and I pointed out the guest room. Martin smiled at me.

"Isn't there another room?" he asked.

"Yes," I said. "My room." As his eyes met mine, we both knew where he was going to sleep that night.

We drew close to each other. "Senator . . . ," he

murmured as I moved into his embrace. He was warm and passionate. He wanted compassion. He wanted to be cuddled. He slept for a while curled up in my arms. The cares of the day seemed far away.

Later M.L. awoke and said, "I lead such a hectic life. My time is not my own. Sometimes I wish I could lead a normal life, pastoring a church and teaching a few classes in theology."

"Do you think there will come a time in the future when you can slow the pace down?" I asked.

"I would like to think so, but it will not be soon." He gradually slipped into a peaceful sleep.

Glancing out the window the next morning, I saw a plain white van parked out front with two White men sitting in it. I woke M.L. "G-men are waiting across the street," I said. He looked out at them, and then back at me, communicating without words his desperation.

There was constant talk among leaders of the movement about the FBI trying to dig up dirt on M.L. We both knew we were under surveillance. I was concerned, of course, but I didn't know anything I could do about it short of stopping our meetings, and I wasn't willing to do that. Obviously, neither was he.

12

MARCHES AND PRIMARIES

Despite the defeat of the proposed open housing measure, those of us dedicated to its principles vowed that the marches for open housing would continue. When the city issued an injunction against us, we marched anyway and were arrested. Many of the adult demonstrators spent the night in jail.

We continued the marches in Louisville until August, when we stopped, so that everyone could work on a voter registration drive. We were determined to vote those out of office who would not vote for our rights. Eleven of the aldermen were defeated. Only Louise Reynolds, who had actively worked for an open housing law, was reelected. A Democrat, Harvey Sloane, was elected mayor. I realized then how the power of the vote, combined with nonviolent action, could produce dramatic results.

Sometimes I wonder why elected officials are so slow to learn. This election was a repeat of the 1961 Louisville elections when Black voters had been the deciding factor in electing Republican Mayor Bill Cowger and Republican County Judge Marlow Cook after the Democratic Board of Aldermen refused to pass an ordinance outlawing discrimination in public accommodations. However, unlike the talk which preceded them, our marches had their desired effect.

Early in December, the newly elected Louisville Board of Alderman finally passed an enforceable open housing ordinance containing penalties for those who violated its provisions. Meanwhile, civil rights leaders in other parts of the state were working to pass local fair housing laws. Bardstown and Nelson County became the first area to pass an open housing ordinance. Covington and Kenton County were next. Lexington and Fayette County soon joined the ranks of those progressive enough to pass fair housing laws.

Six weeks before the primary election, the Democratic Executive Committee met to make endorsements in thirty-five races. A letter was sent out to all precinct captains informing them of the endorsements, which meant they were expected to work for these candidates. The only race in which an endorsement was not given was the Thirty-third Senatorial District—my district.

I felt that not only did the local Democratic officials decline to support me, they were underhanded in trying to defeat me. Since the party had not endorsed anyone in my race, I didn't expect to see either my name or my opponent's name on the sample ballot. Somehow Norbert Blume must have heard what they were planning, though, because he told me to have some stickers printed with my name on them to fit into my slot on the sample ballot. On the eve of the election, several precinct captains called me to say they had received their election sample ballots with my opponent's name stamped in one slot. It was the practice of the party to print only the names of those they supported on the sample ballot. In fact, they had not printed my opponent's name on the ballot, but someone had inserted his name with a hand stamp.

On May 23, election day for the primary, Raoul Cunningham picked me up at my house at 5:45 P.M. We first went to my polling place, which was a half block from my house. The voting machine was in the basement of a home. I walked from the back yard down three steps into the basement. Robbie Wilson, the precinct captain, and her workers were there checking and testing the machine to see that it was working properly.

"Good morning, Robbie," I said coolly. "Would you mind showing me your sample ballots?" She reached behind the table and pulled the rolled-up sheets from a shopping bag. I unrolled one and held it out its full thirty-six inches. "Now, Robbie, you can see that my opponent's name has been stamped in his designated slot," I said, my voice gathering force. "This is one of the dirty tricks Democratic headquarters is playing. It is illegal to do this. As a matter of fact, it is ballot tampering." In reality it was not illegal, but it *was* unethical since it was their sample ballot. Nevertheless, I put the fear of God into her and continued, "I am taking these with me, so you won't get into any trouble. I can have locked up anyone who passes these out to voters."

"Georgia," Robbie said, looking uncomfortable, "I wasn't going to use them anyway. I just hadn't looked at them yet."

I nodded and went on, "Okay. I'm furnishing boxed chicken lunches to the workers this afternoon." I wanted her to know I'd be back.

"On the night of the election, Nicky drove me around to the homes of key precinct captains and workers in the Black precincts and I passed out money to them. The captains with the largest Democratic turnout from previous elections were given anywhere from twenty-five to fifty dollars for their work. Those I suspected of supporting my opponent received only ten dollars. Some took the money and still worked against me.

In the White precincts, Norbert Blume was getting many of his family members to work. He had his brothers, their wives, his wife, Marie, and four or five of his older children passing out flyers door to door and knocking on doors to get the voters out. I could not help noticing a difference of attitude and responsibility in White and Black captains. Not one Black captain refused the money. On the other hand, not one White captain would accept the money. Howard Spears, a gentle, round-faced man said, "Georgia, you don't have to pay me. If I was just doing it for the money, I wouldn't do it." Spears worked in a factory and had been given the day off with pay to work the polls.

A short while later, Raoul and I went to the precinct with the biggest voting pattern. Attorney Darryl Owens was the precinct captain there. The voters in this precinct were upper-middle-class Blacks; most were professionals. Some lived in large, spacious homes on Western Parkway. Others lived on Forty-seventh Street. Their back yards sloped down a hill to the Ohio River.

Darryl was standing in front of the polling place. When Raoul and I appeared, Raoul greeted him and then asked, "Darryl, what did you do with your sample ballots?"

Darryl said, "I didn't bring them, so I don't have to dispose of them."

I broke in, "I wish you had told some of your fellow captains to do the same."

Darryl didn't even comment on my remark. Instead he said, "Don't even worry about this precinct."

We walked a few blocks to another precinct; Stella

Pruitt, a petite woman with dark skin and curly hair, was captain. When we arrived and went into the polling place, she was busy with a line of voters. "How's it going, Stella?" I asked.

She looked straight at me, never blinking. "We've had a very good turn out so far. We've voted seventy-eight and it's only eleven in the morning." She added, "This was the second best voting precinct in the district."

I said, "What about the sample ballots?"

"Don't worry, I've got everything under control."

After visiting the key precincts, I returned home to rest. It was 4:30 P.M. The polls closed at 6:00 P.M. Raoul and William Gatewood kept the headquarters open until then. Afterward they rushed to the armory, where the votes were tabulated, to observe. One of the wise sayings of politicians is, "Many elections are won and lost in the counting." Blume and some of his workers came, as well, to watch how it was being done.

Raoul and Gatewood were given the results by the *Courier-Journal*. They called me. Raoul said, "Well, we did it. You have won by a majority of more than one hundred sixty votes."

Tears came to my eyes. "Raoul, is it really true? I am so excited." The first people I called, after getting off the phone with Raoul, were my mom and pop.

When I got to the victory party at Democratic headquarters later that evening, it was crowded. Henry Ward, who had won the gubernatorial slot, and many legislative winners were there. Walking across the room, I was congratulated by many of the Democratic workers and elected officials. Winning the primary election as a Democrat in the west end was tantamount to being elected. Registered Democrats outnumbered Republicans three to one there.

Never had I been happier. I knew I had cleared the most difficult hurdle.

13

M.L.

A week after the primary election, M.L. called. He said, "Well, Senator," using the name he called me from our first meeting to our last, "congratulations on your win in the primary! I had no doubt you would win. A.D. told me how you slaughtered your opponent."

"Yes," I said enjoying my own success. "The primary was the major hurdle. The staff members did an excellent job in getting the vote out."

"What will you be doing now—taking a rest?" he asked.

I sighed, "We will have a voter registration drive during the summer months, and get into campaigning for the general election in the fall."

"Senator, I'm going to be in Chicago next week for a couple of days. Will you meet me there?"

"I will," I replied.

"Your ticket will be at the airport," he said.

On the appointed day, I arrived in Chicago near seven. It was already dark. One of Dr. King's aides picked me up at the airport and drove me to an apartment house. I had no idea where I was or what part of town I was in. The driver opened the door and let me into the apartment. M.L. was not there. He said, "Dr. King will be here soon. Make yourself at home." Then he left.

I looked around the sparsely furnished apartment that seemed to belong to a bachelor. It did not have one feminine touch. Absentmindedly, I watched some television. When I heard a key being inserted into the lock, I went to see who was there. It was M.L. We greeted each other with a hug, then he asked about my campaign. "What about your opponent?" he wondered. "Was he devastated when you beat him?"

"Yes, he was very hurt that a newcomer to politics defeated him," I said. "It also hurt his ego that a Black woman defeated him."

Martin added, "And a good-looking one at that!" We both laughed.

"By having the backing of the local Democratic Party, he was sure he would win. But he underestimated his opponent," I said.

He looked at me and winked. Abruptly, he changed the subject. "Is A.D. doing better with his drinking problem?"

"Not really," I responded.

Martin frowned, "Is he getting worse?"

"Worse than what?" Again we laughed. I was purposely trying to lighten the mood. I didn't tell him how bad things had gotten with A.D. lately. After all, I wondered, what can M.L. do about it with his busy schedule?

"What is A.D.'s relationship with that woman he's always with?" Martin asked. "I'm not sure we should trust her. When A.D. is drinking, he could tell her anything."

"You're probably right about *that*," I said, looking away and avoiding the question about A.D.'s relationship with Lukey. Trying to get his mind off A.D. I asked, "How is the movement going in the North?"

M.L. frowned. "About as rough as it can be. Everything is in turmoil."

I sensed he didn't want to spend that night talking about the problems confronting him, and he confirmed my feeling, saying, "I just want to spend a quiet evening with you. I have a round of meetings to attend tomorrow. While I'm gone, make yourself comfortable. Don't fret if it gets late. I don't know how long it will take." We went to bed. The night went quickly.

Early the next morning he left. I spent the day studying some campaign reports, drinking coffee, watching television, and waiting around. I found some crackers and soup and sat at the table having a light lunch. On the table were some papers and a utility bill with the name of one of the SCLC attorneys, Chauncey Eskridge, printed on it. Later Chauncey phoned looking for M.L. "He's not back yet," I told him.

When M.L. returned in the early evening, he apologized for being late. "I've been with Mahalia Jackson. She's having some domestic problems."

I laughed, "I know you are a lot of things, but I didn't know you were a family counselor, too. Were you able to solve *all* her problems?"

He gave me a mischievous look, and said teasingly, "She served up some good soul food. Did you eat anything?" he asked.

"Yes," I nodded.

As I watched him, I could see he was tired and his mood had turned melancholy. I felt rather down myself; this was our last night. Suddenly M.L. said, "I'm just as normal as any other man. I want to live a long life, but I know I won't get to," he said.

I asked, "Do you think we can change the course of our lives? I often wonder if our lives are not predestined by God. Was it predestined for me to be here with you tonight?" He did not answer my first question, but said, "Definitely. You are destined to be here right now with me," and smiled, looking into my eyes. Later he slept quietly and peacefully as I held him.

The next morning, an aide came to take me to the airport. Martin immediately became more formal. "Thank you for coming, Senator. I'll be keeping up with your campaign for office," he said, shaking my hand.

A few weeks later, A.D. called to tell me M.L. would be in Chicago and wanted me to meet him again. I told him I would. "Good," A.D. replied. "I will make the arrangements. He wants you to come to Robert's Fiftieth at the Lake Hotel."

I thought this a strange name for a hotel. "Robert's what?" I asked.

A.D. explained, "Robert's Fiftieth. It's a hotel on Lake Michigan that's owned by a Negro whose name is Robert."

"I've never heard of it. But then, I'm not familiar with Chicago."

I arrived at 11:30 A.M. It was a beautiful day. The sun shone strongly and a soft wind blew off the lake. One of Dr. King's aids met me at the airport and drove me to the hotel. M.L. was there, but was getting ready to leave to make a round of appointments. He greeted me warmly, "I'm glad you could come. I don't know how long I'll be gone, but I know you will find something to do to occupy your time."

I nodded, "Yes, I'll read and probably take a walk along the lake. Don't worry about me—just don't forget I'm here!"

He laughed and said, "I *can't* do that."

After he left, I couldn't stay inside the hotel room; the weather was too beautiful outside. Taking the galley he had given me in Louisville, I wandered outside and looked for a quiet place to sit and read. There was a foot-wide, three-foot-high concrete wall separating the walkway from the lake. I wanted to sit on the wall's ledge, but didn't know how I was going to get up onto it in what I was wearing—a lime green, princess-style, one-piece dress. Somehow, I managed to climb onto the ledge and let my sandaled feet hang over the lake side of the wall. I looked out at the still, blue-green water whose boundaries seemed endless.

Bodies of water have always fascinated me and soothed my mind and soul. Now I gazed at this one, reminiscing and dreaming dreams. I looked at my life and remembered how far I'd come and where I hoped to go. I remembered that only God can make the ocean roar and the lake ripple. It was hard for me to keep my mind on reading, as I just wanted to stare at that lovely lake. My mind was far from the hectic Senate campaign I was waging in Louisville.

When I got tired of sitting there, I just walked and walked. I got back into the hotel after four o'clock. Dr. King arrived an hour later. He said, "I have had one *busy* day. It was hard getting away, but I remembered that you said not to forget you were here, and I didn't intend to. What would you like to eat? They have some good home-cooked barbeque here in Chicago. You can get the ribs or the sliced pork or ham on a bun with potato chips and slaw."

I said, "The ham sounds good to me."

"I think I'll get the ribs," he said, and telephoned one of his staffers to bring the food to us.

Then he motioned for me to sit beside him on the couch. "I just want to spend a quiet evening here with you without worrying about the problems that beset me. I don't even want to think about them," he said, adding, "Did you get to finish my galley?"

"No," I answered, "I found looking at the lake more interesting." We both laughed.

"Seriously, what do you think about it?" he quizzed.

"What, the lake?" I teased.

"No, smarty, the galley," he said.

I became serious, "For one thing, I think you are more radical, but I agree with you that our problems are the result of powerlessness. The White man has it and he is reluctant to give it up or share it. It is our basic challenge to organize and discover how to coalesce our strength in terms of economic and political power."

He responded, "That is the reason it is so important for you to get elected to the Kentucky Senate. That is about power! There is nothing wrong with having power as long as it is not abused."

Our food came and we began to speak of less serious things. He seemed to grow more carefree, and I more frivolous. He talked about the ministers and "leaders" he had to deal with. At times he stood up and mimicked them with voice and actions. I laughed as he portrayed them.

Sitting together on the couch, we watched the late news on television. Afterward he stood up. "Senator," he sighed, "I'm tired. Let's go to bed." I followed him. Later, as he slept, I lay awake thinking. He made me feel very special emotionally, physically, and psychologically on that night, as always. Watching him sleeping so peacefully, however, I could not forget what he had said the last time I'd come to Chicago, about wanting to live a long life and being sure he wouldn't.

Both when I was with him, and afterward, I always looked upon Martin Luther King Jr. as a man, not a god. I believe he was an instrument used by God to do His will, but I never confused the two. M.L. was a man who did great things, a man who had the intellect, the humbleness, and the leadership ability that God needed to bring about social changes in the world. Those who would judge Martin for being human should remember that even Jesus once said, "Father, if it be Thy will, let this cup pass from me."

Some people called him a prophet, and compared him with Jesus. I believe that, in the sense that he was under divine inspiration as a teacher of God's will to the people, he *was* a prophet. However, I did not compare him to Jesus in a supernatural sense, because I knew Martin had all the imperfections, foibles, and passions of a mortal man.

He was a man meticulous about his clothes and hair. He did not like wearing what he called "overalls," and usually wore black silk suits and a dress hat. He enjoyed laughter and jokes. He liked to talk about women, both those he found attractive and those he thought unattractive. He liked barbecued ribs, fried fish, greens, and other "soul foods," including chitterlings. He had a good appetite for life.

At that time, newspapers were reporting that many Black leaders did not agree with King's nonviolent philosophy. The "Black power" advocates such as Floyd McKissick of the Congress of Racial Equality (CORE) and Stokely Carmichael of the Student Nonviolent Coordinating Committee (SNCC) were not as committed to nonviolence as King. Martin told A.D. that when James Meredith was shot leading the "March Against Fear" on June 6, 1966 from Memphis, Tennessee to Jackson, Mississippi, the leaders of several factions met in Memphis to plan a strategy to resume the march. A misunderstanding followed, and Roy Wilkins of the NAACP and Whitney Young of the National Urban League returned to New York. Carmichael and McKissick, who persisted in the advocacy of violence, said they would only remain if King would leave the march.

Of course, they had not studied the great philosophers

as Dr. King had. He was a follower of Mahatma Ghandi. King believed that Ghandi's tactics to free India from British rule—using fasts, boycotts, mass marches, and massive civil disobedience—could be effectively used in the racial struggle in America. Gandhi led a majority against a minority. King, who forced America to pass national laws to bring about equality in housing, education, voting, and jobs, was leading a minority against a majority. Both believed in suffering and sacrifice.

Talking to Lukey and me about Dr. King's feeling on the subject of nonviolence, A.D. said, "M.L. had to convince me. I believed, as most Negroes do, that if you hit me, I'm going to hit you back." Of course, he also became an advocate of nonviolence. A.D. said, "M.L. believes that the church should take a direct and active role in the struggle for social justice. He derived this belief from his study of several great philosophers and leaders."

In between visits, M.L. telephoned me often, usually at night. One night he sounded very upset. "A.D. just phoned," he said. "He was drinking and he told me he was going to kill himself. Will you go over there and try to sober him up?"

I rushed over to his brother's house. His wife, Naomi, took me to their bedroom. "A.D., what's wrong with you?" I demanded. "Why are you worrying your brother with such foolishness? Hasn't he got enough to think about?"

"I was just kidding him," A.D. insisted. "I'll call him now and tell him I'm all right."

He dialed the number and talked with M.L. for a few minutes. "I'm not going to do anything crazy," A.D. assured him.

Then he handed the phone to me. "It's all right," I told Martin. "It was just his liquor talking."

He said, "I will call you later at home."

When I hung up, I gave A.D. a thorough tongue-lashing.

"Get your drunken self into bed and stay there. You ought to be ashamed to pull such a stunt," I chided him. Then I went home to wait for his brother's call. As always, M.L. kept his word.

14

PREMONITIONS

On July 18, 1967, a group of sixty-two people from ten organizations met to discuss and organize a voter registration and education drive. We called it the All Citizens Nonpartisan Voter Registration and Education Crusade. We elected a board of directors with members C.C. Richardson, pastor of Trinity AME Church, chairman; Raoul Cunningham, executive director; W.C. Young, of the Kentucky State AFL-CIO executive board, vice-chairman; Verna Donaldson, director of activities of the Women's Division of the AFL-CIO Committee on Political Education (COPE); and I, at that time, chairman of the Presbyterian Social Action Committee. Raoul and William Gatewood organized the office and solicited volunteers. Raoul drafted teenage members from his Green Street Youth Choir.

The committee sent 150 letters to ministers, asking them to declare two Sundays in July as "Voter Registration

Sundays," and to take special offerings to support the crusade. We set the starting date for August 3 and I contacted Dr. King. He agreed to come to Louisville and launch the voter registration drive.

At the headquarters Raoul, Gatewood, and I worked very hard. Everybody involved knew I was a candidate for the Senate. The drive served a dual purpose for me: I met a lot of grass-roots people and got out into the community to be visible and become known. We kept a record of the new registrants so that we could contact them before election day. The Thirty-third Senatorial District encompassed the Forty-first, Forty-second, and Forty-third Legislative Districts. The three Democratic candidates for the House of Representatives in those districts were Mae Street Kidd, Hughes McGill, and Norbert Blume.

A full day was planned for Dr. King on August 3, including a noon luncheon with local ministers, a press conference, a motorcade ride through the city, and an address to a mass meeting at Green Street Baptist Church in the evening. The volunteers passed out flyers in various neighborhoods announcing King's coming, the motorcade, and the rally. Flyers were placed in the west end churches on the Sunday prior to the registration kickoff. Announcements were made about the "big day" on the one radio station directed to the Black community, WLOU.

He was due to arrive at 11:00 A.M. A.D. had designated persons to meet Dr. King and bring him to Stouffer's Louisville Inn for the luncheon with ministers only. A.D. wanted to be there in order to greet the guest ministers as they came. Leaving, A.D. said, "I will bring Martin back with me to the office." The rest of us kept busy making signs to go on cars for the motorcade, which was to start at 6:00 P.M.

After the luncheon, A.D. and Lesser returned to the headquarters alone, looking very disappointed. A.D. said,

"M.L. missed his flight. I had to fill in for him at the luncheon."

Not wanting A.D. to lose all his enthusiasm, I asked, "What did you talk about?"

"It went all right. We discussed the importance of getting the voter registration numbers up and educating the voters on the candidates."

"Good, but I wonder what happened?" I quizzed.

A.D. said, "I'm worried about M.L. It's not like him to miss his flight. I'm going to call and find out what happened." He talked to Martin, then told us, "M.L. has a fever and is sick. He is going to rest for a while and if he feels better, he'll get a later flight."

Worried, I asked, "What will we do if he doesn't make it?"

A.D. answered, "We can manage the motorcade, but I'm just hoping he will be here. I can get one of the local preachers to speak, but the people are expecting to see M.L." We urged A.D. to call at 4:00 P.M. to see how Martin was feeling. "M.L. will be in at six o'clock," A.D. told us. We breathed a collective sigh of relief.

Someone would be at the airport to meet Dr. King and bring him to where we were. Many candidates, even those who were running statewide, would be riding in the motorcade and attending the mass meeting. The Democratic candidate for governor, Henry Ward, and some other statewide candidates had also been invited, but they had turned down the invitation, not wanting to be seen on television attending a predominantly Black affair. They did not want to alienate their White constituency or be associated with Blacks, as Blacks were a minority in their districts. Only Kidd, McGill, and Blume attended the rally.

On schedule, the cars began lining up in front of headquarters at Thirty-eighth and Broadway. We had a parade permit and a police escort. The motorcade planned six stops at two schools, one shopping center, and two housing projects. Because of all the cars, the motorcade left a half-hour late. A.D., Martin, and J.V. Bottoms, pastor of Green Street Baptist Church, sat on the back edge of a convertible with the top down. Their feet were on the back seat. The motorcade snaked through the different streets and was on the fifth stop, at Beecher Terrace Housing Project, when Dr. King was brought to meet us. Even though he was seven hours late, we were glad to see him. So were the onlookers who circled the convertible. The crowd roared when he appeared. There was so much jubilation, he could hardly be heard.

Bernard Lee, a young minister who accompanied Martin almost everywhere, did not come to the motorcade but joined King at the church. Martin spoke through a bull-horn, urging the people to register to vote. He urged them to join the motorcade and to come to the later meeting. He looked very tired to me, but I was not close enough to him to say anything.

The rally was billed to start at the church at 7:30 P.M. and it was already that time. Beecher Terrace was only a mile from the church and we still had a stop to make at Sheppard Square, a housing project three blocks from the church. After this last stop, the motorcade arrived at the second oldest Black Baptist church in Louisville, organized in 1844 and located on East Gray Street. The building, made of brick and stone with three white Doric columns across the front, had wide steps leading up to the red, triple front doors. Hundreds of people waited outside.

As we walked in, I first noticed the stained glass windows and then the choir which surrounded the pulpit. Inside another seven hundred people were seated and many more stood in the street trying to hear Dr. King. Abernathy gave him a rousing introduction. The crowd was stirred up emotionally. When King approached the podium, the people received him with a standing ovation. He had no prepared speech or notes. He just started talking about some recent experiences, which led him into the bulk of what he wanted to say.

"We are entering deeper nights of social disruption in our country. We have the resources to solve our problems. But the question is, do we have the will? I am worried about our national will. Either the Negro must be granted freedom, or he will have to be exterminated," Dr. King declared.

He spoke about the ineffectiveness and unsoundness of rioting. "Everybody is shouting, 'Get Whitey!' but they burn down the places where 'Whitey' is nonexistent. Whose children suffer? Who gets killed?" he asked.

Referring to the Detroit riot, he talked about the fact that, of the thirty-eight who died; thirty-six were Blacks."

He urged Blacks to seek public offices of prominence, where they would be in control, and could rebuild the inner cities.

He called upon Blacks to, "Get up from your stools of do-nothingness and complacency and do something for yourselves and the nation."

Finally, he urged Black people to "Build, baby, build—and vote, baby, vote—instead of burn, baby, burn."

After he concluded, the crowd rose to their feet and applauded for what seemed like five minutes. The twenty ministers seated in the pulpit surrounded him and showered him with hugs and admiration. Lukey and I sat in one of the front pews facing the pulpit, looking on.

After the program, we went with A.D., Martin, and Abernathy to the Colonial Inn Hotel in Jeffersonville, Indiana, across the Ohio River.

A few weeks before he came to Louisville, Dr. King spoke out about the injustices he thought were going on in Vietnam. However, he did not include these thoughts in his speech at Green Street. Lukey asked him, "Do you think directing attention to the injustices in Vietnam will reduce the effectiveness of the civil rights movement?"

He replied, "There have been three evils—racism, poverty, and violence—and I am including another." In explaining his opposition to senseless war and violence, he said, "I am calling for a negotiated settlement in Vietnam. The war is accomplishing nothing. People have been debating in their own minds whether we even had any business taking a position on the war. Many Blacks, including myself, have thought, that we have enough to worry about right here, which I later realized was just selfishness, once I thought about all the lives being lost."

Everyone was hungry and we wanted to order food, but the dining room had already closed. We could only get coffee from room service. A.D. asked, "M.L., what happened to you earlier today? Were you sick or exhausted?"

M.L. answered, "Yes, both sick *and* tired—of a lot of things. There are some people who feel nonviolence is not working. It is sapping all of my energy trying to convince them that the SCLC and I will always stand for nonviolence. I advocate this approach for the whole world. The nonviolent philosophy is not progressing fast enough for some of the militant leaders. But it *is* the only way." He looked dispirited and was obviously feeling down.

Ralph said, "If something isn't done soon to deal with the economic problem in the ghetto, the talk of guerrilla warfare is going to become very real."

Looking at M.L.'s melancholy face, I wanted to lighten his mood by changing the subject. I said, "M.L., you promised me a copy of your book. Did you bring it with you?" He smiled, as I had hoped he would.

"I know you are surprised, but I did." He reached into his bag and pulled out the book.

Excitedly, I asked, "Did you inscribe it?"

"I will right now," he said. He reached for a pen and wrote, "To My Friend, Georgia Davis, for whom I have great respect and admiration," and he signed it, "Martin Luther King Jr."

As I read the inscription, I said, "These words are very meaningful. I will read the book and give you my opinion the next time I see you."

Looking into my eyes he nodded. A short while later A.D. and Abernathy began complaining again that they were hungry. A.D. said, "We should have stopped somewhere and eaten before we came to the hotel."

Lukey intervened, "There are several places we can go to, either in Jeffersonville or in Louisville."

Ralph said, "I sure would like to have some ribs or chicken, but I guess it's too late now."

M.L. sighed and looked over to me, "I'm not that hungry," he said. "I would rather get some rest."

A.D. turned to Ralph and said, "Why don't you go with us to find a place to eat." While they were gone, M.L. and I finally had a chance to be alone.

I smiled at Martin, then became serious. "I have two months to campaign hard," I said.

He nodded, "Are the Negroes supporting you?" he asked.

"I have the support of the majority of Black ministers and the Black grass-roots community people," I said. "There are a few so-called leaders who are opposed, but nobody listens to them anyway. They have imagined political power."

We both laughed. We were able to spend a couple of hours together before the others returned. That short time was precious and sweet for us both, a haven from life's troubles. Later Ralph brought some food for Martin. I stayed another hour with the two of them, but A.D. and Lukey left.

"I'll pick you up," A.D. offered.

M.L. picked over the chicken and potatoes and left most of it on the plate.

"It's getting late," I finally said, yawning. "I have to get some sleep. I will see you in the morning."

The next morning, after A.D. came for me, we went to get M.L. and Ralph at the hotel and take them to the airport.

15

SWEET
VICTORY

The work at campaign headquarters accelerated. We continued to register people to vote in the general election. I was running against Clifton Loeffler, a short man with black hair, brown eyes, and an ivory complexion, who was the publisher of a small community newspaper, *The Star*. He was a reserved man who didn't give the impression he was serious about the race. He did no campaigning, and I never saw any of his posters or leaflets distributed. Despite this, I was not going to take him for granted. I spoke to groups in schools and churches, explaining my platform and what I wanted to accomplish, if elected.

The registration kickoff by Dr. King had given us the impetus we needed to escalate the drive. The last time we spoke, I had drawn him aside and said earnestly, "Dr. King, I need some of your field workers to come here and help us get the vote out in my district. They have experience doing the same thing in some of the Southern states. That is what we need."

Obviously sympathetic to my request he replied, "I will send you some help about a week before the general election. My workers will knock on doors, coerce, cajole, persist, and insist voters come out to vote. They know how important it is."

On September 9, the day the books closed for registering new voters, we tabulated the numbers and found we had registered more than nine hundred new voters in the city. A total of more than nine thousand new voters were added to the rolls during that same period city-wide. The voter crusade ended, and my campaign moved into the period just before the general election.

Anxious for a favorable outcome, and with only two months to campaign, I spoke wherever I was invited to do so. I continued to make campaign speeches at the Black churches and to small groups of people. The Social Action Club of the Third Christian Church, located around the corner from where I lived, invited me to speak at their program. That evening I greeted the audience and thanked them for inviting me. Then I said, "Folks, my platform is simple. I want equality for all people, and electing me to the Senate will assure you a voice in Frankfort. As most of you know, I have been marching in the streets of Louisville in support of a local open housing ordinance, and at the same time campaigning. I have attended the Board of Aldermen meetings on Tuesdays, urging it to enact an ordinance. If I get elected, the first bill I plan to introduce is an open housing bill. I want to increase the funding for Aid to Families with Dependent Children, allowing unemployed fathers to remain in the home if they must."

They seemed to be listening intently, so I went on with my list of priorities. "I am opposed to the redlining of real estate in the west end by the insurance companies. The minimum wage in Kentucky is now seventy-five cents an hour. I want to increase it. Children need free immunization. Black people are prone to having sickle cell anemia, which can kill you at an early age; we need research done in this area to develop a cure. Women cannot get a line of credit without the signature of their husbands. What if they don't have a husband or don't want them to know?" The audience chuckled. "I want the category of race eliminated from automobile operator's license. What does driving a car have to do with race? There are also the issues you have that you are concerned with. In me, you will have someone in the Senate who will listen and help, if at all possible. I urge you to come out and vote for me on election day and to urge your friends and relatives to do the same." I paused as they applauded, then continued, "If anyone has any questions, I will be glad to answer them."

A tall, well-tanned man in his forties stood up. I acknowledged him.

He said, "My name is Melvin Jones and I am a member of this church. My question is, 'What makes you think that we should vote for you, a woman?'"

He got my ire up, but I had to keep my cool and I answered in a calm voice, "Mr. Jones, God gave me a mind and soul just like he gave men, and I think he intended for me to use it." Hearing this, the women applauded loudly and a few men applauded politely.

One petite, gray-haired woman got up and asked, "Mrs. Davis, I don't want to seem stupid, but what is the job of a senator?"

I replied, "That is a very good question. There are probably others here who want to know, too. There are three branches of government in Kentucky: the executive branch, which is the office of the governor; the judicial branch, where justice is supposed to be dispensed by the courts; and the third branch, which is made up of two legislative bodies—the House of Representatives and the so-called upper House, the Senate. By the way, the members of the House of Representatives never like you to call the Senate the upper House, because that would make them members of the lower House." Once again there was scattered laughter. "These two bodies make the laws for Kentucky. A bill can be introduced by either body and must be passed by both. Once passed, a bill then goes to the governor, who can do one of three things: sign it, veto it, or let it become law without his signature. And that's a short lesson in government." I smiled and sat down.

After the meeting, I was invited to stay for a reception in the adjacent hall. People came up to me and shook my hand, greeting me warmly and saying, "We're going to vote for you," and, "Thank you for coming." I hoped they would not change their minds. Every vote for me counted.

A week before the general election, just as he'd promised, five of Dr. King's best fieldworkers arrived in Louisville. "We're here to get you elected," they announced. "Dr. King told us not to come back unless you win."

I laughed and said, "Well, in that case, we'd better get started." We worked eighteen-hour days that week.

On the day of the election, I visited the key precincts. Tired, I returned home at 4:30 P.M. to rest before going to the Democrats' victory party. Raoul and Gatewood stayed. They were young and could go straight through the evening without taking a break. I knew we had done all that we could. They closed the headquarters the same time the polls closed, 6:00 P.M., then rushed to the armory where the votes were being counted. We knew we had to have observers to see to it that there were no more dirty tricks played. There were hundreds of card tables on which several tabulators were transferring figures from the machine sheet onto charts. Blume and some of his workers were there. Blume, who'd been involved in local politics for twenty years, knew what to look for. The transferral of the numbers could make the difference between winning and losing. I was confident we had all the bases covered.

I took a long bath and dressed for the evening in a black, fitted wool dress with long sleeves and a gold border circling the neckline. I slipped on some two-and-a-half-inch heels and looked in the mirror. The shoes made me appear taller and thinner, and I could take long strides when I walked in them. I had bought a special coat to wear. It was an imitation broadtail with a full white mink collar circling my neck. Trying it on, I felt good. I took it off again and sat down to wait. Finally, Raoul called me from the armory to let me know that the television results were showing I was the winner. I was elated, but became so nervous realizing that I really was a state Senator that I could hardly sit still. My brother Lawrence picked me up at 8:00 P.M. and took me to the Victory Party at the Seelbach Hotel.

As we walked in, John Kelly, the doorman, said, "Miz Davis, congratulations on your victory." Kelly lived in my area and I had known him from the years I worked in campaign headquarters. I smiled and he went on, "You're the star tonight. They're waiting for you to arrive." Touched by his words I said, "Thanks very much, John, for your vote and your help."

When the elevator opened on the tenth floor, I got out and saw the huge hall in front of me filled with balloons, banners, and people. Some happy and some not-so-happy people were standing, cocktails in hand, or seated at one of the hundred tables. The Democratic candidate for Governor, Henry Ward, had been defeated by Republican Louie Nunn.

Many of the people present were precinct captains and inside poll workers; few were elected officials. The men and women seemed happy as I passed between them. Many hugged me or patted me on the back, shook my hand or called out greetings.

According to the *Courier-Journal* the next day:

> Mrs. Norman F. Davis could hardly get from the elevator on the tenth floor back to the ballroom where the election returns were being posted for all the hugs, greetings, and congratulations.
>
> Mrs. Davis has become the first Negro woman elected to the State Senate and also the first woman elected in a regular election to the Senate.

They quoted me as saying: "I think we're late in having a Negro woman, or more women of any race serve in the Kentucky Senate." Other women who had served in the Senate were appointed or elected in special elections to serve out their husband's unexpired terms.

I had won by a majority of nearly 4000 votes. The count was 10,548 for Davis and 6,778 for Loeffler. I received a generous note from Clifton Loeffler after the election. "You will make a better legislator, because you will give it full time," he wrote.

But not everyone was happy with my victory and the big Democratic sweep of city hall. Republican Mayor Kenneth Schmied charged voter fraud. He said he believed the signatures of some registered voters were forged at the polls and demanded a recount. The Democratic county chairman made a countercharge, stating that a group of Republicans checking signatures, led by Schmied and City Law Director Eugene Alvey, "are ransacking the records at will," and that all Democrats "have been barred from this pillage." An order by the city's Board of Registration Commissioners, of which Schmied was a member, barred Democratic Party workers from watching the GOP signature check. The Democrats got a temporary restraining order to prevent any examination of the records until the court could determine a proper method of inspection.

Thomas Carroll threatened suit against the registration board, saying, "We are not going to permit the mayor of Louisville to disenfranchise the Negro voters of this city." Fifty-three of the fifty-nine precincts involved in the vote check were predominantly Black. I was quoted as saying, "This is a debased approach to disenfranchising the Negro voter. The heavy Democratic vote in the west end was a result of the Negro community going to the ballot to show their disapproval of the actions of the mayor and the Board of Aldermen, not because of any fraud."

A forty-member organization, chaired by Darryl Owens and called Democrats for Better Government, denounced the mayor for "not keeping faith with the Negro community," and declared, "Mayor Schmied indicated his lack of understanding of the desires and aspirations of the Negroes in this community."

In spite of opposition from party heads, party regulars, and other elected officials, I had won election to the Senate. My victory was sweet.

16

SENATOR
GEORGIA M. DAVIS

As far as I know there are no schools for senators, and I had neither experience nor a mentor. Therefore, it was no wonder that my stomach churned and my heart beat so loudly I was sure Raoul could hear it when he arrived at my home that January morning in 1968, to drive me to the state capitol. It was the opening day of the General Assembly and I would be sworn in as a freshman legislator. Like most freshmen, no matter what the educational facility, I was naive and nervous, but eager to learn.

Frankfort, Kentucky's state capitol, is a small city on the Kentucky River located between two major cities, Louisville and Lexington. From Louisville, a highway winds its way down to the capitol. From Lexington, the highway crosses the river to Capitol Avenue, a tree-lined boulevard leading up to the capitol building. Perhaps one of the most beautiful edifices in the United States, around it are thirty-four acres of lush green landscaped grounds. Seventy Ionic columns of Bedford stone and Vermont granite surround the exterior.

In the designated lot, Raoul parked his car. We got out and walked over to a series of steps winding through the brick terraces and flower beds leading to the front entrance. Climbing to the top, the excitement and nervousness I felt grew even more pronounced. Raoul opened the front door and, stepping inside, I was immediately surrounded by walls and stairwells of pristine white marble. Entering the reception area, we walked a few steps into the rotunda. There were statues of Lincoln, Lee, and other dignitaries. We took the elevator up. Getting out, I identified myself and introduced Raoul to the guard on duty. Then we walked along the resonating corridor, stopping at a double set of oak doors with a plaque reading, *The Senate*.

I took a deep breath, and opened those doors. Entering the senate chamber, I stood at the entrance a few seconds, marveling at the beauty of the room. A leaded glass, domed ceiling of jeweled colors let the sun shine through. I faced the raised podium. Behind it loomed a golden granite backdrop upon which was mounted the state seal. There was a long table the width of the room just below the podium where the constitutional employees were and then a divided aisle where the senators sat. Looking to the side, I saw my mother and father, my brother Jimmie, and his wife, Marie, who had come to see me sworn in.

I walked slowly toward seat number fifteen, which I had already chosen. It was in the second row, the second seat from the outside aisle. I purposely did not choose a seat in the back, never having forgotten my humiliating experience on the bus to Texas.

Reaching the seat, I saw that a bronze nameplate with

SENATOR GEORGIA M. DAVIS printed on it had been installed on the front of my desk. Beaming, I looked over at my mother and father, who were now sitting on a heavy, leather couch by the wall near my seat. They were as thrilled as I was. As we made eye contact, they stood up and came over to me. My father said, in a voice filled with pride, "Georgia, we are so proud of what you have accomplished. With God's help, you made it. We are behind you, and whatever we can do to help you to do your job, we will." I embraced them and they went back to their seats. Then, for the first time, I sat down in the high-back swivel chair covered with black leather and imprinted with the Kentucky symbol of two men shaking hands.

The president of the Senate, Wendell Ford, who was also the lieutenant governor, banged the gavel and announced that the Senate was ready to do business. He asked the invited minister, who was seated in a chair next to the podium, to open the session with prayer.

On the other side of the podium sat a black-robed judge. After the prayer, the president called him forth to swear in the newly elected senators and administer the oath of office. Then the president said, "Will all the newly elected senators come to the front and line up with your backs to me?" I looked over again at my mother and father and gave them a big smile. Then I walked to the front of the room.

The judge stood before us and said, "Please repeat after me: I do solemnly swear that I will support the Constitution of the United States and the constitution of this common-wealth, and be faithful and true to the Commonwealth of Kentucky, so long as I continue a citizen thereof, and I will faithfully execute, to the best of my ability, the office of senator according to law." In addition, we swore that we had never fought a duel with deadly weapons nor acted as a second in a duel. At the time, this clause seemed to be an anachronism left over from the South's romanticized past, but later, caught in the fray of legislative battles, I thought they were probably wise to retain it.

After I was sworn in and took my seat again, I looked around at my fellow senators—thirty-seven White men. It was the first time it really hit me that I would be the only woman and the only Black senator.

"What have I gotten myself into?" I murmured to myself. I was not intimidated at the prospect of working with men, even White men. However, I suddenly realized that I didn't know what I was supposed to do, much less how to do it. Never had I felt more apprehensive, and to calm my nerves I began to pray softly.

"God, I'm depending on you to help me to know what I should say and what I should not say, what I should do and what I should not do."

A short while later, the officers of the two legislative bodies were proposed. A blond, small-framed thirty-six-year-old lawyer from Madisonville, Richard Frymire, was voted Democratic floor leader. He would be responsible for steering the bills to be voted on. Walter D. Huddleston, or "Dee" as he was called, an easy-going person with a gentle aura about him, was voted Democratic caucus chairman. Six years later he would become a United States Senator.

All through the Senate's proceedings, television cameras swept over the scene and the clicks of newspeoples' pens could be heard. The Senate was only in session an hour. Afterward, reporters surrounded my desk, and one asked the questions many had in mind, "How does it feel to be the first Black senator to serve in this body?"

I kept my voice steady and clear: "I did not know until I got here that I was the first Black, woman *or* man, to be elected. I am happy the people of the Thirty-third District have sent me here to represent them, and I plan to do just that." Another asked, "What plans do you have for introducing legislation, and do you have any specific legislation you will introduce?"

I nodded, "Yes, I plan to introduce several bills in the area of civil rights, equal rights, and education."

Then, having given my first interview as the senator from the Thirty-third District, and feeling wonderful, I left that venerable gathering for a celebratory lunch with my friends and family before they all returned to Louisville.

My good mood changed abruptly later that day, however, when I inquired at the local hotels for a room to stay in. I did not want to have to commute sixty miles each way. The Holiday Inn was the favorite hotel of the legislators. The lobbyists—or "registered agents," as they preferred to be called—who represented special interest groups liked to stay at the Holiday Inn too, in order to be close to the legislators. The Holiday Inn had a lounge with a bar and a dance floor which the legislators frequented nightly. When I inquired there, they said they were booked for the next three months. Next I went to the Southern Hotel, an old-styled hotel where you walked from the sidewalk right into the lobby. They said they were booked for the duration of the session. My last hope was the Ramada Inn, which was located on the other side of town. I checked with them and, like the others, the clerk said they were full.

The second day, as I was leaving the capitol to return to Louisville, I saw Marlene Tentman, a petite Black woman with saucerlike brown eyes. We had met several years before at a reception. She had been an executive secretary for Lt. Governor Wilson Wyatt at that time. When Wendell Ford was elected Lt. Governor, she stayed in the same job with him. Marlene was a single mother who had moved to Louisville and then to Frankfort from Harlan, Kentucky. She attended Kentucky State College and worked, as she said, "In the White folks' kitchen," to send money home to take care of her daughter until she got her college degree.

Marlene lived in a three-room shotgun house at 221 River Street. It was half of a side-by-side duplex. I explained my problems to her and she said, "Georgia, you don't have to stay in a hotel that doesn't want you. You can stay at my house. It isn't much, but you are welcome there."

I was touched by her kindness and her offer. "Marlene," I said, "I don't want to put you out, but I may not have a choice." As it turned out, the choices I had were meager, so I chose Marlene's small but well-kept house in which to stay. Marlene, a talented country cook, served fresh greens twice a week seasoned with what she called "country meat." She had corn bread and peach cobbler everyday. I'm very sure that her good food contributed to my effectiveness in the Senate.

During those early days I got help from people I knew and trusted. My friend and former campaign manager, Raoul Cunningham, had been hired by Speaker of the House Julian Carroll as the first Black reading clerk; his job was to read the titles of the bills as they were working their way through the legislative process. As a minority, he also was experiencing discrimination problems. When Raoul first reported to work, the chief doorkeeper would not let him enter the Senate Chamber because he was Black. Julian had to instruct the doorkeeper to let Raoul in.

After the sessions Raoul, Marlene, and I would read the day's bills and discuss them all. It never occurred to me *not* to read the bills. I felt like a student who was afraid of being called on while unprepared. Marlene and Raoul gave me their advice on whether I should support or oppose the proposed legislation and then I made up my mind. We wrote up my positions and Marlene typed them for me, often after I went to bed.

In short order, I was named vice-chairman of the Health and Welfare Committee; Republican Senator Walter "Stu" Reichert was named chairman. On the Health and Welfare Committee, I quickly saw that I would be supporting unpopular causes. The first issue to separate me from most of the other committee members was my support for bills that would allow denturists (the people who actually make dentures) and chiropractors to be paid through health insurance.

To me, these practitioners were the underdogs, opposed by the well-financed state medical and dental associations. I think some of the other senators agreed with me, but they wouldn't vote against their personal physicians and dentists, who asked them to oppose the measures. My physician, Dr. A. B. Harris, didn't take a position against the chiropractors, perhaps because he was not then a member of the Kentucky Medical Association. My dentist, however, let me know he opposed the bill—while he had the drill in my mouth!

Chairman Stu Reichert and I had a good working relationship. As vice-chairman, I had a little more power than the other members. I continued to take unpopular positions, although I worked with the other members on whatever I could support. Our discussions were always congenial, however. My fellow committee members could afford to be cordial—they always had the votes.

I also was appointed vice-chairman of the Labor and Industry Committee. Here, too, my views were often at odds with the other members, most of whom were business-oriented. I tended to side with organized labor. In this, I was influenced by my father, who was a strong union member. In addition to my father's influence, my involvement in the civil rights movement had exposed me to the labor movement, since the two movements usually worked together.

The other committee I served on was the Cities Committee, a logical choice since I wanted to influence legislation that affected Louisville. The issues in that committee often divided along rural-urban lines, and the urban members were in the minority.

My fellow Senators were friendly, courteous, and polite to me on a personal basis. However, they had no compassion for me, just because I was a woman or because I was Black, while we were debating legislation. After a defeat I sometimes felt like crying, but never did. I told myself, "The day you shed tears over a defeat is the day you resign from this august body."

One day the death penalty was up for discussion. I argued against it, asserting, "We do not have the right to take a life. Furthermore, it has been proved that the death penalty does not deter crime. Blacks and poor people are the ones who disproportionately receive the death penalty." I referred to the Bible by quoting one of the Ten Commandments, "Thou shalt not kill. There are twenty-eight senators who profess in the Senate directory that they are Christians. I just hope the Christians will uphold their beliefs." I could see the die was cast, however. Again they were disinterested in what I was saying, their minds were made up. The bill passed thirty-five votes to three. My seatmate, tall, dark-haired David Karem, who became a good friend, voted against it. He was Catholic and also opposed all abortion rights bills. The third "Nay" vote was cast by Walter Strong, a minister in the Church of God faith. A Democrat who only served one four-year term, he said, "My conscience will not let me vote for this bill."

Even though I had entered a male arena, I was not tempted to try to be "one of the boys." I have known some "liberated" women who try to do that, even using the vulgar language that some men use with other men. It seems to me that using four-letter words is a foolish way to prove your equality with men. I treated my fellow senators with respect and friendliness, but had my own agenda and wasted no time in pursuing it. I was there to represent the residents of my district, the great majority of whom were poor. Although there are many Kentucky legislators who represent poor districts, since Kentucky is considered a poor state, I didn't find many who were actually working for the poor.

Later I learned that freshman legislators often assume a low profile and try to become accepted by more senior members before attempting to lead in passing or blocking legislation. This wasn't my approach for two reasons: it was not my nature to take a back seat, and it was soon obvious to me that it was unlikely I would ever be accepted by the majority of Kentucky legislators; therefore, I plunged right in. It was my intention to introduce legislation on issues I had advocated during my campaign—statewide open housing, a public assistance measure to increase welfare payments to 100 percent of need, election reform to increase pay for poll workers and reduce the residency requirement for voting, improved services for those with mental handicaps, and labor legislation in the area of workmen's compensation. I didn't like the term "workmen's." Women are an important part of the work force, I told all who would listen, and the program should reflect that. A bill I later introduced changed the name to "worker's compensation."

I also decided to tackle my most controversial goal, legislation to ensure open housing, that very first session.

17

THE LADY
FROM
JEFFERSON 33

My zeal to do something about housing discrimination had become a personal crusade. Until then, although I was keenly aware of the problem, it had not affected me personally. I had a comfortable home in the west end of Louisville and no desire to move to another part of the city. But as a senator, when I sought a place to live in Frankfort, I had to look housing discrimination square in its ugly face.

The insidious nature of discrimination is that it cannot be combatted through individual achievement. To a racist, it doesn't matter how educated you are, how important the position you hold is, or what you have accomplished in life. If you are Black, get back, as the saying goes. The Frankfort motels and hotels that turned me away fueled the fire already burning in me to strike a blow against housing discrimination.

On February 8, a little more than a month after I took my Senate seat, I introduced a statewide open housing bill which Galen Martin, the first executive director of the Kentucky Commission on Human Rights, had helped draft. I had first met Galen, who had blond hair, a lean face, and a ready smile, during the 1964 March on Frankfort. Under the leadership of Governor Bert T. Combs, the legislature had passed several civil rights laws: a prohibition of discrimination on the basis of race or ethnic origin in employment under the newly created State Merit System, adoption of a public policy against discrimination, and creation of the Kentucky Commission on Human Rights. When the latter bill first came up in the House, it failed to pass. Its supporters then regrouped and obtained the necessary votes.

The function of the Commission was to "encourage fair treatment for, to foster mutual understanding and respect among, and to discourage discrimination against any racial or ethnic group or its members." The legislature gave the Commission no enforcement powers and a budget of only $12,500 a year to carry out these responsibilities. Governor Combs said to its members, "We want you to understand we are looking to you to take the initiative and to show the way to us, as to all other Kentuckians. I hope that whatever approach you have to your job, you will be positive and take the initiative. I hope you lead the way in this field. I want to say to you as governor I will give you full support, this administration will, and I think the people will."

I relied on the Commission to keep me abreast of civil rights issues and to give me information and technical assistance to advance the causes of Blacks in Kentucky.

In addition to active opposition from some legislators, the Commission worked in a climate of indifference on the part of many, if not most. However, the Commission and Black leaders were able to join together on the issues and force legislators to take a stand. Even though many of the legislators weren't interested in the progress of Blacks, they didn't want to be publicly on record as racists. It was our skill at thwarting legislators' efforts to hide out that enabled us to pass strong civil rights legislation.

The open housing bill would make it illegal for a person to refuse to sell or rent housing on the basis of race, religion, or national origin. It would also forbid mortgage institutions from discriminating against minorities. The bill gave broad powers to the Kentucky Commission on Human Rights to investigate complaints of discrimination, try to conciliate grievances, and, if necessary, issue orders and seek the aid of the courts in enforcing them.

When I stood to introduce the bill, the president of the senate, Wendell Ford, said, "I recognize the lady from Jefferson 33."

Asking for co-signers for my bill, my strategy was to appeal to their pride in Kentucky as a Border State not guilty of some of the abhorrent practices of states in the Deep South. I also appealed to their obligation to Black men and women who had served their country, and finally, I tried to prick their consciences on the basis of their publicly-declared religious affiliation:

"Mr. President, gentlemen of the Senate, I rise to make a request that Senate Bill Two-sixty-four will place Kentucky in the forefront of progressive states in the nation. This Commonwealth has an enviable record among states in its geographical location for certain significant examples of leadership. The right to suffrage for minorities in Kentucky has never been seriously challenged or restricted by ingenious devices employed to deprive them of their privilege of voting, and integrated collegiate education existed in the state at Berea College until the early part of the twentieth century.

GEORGIA DAVIS POWERS

"The 1968 General Assembly can, and I am sure, will enhance this distinctive leadership by eliminating discrimination in the sale and rental of housing because of race, color, religion, or national origin. This practice of depriving some citizens of opportunities while according them to other citizens clearly contradicts that single-standard status guaranteed in the U.S. Constitution. As such, this denial of equality stands out as a national and international disgrace. There is no section of this state where this problem does not exist. The refusal to sell or lease real property to anyone simply because of the color of his skin is an affront to human dignity and an insult which is conducive to strife and domestic unrest."

In my speech I also reminded my fellow legislators that equal access to housing was essential, because it affected so many other aspects of people's daily lives, where their children would go to school, and where they would find employment. I stressed to the members that it was their constitutional duty to protect the health and welfare of Kentucky citizens—including Black citizens. Much of what I said protested the injustice of asking women and Blacks to serve and die for their country and then denying them housing opportunities. I closed my pleas for the other senators' support by appealing to their Christianity.

"I was particularly impressed when I checked the church roll call of the members of the Kentucky State Senate to find that thirty-four of the thirty-eight senators of this august body profess a belief in the teachings of Christ. With faith in Him, no one should be afraid to provide justice.

"Mr. President, gentlemen of the Senate, I summarize my request and appeal for your signature by quoting the Holy Scriptures, this passage found in First John, chapter two, verses seven through nine: 'Brethren, I write no new commandment unto you, but an old commandment which ye had from the beginning. Again, a new commandment I write unto you, which thing is true in him and in you: because the darkness is past, and the true light now shineth. He that saith he is in the light, and hateth his brother, is in darkness even until now.'"

I sat down. There was a smattering of polite applause from those still there. I hadn't noticed, but many of my colleagues had left the chamber while I was speaking. No one went to the table to co-sign the bill.

I felt discouraged but not defeated. I had learned yet another lesson. Racism could not be fought in the political arena with appeals to logic or a sense of justice. It had to be fought the way most political battles are won—through "horse-trading." I had to have something the other members wanted, and I had to use it to get what *I* wanted.

A bill remains at the clerk's desk for a day before it is reported to the proper committee. In this case, my bill was sent to the Judiciary Committee, chaired by my seatmate to the left, Tom Garrett. After the Senate adjourned, five senators co-sponsored the bill: Robert D. Flynn, Walter D. Huddleston, William L. Sullivan, John Turner, and Carl T. Hadden Sr. Bobby Flynn, who liked to talk to me about his son playing professional baseball with the Cincinnati Reds, was a Republican from Lexington. Walter D. Huddleston, the sociable and slow-talking Democratic caucus chairman, would be helpful to me in getting my legislation into the right committees. William L. Sullivan, an attorney and Democrat from Henderson who was a veteran Air Force pilot and the president pro tempore, loped when he walked and seldom spoke on bills. John Turner was a forty-seven-year-old Democrat who had a sense of humor, drank quite a bit, and came from a very political family in Jackson.

At the time, Tom Garrett was leading the effort to have Kentucky go on daylight saving time. Every day he would say, "Georgia, how do you plan to vote on daylight saving time?"

Every day I would answer him the same way. "Tom, I really don't care what time it is. All I care about is open housing. I want my bill out of your committee."

"Georgia, I can't get a quorum," he kept saying, which meant not enough senators were attending the meetings.

Finally I told him, "If you'd bring it up at the beginning of your committee meeting instead of at the end, you might have a quorum."

He shook his head, "When I try to bring it up some of the members walk out. I can't get your bill out; even if I did, it wouldn't pass," he answered. He had every excuse in the book. I got angry.

"Just get it out, Tom. And watch me pass it!" I said.

Instead of replying, he just brought up his own bill again. I knew that the *Frankfort State-Journal* had polled the Senate on the daylight saving time bill and reported that, "The three new senators from Louisville are split on the issue with Senator Henry Beach for it, Romano Mazzoli against it, and Georgia Davis feeling she 'would have to give more profound study and consideration' before making up her mind." Actually, I never studied it, never intended to study it, and didn't care one way or another whether it passed. I wondered, however, if I could use my vote with its sponsor, Tom Garrett, to get my open housing bill out of committee.

The two bills—daylight saving time and open housing—were both languishing. Tom needed twenty votes to pass his. He finally got eighteen commitments, but the opposition had nineteen, and he realized he had to have my vote. "Georgia," he said quietly, "if I get your open housing bill out of committee, will you vote with me on daylight saving time?"

"If you report it out 'with the expression that it should pass,' I will give it serious consideration," I said.

The next morning he greeted me excitedly, saying, "Georgia, I had a call meeting of my committee this morning and we reported your bill out. Now will you vote with us?"

"First, I must check with the clerk's office to see if it came out with the expression that it should pass," I said.

Tom followed me to the Senate clerk's office, and when I found everything in order, he said, "Now, can I count on you?"

"On one condition," I said.

"*Now* what?" He was getting exasperated.

"Take the roll call sheet and get commitments from your eighteen people who are voting for daylight saving time that they will vote for open housing," I answered.

"I can't do that!" Tom exploded.

"That's the deal," I said calmly. "Take it or leave it. It would do me no good to get my bill out and not have enough votes to pass it."

Finally, he agreed to my terms, and I promised to vote for his bill. Once he had the votes for passage, Garrett wasted no time in getting the daylight saving time bill through. The bill was posted for passage and was debated on the floor for an hour. When the roll call was taken, the vote was tied—nineteen to nineteen—which meant the president of the Senate, Wendell Ford, would have to break the tie.

Some of the members opposing the bill approached me and urged me to change my vote. "You have consistently said you didn't care what time it is, so why don't you change? You know it will be bad for Wendell whichever way he votes."

"Better him than me," I said. "I gave my word and my reputation is on the line."

Despite my words I didn't want to upset Ford because my good friend, Marlene Tentman, was an executive secretary in his office and kept me informed of what was going on.

Luckily Wendell Ford did not hold my vote against me. I have had a good relationship with him over the years as he went from the Kentucky Senate to becoming Kentucky's governor, and then on to serve in the United States Senate. We don't agree on everything and sometimes we've had confrontations, but I think he is an honest person and we have always remained friendly.

Ford broke the tie on the daylight saving time bill by voting for it. Next, my open housing bill was received by the Senate, had its second reading, and was sent back to the Rules Committee. That committee would make the decision about when to send it to the Senate for its third reading, to be placed in the Orders of the Day.

Hardly anyone thought the bill would pass.

The open housing bill was controversial, because many White people did not want Blacks to move into their neighborhoods. However, one of the most basics question for every family is, "Where shall we live?" The vast majority of Kentucky Black families had limited choices with which to answer this question. Most towns had certain areas where Blacks were allowed to live and other areas where they could not live. There was no law requiring housing segregation, however. In 1917, the Supreme Court case of Warley v. Buchanan, which originated in Kentucky, had established that housing segregation of the basis of race is illegal. Nevertheless, segregation did exist and was enforced by an unwritten understanding. In addition, landlords charged unusually high rent to Blacks because they knew their choices were limited.

I believed the opportunity for equal access to housing was the greatest need Black people then had, because housing so intimately affects all other aspects of equality. Without equality of opportunity in housing, schools remain segregated. Without it, employment and public facilities preserve and extend the practice of discrimination. Without it, the people of this nation and this state would become increasingly suspicious of, and hostile toward, their neighbors. Blacks do not necessarily want to move out of their neighborhoods. They want to be able to do so if they wish, however, as would any other citizen.

The Blacks who move into integrated neighborhoods would be on the same level as their neighbors whether these people are persons of substantial means, persons of average income, or persons of limited earning ability. If Blacks, Whites, or people of any race, disturb the peace, constitute a menace to health, or permit his or her home to become a fire hazard, there are enforceable laws to correct all of these objectionable circumstances.

The Louisville *Courier-Journal* carried the following editorial supporting my bill:

> Kentucky needs an open housing law, and the legislature now in session has an opportunity to pass one, and settle the matter once and for all, without having the issue fought city by city and county by county. In submitting the Senate bill, Senator Georgia M. Davis of Louisville raised a simple question: How can we justify sending our Negro citizens to shed their blood and risk their lives overseas for this country, and then when they come home—those who do—deny them the free choice of housing that other citizens have? It's a fair question and it deserves an honest answer, not evasions and phony rationalizations of discrimination.

Others worked hard on getting people from all over the state to lobby their representatives in the legislature. Representative John Hardin, of Hopkinsville, urged passage. He called it "a fine step toward the eradication of this sickness that we call discrimination." Representative Bernard Keene of Bardstown also spoke in support of the bill.

The open housing bill was finally posted for passage on March 12, which left only three days to get it through the Senate and the House before the General Assembly adjourned on March 15. Senator Carroll Hubbard from western

Kentucky told me, "It will hurt me in my district if I vote for open housing. Do you mind if I step into the hall? That way I won't have to vote against your bill?"

I nodded. "If you can't vote for me, at least don't vote against me," I pleaded.

I talked to each senator I thought I could influence. Fellow Louisville Senator Romano Mazzoli (now a member of the U.S. House of Representatives) was one who would not commit to vote for the bill. When I brought it up, he vacillated.

When the roll call was taken, Mazzoli passed on voting. At the end of the roll call, when he realized the bill was already passing, he stood and voted for it. The vote was twenty-seven to three, with eight abstentions. Eighteen Democrats and nine Republicans voted for it; two Republicans and one Democrat voted against it. The others were absent or hiding out. I had been sure the bill would pass if I could only get it to the floor of the Senate. I was jubilant.

The bill then went to the House of Representatives, where a weaker open housing bill had been introduced by Representative Hughes McGill. A companion bill to mine had also been introduced by Representative Mae Street Kidd. Instead of continuing to fight for her stronger bill, Mae had decided to co-sponsor McGill's bill, House Bill 242.

When my bill, Senate Bill 264, went before the House Judiciary Committee, they replaced it with McGill's bill. Thus, we had three Black legislators rivaling each other to pass an open housing bill. I didn't care whose name was on the bill and who got the credit; I just wanted the strongest bill passed, and I knew mine was strongest.

Norbert Blume acted as an intermediary, persuading Kidd and McGill to go along with Senate Bill 264. He told them if they didn't agree it was very possible no open housing law would be passed in the session.

The day for the voting in the House had arrived. An editorial in the *Courier-Journal* called it:

The day of decision on opening housing. The Kentucky Senate has passed an amended but a strong open housing bill and if the House follows suit today, this legislature will occupy a proud place in the history of the Commonwealth. The Senate bill added Kentucky to the list of more than 20 states that have acted to break down the racial barriers in housing, and made this state the first below the Ohio River to do so.

It would be a shame if open housing fails to pass because of a procedural snarl. If this happens, Representative McGill of Louisville cannot escape some of the blame for he engineered a different and weaker open housing bill in the House. If the procedural obstacle is overcome, then it is squarely up to the House to act with the same enlightened sense of responsibility the Senate displayed and give Kentucky an open housing law.

Apprehensive but hopeful, I went to the House of Representatives to observe the vote.

Standing in the back of the House Chamber I looked for the four women representatives—Mae Street Kidd, Marge Cruse, Ruth Wolchick, and Nell Guy McNamara. It was easy to pick out Mae, as she was 5'9" tall and blond. She stood out in a crowd.

The House was busy and noisy that day, as it usually is. People walk around and visit from one desk to another. At times, it seems like all one hundred members are talking and walking at one time. The Speaker has to keep hitting the gavel for quiet. Despite the confusion, the members say they like it better in the House because of the excitement. They say the Senate is "dead" and there's not enough action. That day the excitement was palpable.

The House has electronic voting machines, unlike the Senate, which votes by voice. I kept in touch with Kidd, McGill, and Blume on how the votes were lining up and the number of solid commitments Blume had. They were confident. Carroll, the Speaker, waited patiently for the red and green lights to settle down. When he saw enough votes to pass the bill, he locked the voting machine and announced the fifty-four to seventeen vote. Then he flashed me a "thumbs up" sign. The House voted the title of the bill, "The Georgia M. Davis, Hughes McGill, Mae Street Kidd Civil Rights Act of 1968." Newspapers later reported, "The title was calculated to soothe the bruised feelings that have resulted from competition over the sponsorship of open housing legislation."

Representative Kidd, in tears, rose to thank the House after the vote. The Democratic floor leader, Fred Morgan of Paducah, added that John Hardin and Foster Pettit of Lexington "have worked far beyond the call of duty to work out this matter."

Many legislators came over to congratulate me, and I congratulated the floor managers for their diligence and hard work. Now I was hoping Louie Nunn, the Republican governor, would not veto the bill. Nunn, an attorney from Glasgow, had the build of an athlete, was always impeccably dressed, and had a stern look. He had campaigned against open housing, so I was worried. But he let the bill become law without either vetoing or signing it.

The passage of my bill was generally regarded to be the great surprise of the 1968 legislative session. More than anything, I had wanted to pass a strong, fair housing bill. Accomplishing that goal energized me for the future battles ahead. I didn't realize then just how much I was going to need that energy.

18

R & R

It was the sixtieth day of the session, March 15, 1968. The General Assembly met into the wee hours in the morning. At midnight, the clock on the wall was stopped, so the Senate could continue doing business. The Kentucky Constitution allowed the General Assembly to meet for sixty days every other year. Stopping the clock was circumventing the law. Conference committees were appointed by the president of the Senate and the speaker of the House for the purpose of resolving the difference in House bills and Senate bills. Those who were not on a committee sat and waited for the bills to be reported out and voted on again. There was a party atmosphere while the waiting was going on. The men kept slipping out to their restroom, which was right outside the chamber door, to drink. They offered me some liquor, but I politely refused.

Dark circles had formed under my eyes from the pressure and long hours during the last days of the session. I had worked hard and felt good about my accomplishments in my first session, though. The General Assembly finally voted *sine die* at 4:00 A.M.

The next day I drove home feeling very tired but satisfied. I tried to rest, but both small and large matters needed my attention. A.D. called and said, "I talked to M.L. He's going to call you tonight."

"I'll be home," I replied.

M.L. called. It was a short conversation. He asked how the session went, and he ended with, "You've kept the men off you, haven't you Senator?"

"Not to worry!" I teased. "I took care of myself."

I hadn't seen Lukey at all during the session. She sent me notes of congratulations when there was something in the paper about me or when she had seen me on television. But the day after I came home, she called and said, "How about going to Florida with me? You deserve a vacation." I didn't even have to think about it. Never had I been more glad to receive an invitation.

"When are we leaving?" I asked.

She said, "We can leave on the eighteenth. I'm going to drive my car."

"Fine with me. I'll be ready as soon as you want. How long will we be gone?" I said.

"We'll stay a month."

"What will we do for a whole month?" I asked.

"I want to do some writing," she answered.

I laughed, "When did you become a writer? Never mind, I'm going."

Lukey and I drove down in her pale blue Cadillac convertible. Still feeling exhausted, I slept for the first leg of the trip. When I awoke, Lukey said, "I'm so proud of you. I still don't understand how you got that open housing bill passed. I heard from A.D. and the newspaper that you had some problems with McGill in the House."

"Aha—it was my intellect," I teased. "Yes, McGill wanted to substitute his weaker version of open housing for my stronger one. Blume had to go to him and tell him, "Now, boy! You had better go along with Georgia's bill since this is the last day, or you will be responsible for losing the whole thing." Lukey laughed.

As we drove along the highway, we joked about the different people we knew; especially the preachers, but not sparing ourselves either. At one point I said, "Remember the appointed position Frank Stanley Sr. had under the Breathitt administration? He was supposed to go to the predominantly Black high schools and talk to seniors about the state scholarships that were available. I ran into him in Frankfort and asked, 'Frank, how successful was the recruitment program you directed for seniors? How did you go about recruiting?' He laughed in his ebullient way and said, 'That was no job, that was a gift from Ned Breathitt for my support of him when he ran.'"

Lukey wrinkled her nose and declared, "He's a pompous ass."

"But, look at all the deserving students who probably missed out on an education because of his attitude," I said, pausing to consider the consequences of Stanley's inaction. I continued, "Lukey, that's the thing that irritates me the most! When Black people get into a position of power, very often it is wasted by someone who is only interested in self-aggrandizement. They are really not committed to improving the life of anyone but themselves."

"White people do that, too," she sighed.

When we stopped in Jackson, Mississippi to get gas, all the horror stories I had heard about that state crowded into my mind. Suddenly I felt afraid and slid down in the seat, pretending to be asleep. Lukey giggled and said, "Every shut eye ain't sleep."

Sitting up I nodded, "Okay, do you want me to drive this buggy?"

"No, I'm alright." Lukey said.

"Good! Now drive on—and hurry!" A few minutes later I added, "I don't know why I'm worried; with your dark complexion, you're 'blacker' than I am. Are you sure something didn't happen in your ancestry, the famous Baldwin family of Scarsdale, that you haven't told me about?" We laughed.

"You never know," she replied.

In Birmingham we stopped overnight at a Holiday Inn. "You go in and get the room," I said. "They may tell me, 'No vacancy.'" We ate dinner that evening and breakfast the next morning in the hotel restaurant before continuing our trip.

Early the next evening, we approached Fort Walton Beach, Florida. The sun was high, the weather was beautiful, and I was looking forward to the rest and relaxation. This was my second trip to Florida. In 1930, when I was seven years old, my father had driven the family to Sanford for a church conference. He took his mother, Grandma Annie, Mom, and six of us children. Phillip was the youngest. We had stopped in Birmingham and spent the night with a family, Bishop and Mrs. Cromartie, who were members of the Triumph Church. I remember playing in the warm sand in their front yard.

I visualized Florida as a place where rich folks went after Christmas and stayed until springtime. Since the National Public Accommodations law had not been in effect very long, I did not know what to expect in a state of the Deep South after the "no vacancy" treatment I had received in Frankfort just two months before.

I Shared the Dream

Lukey drove around and we looked for a place to stay. We saw a complex of unattached, one-story brick houses that were located on the beach on the Gulf of Mexico. Lukey went in and rented a nicely furnished apartment with two bedrooms, a living room, a kitchen, and a bath. There was a balcony facing the ocean. We decided to share the expenses. After we unpacked our clothes, we went shopping for food, stopping at a chain store to buy the staples, and a fresh seafood stand to buy two pounds of fresh shrimp in the shell and several bottles of cocktail sauce. That evening we watched some television and relaxed.

The next morning we put on our bathing suits and walked up and down the beach. "This is just about perfect," I murmured. "The sun, the sand, and the sea. What more can I ask for?" Every morning from then on we walked on the beach, enjoying the ocean breezes and searching for different kinds of shells. In the afternoon, we sat on the porch and read or sunned on the beach, listening to the ocean's roar.

During those first days I felt like I would be content in that atmosphere forever. However, after a week of such idle tranquility, I began to miss the excitement of my regular life.

On March 28, we were watching the evening news when I saw the disruption of the March on Memphis. Dr. King was in the front of the march when turmoil erupted in the rear. Seeing him there, I knew where I wanted to be. I turned to Lukey and said, "I need to go to Memphis, and I'd like to leave next week. I'm getting tired of this routine of just walking on the beach. I'm just not used to having nothing to do and, besides, I can't take too much of this sun all at once. It's drying my skin and I'll soon be as tan as you."

"That wouldn't be too bad, would it?" Lukey kidded.

"What, the drying or the tanning?" I kidded back. The truth was, I felt guilty relaxing when so much still needed to be done in the civil rights struggle. Each day the situation in

Memphis worsened. A demonstrator had been killed. I telephoned the SCLC office in Atlanta and left a message for Dr. King. He returned the call from New York. Not knowing who he was with or where, I spoke to him formally. "Dr. King, I have been in Florida on vacation for the past two weeks."

He laughed and asked, "Are you getting a tan?"

"I needed the rest more than anything. A.D. is coming down on Monday for a couple of days," I went on.

"Have him call me when he gets there." He paused and then added, "Senator, please come to Memphis, I need you."

"Well," I said, "I was thinking I'd had about enough sun. I will be there Tuesday or Wednesday."

"I'll have a room reserved for you at the Lorraine Motel," he replied.

When I hung up I asked Lukey, "Will you drive me to Memphis next Tuesday?" I had no idea how far Memphis was from Fort Walton Beach.

"I had planned to stay two more weeks," she mused, "but I'll think about it."

"You can always come back here," I said. "If you don't want to drive me, though, will you take me to the airport so I can fly there?"

"Let's wait and see," she responded pensively, then added, "Let's telephone A.D. and see what's going on."

"Go ahead; call him now," I said.

She made the call to A.D. "Georgia's starting to think about going to Memphis, but we've been having such a great time resting, eating, and enjoying the ocean."

He said, "I think I'll come down to join you two. I need some of that sun. My tan is getting pale."

"Come on down; we don't mind. When can you come?" Lukey asked.

"I have to preach this Sunday," he said. "It will have to be after that."

Lukey said, "What about Monday, April Fool's Day?"

I reached for the phone and said, laughingly, "A.D., that would really be an appropriate time for *you* to come. We'll be expecting you."

He said, "Okay, I will let you know what flight I'll be coming in on." We picked him up at the airport; he had been drinking heavily. The smell of liquor was strong on his breath. I teased him, "A.D., you must have missed us so much you couldn't take it without us. Did you hit the bottle, or did the bottle hit you?"

He laughed and responded, "There you go again."

The three of us went out on the beach early the next morning. Most of the day, we played in the ocean, taking turns dunking each other and throwing around a beach ball. We had a good time, acting like kids. When I got tired, I went up and changed, then I went out on the balcony and sat watching A.D. and Lukey play in the water. I looked out at the ocean cresting in white-capped waves onto the deliciously hot, beige beach, my body feeling like it was in a sauna. Nevertheless, I couldn't help but think how White men had deprived me all these years of enjoying these natural elements that belonged to God.

That evening I said to A.D., "I talked to M.L. last Wednesday, and he asked me to come to Memphis. I think he needs us and I want to go tomorrow."

He replied, "Wait until Wednesday and I'll go with you."

Lukey spoke up and said, "I'll just leave my clothes here and drive you both to Memphis. Then I'll come back."

A.D. called M.L. and confirmed we would be there Wednesday evening. I didn't talk to him myself.

We left Fort Walton Beach early Wednesday morning. I was anxious to see M. L. again. Though we took rest stops, we traveled all day. A.D. sat in the front seat with Lukey and I stretched out and slept in the back seat. We teased A.D. about having to stop so often to go to the bathroom. I asked him, "Do you have a leak in your bladder?"

He snapped, "No, but I do have to *take* a leak."

As we drove on, A.D. admitted, "I am very concerned about my brother. He is exhausted and does not seem able to take a break. I wish he would take a year away from the SCLC." He paused, and then said, "There are also the constant threats on his life that deeply trouble me."

Lukey said, "The ones who make the open threats are not the ones you have to worry about. It's the ones who you never hear from who are the danger."

"When will we see the end to the turmoil in this country?" I questioned.

A.D. shook his head. "We won't see it in our lifetime, I'm afraid. It's all about power. Those who have it will not give it up, nor will they share it. The pressure will have to stay on until there is equality for all races."

"The younger generation seems to be more tolerant of other races," I interjected. "They're going to school together and, at least, they're getting to know each other." I rolled up the pillow, curling up in a fetal position so I could drift back to sleep. A.D. stayed awake to talk to Lukey. He offered to drive, but she said, "No, I'm okay." We went through Montgomery, Birmingham, and on into Memphis.

It was dark and raining when, at about 11:00 P.M., we arrived at the Lorraine Motel. The building, I noticed, was L-shaped, having two stories and a balcony. As we entered the courtyard, two or three fellows were standing under the overhang on the sidewalk. A.D. asked, "Where is the mass meeting being held?"

One said, "It's at Mason Temple." The man came closer to the car and gave directions to A.D. and Lukey. We drove to the building, but it was now dark. Back at the Lorraine, we went into the office and checked into two rooms. My room was on the first floor, on the left side at the small end of the "L." I unpacked, then went to find Lukey and A.D.

Outside it was damp and humid. There was just a fine rain coming down. They were sitting in his room with the window open and the television on. We called room service and ordered coffee. Before long, a taxi entered the courtyard. "It's Dr. King, Ralph Abernathy, and Bernard Lee," said Lukey, looking out the window.

A few minutes later, I heard M.L.'s deep, resonant voice asking, "Where's the Senator?"

He and Abernathy came into the room. We were anxious to know how the demonstration was going. M.L. said, "City lawyers have gone into federal court seeking a temporary restraining order for ten days banning us from marching. The judge has signed it."

A.D. said, "What are you going to do if it's not lifted tomorrow?"

"Next Monday, April 8, I plan to go on with the march whether the court order is modified or not," M.L. answered decisively.

Abernathy added, "We'll know something tomorrow after Andy Young and Eskridge go to court."

Martin looked over at me. "I would rather have been in Florida getting a tan than here in the middle of turmoil."

I smiled. "You are invited."

He shook his head wearily. "We've got some young militants who have admitted they purposely started the disruption in last week's march," he said. "They call themselves the Invaders," he continued.

"They had the right name, didn't they—or maybe they should be called the Disrupters," I sighed. We talked for hours. Finally, too tired to continue, I excused myself. Within seconds, Martin followed me. I didn't know, of course, that this would be our last time together.

19

THE
LAST
NIGHT

As I walked toward my room I could hear his footsteps echoing on the concrete walkway. He was right behind me. We didn't speak to each other; we didn't know who could be watching. Turning the key in the lock, I entered my room, leaving the door slightly ajar, so he could follow. Once inside, he said to me softly, "I've never been more physically and emotionally tired, but what an uplifting experience it was to see the attitudes of all those people in the church change from apathy to commitment to our cause." He sat down on the edge of the bed. "Senator, our time together is so short," he said, opening his arms.

M.L. left my room while it was still dark, telling me, "I have a meeting with my staff around 8:00 A.M., but I'll meet you back here at about noon." From my window I could see the door to his room, and I watched as he went inside.

I felt restless. Even after a long bath, I still couldn't sleep. Lying on the bed, I watched people filter into Dr. King's room for the meeting with Dorothea Cohon, Hosea Williams, Bernard Lee, and others. At 12:30 P.M. he came back to my room with Abernathy. A. D. and Lukey followed soon afterward.

We were waiting for Andy Young and Chauncey Eskridge to return from court where they were trying to lift the temporary restraining order against the demonstrators. Chauncey Eskridge, a Black lawyer, was one of SCLC's attorneys. Andy Young was active in the civil rights movement, an intellectual and moral advisor to Dr. King. He was a noble man who never sought to promote himself.

M. L. asked me, "Well, Senator, how did your first session go? Were you able to accomplish anything in a hostile environment?"

I said, "It was quite different from what I expected. I was shocked to find thirty-seven White men and no women in the Senate. I knew then that my work was cut out for me."

He laughed and said, "That must have been like a woman going to the hospital and having a baby, but not knowing she had even been pregnant."

"Yes, it was a total surprise," I said, "but I held my own, even though I was outnumbered and outmanned, no pun intended. I stuck to my own agenda."

He said with respect in his voice, "A. D. told me how you passed that open housing law."

A. D. nodded, but his mind was on more mundane things, "I need to get my pants pressed and find something to eat."

"I'll find a dry cleaner close by and pick up some snacks," Lukey offered.

Abernathy wryly commented, "A. D., you must be mighty close to Lukey for her to take your pants and get them pressed."

To which A. D., tongue firmly in check, replied, "She is a great volunteer for the cause of justice."

M. L., lying on one of the beds in the room, joined in the laughter. He interjected his thoughts, saying, "I know one thing. For the last three years, she's has been my brother's constant companion. Every time I see him, she's there."

Lukey returned shortly with the pants, bags of potato chips and pretzels, bottles of soda, and some beer for A. D. He took one, but did not engage in his usual heavy drinking that day. He knew it embarrassed his brother.

M. L. brought the atmosphere from jovial to somber by saying, "The decision has been made to march on Monday. Regardless of the outcome of today's hearing, we *will* march on Monday. We cannot give in now."

Abernathy, not ready to relinquish the fun, said teasingly, "Doc, aren't you afraid to march if the injunction isn't lifted?"

M. L. answered slowly, "I'd rather be dead than afraid."

We waited for the others to return. A.D. and Martin talked on the phone to their parents for a long time. After hanging up, M.L. made an effort to join in the conversation with everyone, but I noticed he seemed lost in thought. For the rest of the afternoon, he continued to lie on the bed just staring at the ceiling. He was withdrawn and meditative, almost prayerful.

About 4:30 P.M., Eskridge and Young returned. They knocked on the door and came in, smiling. Eskridge said, "The judge has agreed to modify the order and allow the Monday march."

Martin's face wore a determined look, "We were going to march regardless of what he said."

Despite such conviction, there was an air of relief in the room. Abernathy was the first to leave after receiving the news, but not before a small pillow fight had broken out.

This seemed to enliven even M. L.'s somber mood. He got up and walked towards me.

"Senator, how would you like to go to Billy Kyle's house for a soul dinner? Do you like chitterlings and all the trimmings?"

I smiled, "Do you mean Kentucky oysters?"

A. D. interjected, "In the Bluegrass State, that's what they're called."

Nodding, I said, "Yes, I'll go."

"What about you, A. D.?" Martin asked.

"No, I'll skip it," A.D. said. "I'm tired and need some sleep." He and Lukey left.

On his way out the door, M. L. brushed past me, "I'm looking forward to a quiet and peaceful evening," he said softly. "Don't make any plans. I'll knock on your door when I'm ready to leave. I want you to ride over and back with me."

"I'll be ready," I replied.

He went up the stairs next door to my room and out onto the balcony. I could hear him talking to Jesse Jackson and some others standing in the courtyard.

I was standing in front of the dresser mirror patting my hair when I heard the shot. A woman screamed, "Oh my God! They've shot Dr. King!" I rushed to the door of my motel room and flung it open. Uniformed policemen were entering the courtyard. Where had they come from so fast, I wondered? Later I learned that the police station was just seconds away on the corner.

Someone was pointing to the second floor. I looked up to my left and gasped. One of Dr. King's knees stuck straight up in the air and I could make out the bottom of one foot. People in the courtyard had scattered to take cover. Without pausing, I hurried up the stairs closest to my room. Reaching King's room, I stepped inside and saw Andy Young and Ralph Abernathy, their faces grim, feverishly telephoning for an ambulance. They hardly noticed me, and I went out on the balcony.

Alone, I walked over and looked at Dr. King. He was lying in a pool of blood that was widening as I stood there staring. The bullet had pierced the right side of his neck. His tie had been severed about an inch from the knot. Both the knot and an inch of tie were sticking up. It is a picture permanently imprinted in my mind.

A siren wailed. I went over to the iron railing and looked down. A black ambulance, looking more like a patrol car, was making its way in. By this time the courtyard was crowded with people, many crying or praying.

Two medics from the ambulance hurried upstairs. They lifted Dr. King onto a stretcher, then brought him down to the courtyard. I hurried after them. Andy Young and Ralph Abernathy did the same.

I had always been terrified of being exposed. Only once did I put such thoughts aside. When they put Dr. King into the ambulance, I instinctively began climbing in to go with him. Andy Young gently pulled me back. "No, Senator," he said, "I don't think you want to do that."

After about fifteen minutes, I realized that A. D. and Lukey were still in their room and didn't yet know what had happened. I rushed there to tell them. A. D. was sleeping, but Lukey was awake and I gave her the news.

"Let me tell him," she said quietly. She called to A.D. and when he didn't awaken, she shook him gently. "A. D., your brother's been shot," she said softly, handing him a cigarette. She hadn't said Dr. King was dead. I knew he was, but I didn't correct her. We turned on the television and when they announced that a White man was suspected of the shooting, A. D. started cursing and going to pieces.

I couldn't stand to watch A. D. fall apart, so I left the

room. I went outside and saw television cameras pointed toward the door of A.D.'s room, waiting for him to come out. I told the staff to hold the television reporters off and went back into the room to calm Dr. King's brother. "A. D., I know what you're feeling, but the television people are waiting for your statement. You can't go out there and curse the world. Dr. King would not have wanted that," I told him.

After a bit, he said, "I'm ready," went out and spoke briefly to them. I don't think A. D. ever forgave himself for not hearing the shot and not knowing what had happened until after it was all over.

After A. D. talked to the press, he, Lukey, and I went to Bill Kyle's house to make phone calls. All the lines out of Memphis were tied up, but we were able to get through by saying we were placing calls for Dr. Martin Luther King Jr.'s brother. We didn't want to stay at the Lorraine that night, but we couldn't get a reservation at the Holiday Inn or anywhere else. All of Memphis was in chaos.

Finally, we had no choice but to return to our original rooms. When I got to mine, the sound of metal scraping against concrete drew me to the window. A lone workman was removing the blood from the second floor balcony with a scraper that resembled a putty knife, only much larger.

As he drew the metal back and forth, I began to shake. I couldn't stop. The sound of the scraping grew louder and louder and synchronized with the movement of my shaking body. The sound became a roar in my ears. I was on a train, moving faster and faster toward a dark tunnel. I am going mad, I thought. A newspaper headline flashed before my eyes: "SENATOR DAVIS FOUND INCOHERENT IN MEMPHIS MOTEL WHERE DR. KING ASSASSINATED."

I lay down, still shaking. I looked over at the pillow where his head had lain less than twenty-four hours ago. Last night, and every other time we had been together, he had said, "Our time is so short." Now these words joined the roar in my ears—so short . . . so short—they blended with the rhythmic sound that was like a train in my head, rushing headlong until both sounds became a single blur of noise, and I was still shaking.

I touched the pillow, searching for some lingering contact, some connection with him, but all I felt were the cold, clean sheets. I had forgotten I was in a motel and the bed had been changed since last night. I lay waiting for the tunnel to swallow me up—waiting for the madness to take me into oblivion. At least then I would be forever free of the pain of seeing him dead on the balcony, sprawled in a pool of his own blood.

Suddenly, the memory of our last telephone call accosted me. "Senator, please come to Memphis, I need you," he had asked. I had come, but it hadn't helped. Nothing had.

Again the vision of his body flashed through my mind. I am descending into hell, I thought. I remembered all the preachers I had ever heard, describing the fiery furnaces of hell. I knew they were wrong; hell is not hot. Hell is cold.

As icy cold as I was now. Was I condemned to live forever shaking, unable to get warm, I wondered, while he lies colder still in his grave? The thought was unbearable. I would gladly have suffered what I had feared for so long—public exposure and the threat to my political career—to have him here beside me now as he had been last night.

At 8:00 A.M. the next morning, Lukey called and said, "You and I should drive to Atlanta. A. D. is flying back on the plane with Dr. King's body." I called my family when I reached Atlanta to let them know I was all right.

The following day, A. D. asked us to go to Dr. King's house. I didn't want to—I didn't want to face Coretta, Martin's wife—but A. D. insisted. We walked slowly through the crowded house and found her.

As I took Coretta's hand, I said, "I'm sorry." Sorry for what? I was sorry she had lost her husband; I was sorry the world had lost a savior, and, on some level, I think I was also apologizing for my relationship with her husband.

Lukey and I stood in line with the thousands of others viewing King's body at Ebenezer Baptist Church on the day he was buried. A. D. had arranged for us to ride on a special bus to the funeral site. Sidney Poitier and his two daughters, Diahann Carroll, Alan King and Bill Cosby were among those with us. I was annoyed with Alan King, because he kept cracking jokes as we rode along.

Why don't you just shut up? I thought. I was in a state of shock and I thought the whole world should be, too. Numbly, I watched as the famous Jackie Kennedy, Hubert Humphrey, and many others, offered their condolences to Coretta. Numbly, I marched with Lukey behind the funeral bier carrying Dr. King in his African wood casket to the campus of Morehouse College, where Dr. Benjamin Mays eulogized the slain leader.

As Dr. Mays spoke, questions, thoughts, and memories flooded my mind. Why had I become Dr. King's lover? Though I didn't analyze it while he was alive, the answer now seemed obvious to me. I was middle-aged and not feeling very attractive when Martin Luther King, the leader of the civil rights movement, the man who fought so valiantly to make the dream of all Black people for equality a reality, wanted to be with me.

How could I *not* have seized the moment, no matter what my fears, no matter what the obstacles? When we were together, the rest of the world, whose problems we knew and shared, was far away. Our time together was a safe haven for both of us. There we could laugh and speak of things others might not understand. He trusted me, and I him, not to talk about it.

Others have speculated about Dr. King's relationships with women. I have no knowledge of affairs he may have had with other women; that was not what we talked about when we were together. I only know that our relationship began as a close friendship between two people sharing the same dream, working for the same goals, and it crossed the line into intimacy.

Looking back, although I regret any hurt inflicted on others because of my actions, I have never regretted being there with him.

V

THE SUNSET
YEARS

20

AFTER THE NIGHTMARE

Dr. King's death devastated the civil rights movement. It was his inspired leadership that had held it together. The troops were still there, but the heart was gone.

Because of his humility, Dr. King had been able to work with all kinds of people. Though he was brilliant, he didn't flaunt his intelligence. When he spoke with you, he addressed you as an equal, talking on your level, but not in any way condescending. He inspired trust in those who worked with him. It was horrible for those of us who followed him to lose our leader in such a senseless, violent way.

After the shock of his death wore off, I was filled with anger. Anger that hate had killed this man who had never himself hated. I saw him endure the vilest epitaphs and physical attacks, and turn the other cheek. I saw him spat upon and hit with rocks. I saw him suffer indignities that even the most passive person would have found hard to endure without fighting back. But he was firm in his conviction that non-violence could accomplish more than retaliation.

It was more than his belief in the power of non-violence that sustained him. I believe the highly evolved state of his spiritual development allowed him to feel only love for those who hated and reviled him. I watched him closely as we marched along together. He was always cognizant of those on the sidelines. He often interrupted his direction to step to the side and shake the hand of some poor soul in a wheelchair, or some mother in rags holding a child. He spoke to them out of love. He was not marching for the cameras; he was marching for justice. And unlike many reformers who become obsessed with their cause and own stardom, forgetting the people they are working to help, Dr. King didn't forget.

Though nothing could bring him back, I vowed to take the valuable lessons I learned from him with me, and to use them throughout my political career to help Black women, the disenfranchised, and the poor of every race.

Many times I have been introduced with these words: "She doesn't forget where she came from." That introduction is especially gratifying to me, because I had resolved never to be too busy to talk with my constituents. I couldn't always help them, but I could always listen. It is easy to lose touch with the people back home when you are bombarded by lobbyists for special interests and pressured by a governor's office. My association with Dr. King gave me a model to strive to follow in resisting such temptations and in the way I related to those who had elected me.

Very soon after his death there was much debate about whether the Poor People's Campaign that Dr. King had planned would be continued. However, A.D. returned to Louisville determined to join with the Kentucky Christian Leadership Conference and carry on M.L.'s campaign to go to

Washington and try to get Congress to pass an economic bill of rights to provide jobs and income for the poor.

However, the KCLC was floundering. And, in addition to their other problems, they had to give up the office next to A.D.'s church, because it was needed for a day nursery. I offered them, without charge, the vacant first floor of a duplex I owned.

Then, ten days after Dr. King's death, I held a press conference in front of KCLC's new office to announce we were reorganizing and had elected new officers. They were: Reverend A.D. King, chairman; Reverend Leo Lesser, president; Mrs. Lukey Ward, executive assistant and Raoul Cunningham, office executive director. Dr. John Claypool, pastor of Crescent Hill Baptist Church, which had a largely White congregation, and I were elected to co-chair the Finance Committee. "We are expecting to recruit more then four hundred people in Kentucky, Indiana, and Ohio to attend the poor people's march in Washington in May," I said. "This is our immediate goal now, but we will be involved in other civil rights activities. We advocate the enactment of an "economic bill of rights to provide an income for the poor."

To solicit funds from churches, businesses, and individuals, we sent hundreds of letters out with Claypool's and my signatures. We raised more than ten thousand dollars. It was a tribute to Dr. King's memory that so many people contributed.

On May 10, we held a rally in northern Kentucky to raise additional money and focus attention on the campaign. At the rally, in the Ninth Street Methodist Church in Covington, Raoul Cunningham spoke to the crowd:

"We ask that we be given jobs so that we can walk proudly down the streets in the Great Society and make it a Greater Society."

The crowd applauded him and shouted, "Amen!".

GEORGIA DAVIS POWERS

According to the *Cincinnati Enquirer*:

The biggest cheers from the crowd, however, were saved for State Senator Georgia Davis, who is credited with steering Kentucky's Open Housing Law into passage during the waning hours of the General Assembly. Her speech received a standing ovation. In Senator Davis's speech she said, "the days of the contented Negro are over. We are living on the outside of an affluent society. We can afford not to have poverty." The Negro woman senator said that the recent murder of Dr. Martin Luther King Jr. awakened a reaction of conscience for all Americans . . . the planned march on Washington where poor people will build a shanty town until their demands are met by Congress is for the benefit of all the nation's poor, not just the Negro.

Reverend W. J. Hodge, pastor of Louisville's Fifth Street Baptist Church and president of the Kentucky NAACP, chided Blacks who "rise in society, but forget their brothers."

More than three-hundred people—mostly Blacks, but Whites too, including a number of Catholic nuns—attended the rally. Some people dressed in blue jeans and sweat suits; others were in expensive suits and silk dresses. One goal was to raise $1,000 for the trip to Washington. We collected $901.16.

KCLC was host to two thousand marchers en route to Washington from the western United States. We had to find them overnight lodging, food, and transportation to Cincinnati. I appealed to Adjutant General Allen Carrell to provide National Guard vehicles to transport the marchers, but he refused. I did not give up on my entreaties to him. "This will give the National Guard an opportunity to improve its image," I further pleaded.

He wouldn't budge, saying he had discussed it with Governor Louis B. Nunn, who had told him to do "only what is authorized under federal regulations."

We held a freedom rally the evening of May 15, at Freedom Hall, where the caravan of marchers would eat and sleep. A.D. King announced that unless sufficient funds were raised for transportation, "these people will be permanent guests." Contributions began to come in. The Catholic diocese provided hot food, the Red Cross brought cots, bedding, and first aid equipment. Many volunteers showed up to work with the Red Cross crews. Gospel singers entertained the eight hundred people gathered to welcome the marchers. The singing groups The Loving Sisters and the Caravans performed for the crowd.

After the marchers from the West arrived, we had another rally at West Chestnut Baptist Church where Reverend Garland K. Offutt was the pastor. In the caravan were many Native Americans. Cesar Chavez, president of the United Farm Workers Organizing Committee, spoke to the crowd.

I flew to Washington and visited Resurrection City, where the poor people were camped out. Most were clothed in rags and were hungry. The poor sanitation conditions gave the place a pigsty smell. Yet people I talked to from Marks, Mississippi said, "This is better than we have back home." I wish I could report that the Poor People's Campaign made a difference. Except for empowering more individuals to act in their own behalf, however, I can't see that it did. It seemed that the nation had developed an ever increasing tolerance for deprivation and were not moved by the plight of the poor— even when we brought them to the nation's capitol.

Ralph Abernathy soon became president of SCLC, but he showed signs of being ill-qualified to be the leader of the organization. Ralph, a heavyset man, was an ordained minister, pastor of West Hunter Street Baptist Church in Atlanta, Georgia. He was considered by many to have been Dr. King's closest associate during the civil rights campaigns of the 1950s and 1960s. Abernathy had been one of the organizers of the Montgomery Improvement Association and the Southern Christian Leadership Conference. He also wanted to be King's alter ego. It was hard, I noticed, to take a picture of King without Ralph's face being in it. I believe Ralph was covertly jealous of King and had an inferiority complex about being second-in-command of SCLC.

I admit it would have been difficult for anyone to fill Dr. King's shoes, but it would have been better if the Board had gone outside the organization and brought in someone else. Ralph portrayed himself differently in his book, *The Walls Came Tumbling Down*, than the person I had known. He was not the pious person he claimed to be. Moreover, he lied in the book about the evening before King's assassination, and exaggerated about having lifted King's body into his arms and spoken to him.

Despite the efforts of his followers to channel into good works the grief felt by so many who cared about civil rights, many cities, including Louisville, had riots after Dr. King's assassination. Among the ones where disturbances broke out were New York City; Washington, DC; Baltimore; Chicago; and Greensboro. In Louisville, Samuel Hawkins and Robert "Kuyu" Simms, leaders of the Black Unity League of Kentucky, organized a rally to be held on May 27, 1968.

They falsely publicized that Stokely Carmichael, head of the national Student Nonviolent Coordinating Committee, would be there to speak. The announcement was a ploy to draw a crowd. The evening of the rally, I was having dinner with several reporters and was scheduled to speak to them about problems in Louisville's west end. After dinner, as I stood up to speak, a man tapped me on the shoulder and whispered, "A riot has broken out at Twenty-eighth and Greenwood Streets." I informed the guests of the problem, left, and went to the Kentucky Christian Leadership

Conference office, which was located just a few yards from the initial disturbance. Raoul Cunningham, Lukey Ward, and A.D. King were already there.

James Rodriquez Cortez, who was introduced as a Carmichael associate, had spoken and inflamed the crowd of four hundred people. City policemen were near the scene, but Chief of Police C. J. Hyde had told his officers to stay two blocks back from the crowd. Suddenly, a soft drink bottle thrown from the top of a building shattered in the area, and a police car immediately drove into the intersection. An officer jumped from the car with his pistol drawn. A second police car followed. This time an officer leaped out of the car and fired a couple of rounds of ammunition into the air. After that, the real violence began. Later, Chief Hyde would publicly state that "there's no question that those police cars, especially the first one, contributed to getting things started . . ."

Most of the violence was contained within twenty blocks. But in Parkland, all hell broke loose as young people roamed the streets setting fires, breaking windows, and looting stores. Police Chief Hyde and Mayor Kenneth Schmied decided they needed help from the National Guard. Governor Nunn activated the Guard, sending in nineteen hundred troops. He also sent in one hundred state police officers to help quell the riot. A curfew was imposed from 11:00 P.M. to 5:00 A.M. The Guard and other law enforcement officers operated from a command post set up in the Brandeis Elementary School, four blocks from the corner of Twenty-eighth and Greenwood Street.

When the National Guard left Louisville nine days later, several hundred people had been arrested, two hundred injuries treated, and two youths were dead. James Groves Jr., a fourteen-year-old, was shot by a policeman who claimed Groves was with a crowd who had looted a store. The other young man, nineteen-year-old Matthias Browder, was shot by a liquor store owner who claimed he shot Matthias after he broke a window and was reaching inside for a bottle of liquor. Considerable doubt was raised about Browder's death. Investigation revealed that he had been next door in a sandwich shop just before the shooting. When he was shot, he still had a partial fish sandwich in his hand and fish remnants in his mouth.

Many more lives would have been lost if authorities had not acted quickly. Nevertheless, most of the White-owned businesses in a ten-block area were destroyed. Business buildings in the immediate area of the riot that escaped destruction included Moon Cleaners, the Metro Lounge, and Little Palace Hamburger Shop (which I later bought). White store owners were too frightened to rebuild their businesses; more than twenty-five years later, the area still looks war-torn.

Earlier in 1968, President Lyndon B. Johnson had appointed a commission on civil disorders, known as the Kerner Commission, to investigate urban rioting and make recommendations for solving the problems of the cities. In their findings, the Commission warned that the United States was "moving toward two separate societies, one Black and one White—separate and unequal."

In June, I helped in the struggle for better working conditions for the sanitation workers in St. Petersburg, Florida. A.D. King and the Kentucky Christian Leadership Conference staff were asked to go there to support the 211 sanitation workers who had been fired from their jobs for going out on strike after the city failed to keep their part of a wage agreement. When they walked out, the workers, whose average age was forty, were earning between $1.82 and $2.27 an hour. They had been promised a raise of twenty-five cents an hour.

A.D. talked to me about the trip. He was severely depressed, still mourning for his brother, and unable to undertake this new struggle so soon. He was also in the process of moving from his church in Louisville to become co-pastor at Ebenezer Baptist Church in Atlanta.

Raoul Cunningham and I went without him. Our first step was to hold a press conference to explain why A.D. King did not return as he'd promised. We didn't want to openly discuss his depression, so I made the following statement:

> It is with deep regret that A.D. Williams King will not be able to be in St. Petersburg this week. . . . This, by no means, indicates a lack of interest or concern for the problems that exist here in St. Petersburg with the sanitation workers. Mr. Cunningham and I were requested to come and give any assistance that might be deemed necessary. We desire to meet with all segments of the community with the hope of bringing unity and understanding and to help resolve this situation that has been brought about by the broken promises of the St. Petersburg City Administration. . . . We are committed to militant, nonviolent methods.

The press conference was held in the Lakeview Presbyterian Church. Those attending included Joe Savage, a long-time leader in the fight for better working conditions for the sanitation workers of St. Petersburg; James Sanderlin, attorney for the workers; Reverend David Havens, president of the Florida Community Development Association; August Vanden-Bosch, director of the Florida Council on Human Relations; Henry Catherill, a sanitation worker; Jesse Epps, the International Representative for the American Federation of State, County and Municipal Employees Union; and a White couple who were supporters, Mr. and Mrs. Albert France from Gulfport, Mississippi.

We stayed at the home of Samuel and Eleanor Adams. Sam was a reporter for the St. Petersburg Times. He asked me, "Senator, are you prepared to go to jail?" Other reporters repeated the question. I always replied, "Whatever I feel is necessary to bring about justice, I am prepared to do."

Demonstrations at the city hall were scheduled for two reasons: we wanted to let city officials know St. Petersburg's problems were a national concern, and we wanted to recruit more people to help in the struggle. Late in the afternoon of the first day, we started out with sixty people from Jordan Park Community Center. There were five White marchers. We marched two-and-a-half miles to the city hall, singing freedom songs the whole way. By the time we reached our destination, the column had doubled in length.

We marched back to Union Street Meeting Hall, a small concrete block building close to the park. Inside, Raoul played the piano and I led the singing—a mixture of freedom and inspirational songs. In that non–air-conditioned building the heat was stifling, and the air was heavy. We kept singing and clapping while the sweat poured off all of us, though.

Joe Savage, a mild-mannered, cigar-smoking man, said Chief of Police Harold Smith would give him a parade permit as long as the march was peaceful and signs were carried by hand instead of on sticks. We asked Joe to get a permit for the second day.

The second morning, Raoul called City Manager Lynn Andrews, who asked for a conference with me. Raoul handed me the phone. Andrews agreed to meet with me at 2:30 P.M. the day before the City Council meeting. When I called back to let him know I planned to bring five or six people with me, he said, "They are welcome to come and sit in my outer office, but I feel the meeting's effectiveness would be lost if we have more than a head-to-head ratio."

I refused to meet with him alone, though. I do not meet an adversary alone; I always bring along at least one witness. Andrews reported in the newspaper that he had "a very pleasant forty-minute phone conversation with the senator. She would not meet with me, but I will probably see her another time."

At the City Council meeting, Councilman Allison posed a question to Police Chief Smith. "Is it your opinion that, for the general welfare and safety of the citizens of St. Petersburg, the city should not issue any more parade permits at this time?"

It was a loaded question, of course, and Smith replied, "Based on the conduct of the parades, [which had been peaceful], the overall situation, the merchants and everyone, [and] the number of calls and complaints, my recommendation is that they be stopped."

Smith told the City Council that the sanitation crisis had cost $94,887 in overtime for police officers alone during the previous thirty days. "Forty-eight uniformed officers and patrolmen have been assigned to the nightly demonstrations. In addition sixteen cars, detectives, nearly all Youth Aid Bureau personnel, and those from the Intelligence Bureau have been diverted from normal duties," Smith added.

Ike Williams, of the local NAACP, disagreed with their negative assessment. "I believe these marches have been a good thing for the community."

No action was taken by the Council—no talk of trying to solve the problems of the sanitation workers. After the meeting, I went up to City Manager Andrews, introduced myself, and castigated him for the city's refusal to settle the strike. The next day the *St. Petersburg Times* ran a picture of Andrews and me at the meeting pointing our fingers at each other.

We received many threats while we were in St. Petersburg. One night a caller said, "If you march tomorrow, you will be bombed."

Raoul replied, "We will be there, come hell or high water."

Most threats such as this are from cowards who don't intend to take action, but Raoul and I knew that because of the strong emotional feelings some held against the marchers, there was the possibility that someone would follow through with the threat.

We demonstrated for days without any apparent results. I was beginning to feel that we needed something more dramatic. "But what?" I asked myself. Then, one day as I sat in the meeting hall after a march, the thought came to me that I should call a meeting of only women.

About fifteen women met with me in a corner of the building. I said, "Tomorrow is Independence Day, and I plan to show my independence. I'm going to Lake Magiorre Sanitation compound and hold a prayer vigil to stop those trucks driven by scabs from coming out of there. I plan to be there at six A.M. The first truck comes out at seven. Those of you who want to join me, meet me there. Those who are afraid, and those who have children, please don't come. Who will join me?"

Seven women raised their hands. Serious-faced, I asked, "Do we have a sister who can moan?"

One woman pointed to another and said, "Mary Frances sure can moan!"

"Good," I said. "I'll see you in the morning."

During the night, a storm raged both outside and within me. I arrived at the park at 5:50 A.M. It was still dark. The other women arrived on time. The concrete driveway from the compound led down a curved hill. Just past the gate was a two-lane street with a six-foot grassy plot in between. At 6:45, eight of us knelt across the exit lane where the trucks would be coming out. We started to pray. At 7:00 A.M. the first truck came rolling down the hill. We heard it coming. While the sisters were moaning and praying, I repeated in a soft, firm voice, "Don't move, don't move, don't move."

Only ten feet away, the driver slammed on his brakes and skidded. When he finally came to a stop, we were still praying—believe me! He called the police on his two-way radio. Within five minutes, officers were there. They lifted us one by one off the pavement onto the grassy plot, staying there to make sure we didn't go back into the street.

Later, A.D. Williams King and Reverend C. K. Steel arrived in St. Petersburg. They joined us in meeting with the union leaders and on the marches which continued. Lynn Andrews called us "professional protesters who have turned a walkout from a labor problem into one of race relations." He added, "Their only purpose is to stir up discord to create a situation which, unchecked, would cause violence to erupt in our peaceful city."

After two weeks in St. Petersburg, Raoul and I went home for two days. While there, I called Norbert Blume to ask how we could go about starting a welfare fund for the strikers whose families needed money for food, rent, and emergencies. He advised me to call Jerry Wurf, President of the American Federation of State, County, and Municipal Employees. I called Wurf and, by the time we returned to St. Petersburg, he had sent a check for fifteen hundred dollars to the local union.

We scheduled a rally in the Gibbs High School auditorium to hear Reverend Ralph Abernathy, A.D. King, Reverend Steel, Georgia State Senator Leroy Johnson, Constable Clarence Huff of Pittsburgh, Alderman Vel Phillips of Milwaukee, and Alderman Louise Reynolds of Louisville, for July 31. We invited national figures. I also spoke, and, as I approached the podium, I received a standing ovation. By that time, the people knew me; they had marched with me, and prayed with me.

The headlines of the *St. Petersburg Times* read: "THE NATION'S LEADING NEGRO ORATORS SPEAK,

AND A THOUSAND RALLY AROUND." Our pictures were on the front page.

The *Atlanta Journal* headlines read: "ABERNATHY WARNS ST. PETE OF HELL IN GARBAGE DISPUTE." Abernathy had said, "We are going to stay here until the walls crack, until segregation crumbles and until the garbage workers get their jobs back." If there was to be any hell, though, it wouldn't come from us; we were demonstrating peacefully.

Labor organizer Jesse Epps refused to speak. He said he hoped "to transform the dispute, with the approval of the garbage men, from a strike run by civil rights activists into a strike which is labor-oriented."

I didn't understand his point. The civil rights struggle is a labor struggle and always has been. The strike was finally settled that fall. The pay increase was granted, and most of the workers returned to work.

After working on the St. Petersburg sanitation strike, I went to the Democratic convention in Chicago and spoke to the delegates. W. C. Young, a member of the Executive Board of the Kentucky AFL-CIO, asked whether I would be interested in speaking on the Vietnam War plank, which was strongly backed by President Lyndon B. Johnson and the supporters of Vice-President Hubert H. Humphrey. I agreed, mostly because I had something to say that I thought the other twenty-six Vietnam War plank speakers wouldn't cover, but also because of my admiration for Vice-President Humphrey.

At the convention, the minority plank, developed by Eugene McCarthy supporters, opposed the Vietnam War. In their plank, great emphasis was placed on the idea that America was not meeting its needs at home because of the costs of waging the Vietnam War. I didn't believe this and I planned to say so publicly.

Andrew Young was also scheduled to speak that night. Young had been an ordained minister of the United Church of Christ since 1955 and had become executive director of SCLC in 1964. Andy had been a disciple of Dr. King. King came to rely on him for counsel and ideas. Andy was quiet in his demeanor, but would debate with King if he did not agree with him. In making decisions about what to do in the field, Andy was one of the cooler heads. King trusted his judgement and often took his suggestions. The staff had terrible ego problems, however. Everybody wanted to be the closest one to King, to be his confidant. There were disagreements among Hosea Williams, Wyatt T. Walker, Jim Bevel, and other staffers. However, when the leaders, King and Abernathy, talked about loyalty they talked about Andy.

Andy escorted me behind the platform to a room where they would make me up. A secretary came in to take down my three-minute speech, and I was assisted by a Humphrey aide.

United States Representative Hale Boggs introduced me, and I began:

Mr. Chairman, fellow delegates, there is one argument in the minority report which needs to be dealt with honestly and bluntly. It is the "but for" Vietnam argument. You all know how it goes, but for Vietnam . . . we would have the resources to rebuild our cities. I say we *must* rebuild our cities and we have the resources to do it even with Vietnam and our current defense budget.

I went on to say that the tax cut of 1964, initiated to boost the economy, should have been less, so that more revenue could have gone to the starving cities:

If Vietnam peace came tomorrow, too many leaders would favor using the peace dividend for tax cuts rather than to rebuild our cities. The point is that we have the resources now, even while the war continues, and we will have them even after the war is over. The crisis of our cities is too serious to fool ourselves with slogans claiming the only reason we are not meeting needs at home is Vietnam. That is why I believe the "but for" Vietnam issue in the minority plank is so misleading and so harmful. It takes our attention away from where it ought to be, on the appropriate domestic policies to meet our domestic needs—enough appropriations to carry out our priority programs and enough revenue to pay the bill. WE CAN AFFORD IT!

When I finished, there were boos from the McCarthy people, and polite applause from the Humphrey delegation. My picture and statement appeared in *Newsweek, Jet, The Louisville-Courier Journal,* and *The Louisville Times.* As always, I had not made a speech to curry favor but to satisfy my conscience, so approval or disapproval was not my goal.

Dr. King's death was followed that November by the senseless slaying of Robert F. Kennedy as he campaigned in California. I was invited to his funeral, along with A.D. King, W. J. Hodge, and Raoul Cunningham. We flew in a chartered plane and, since our plane was not equipped with radar, I sat in the seat by the pilot to watch for other aircraft. When we landed in New York City, after circling John F. Kennedy Airport for thirty minutes waiting for clearance, a limousine took us to the Waldorf-Astoria Hotel. Attending the funeral at St. Patrick's Cathedral momentarily plunged me back into the intense anger, grief, and helplessness I had felt right after Dr. King's death.

I don't know how I survived 1968—King's death, the Louisville riot, the Poor People's Campaign, the St. Petersburg sanitation strike, and Robert Kennedy's murder. It seemed the world had turned upside down.

21

HARD WORK
AND
DESPAIR

Practical problems have a way of intruding and blocking out larger concerns. Perhaps that is a fortunate thing for those who pass through a period of despair. At least I found it so in that first year after Dr. King's death. The time constraints imposed by the demands of my political career and civil rights activities left me few idle hours. I tackled those two activities with a fervor born of the desire to bring about social changes, the changes Dr. King had fought for so courageously and in which I believed wholeheartedly.

However, it wasn't very long before I realized that, though my political career and civil rights activities were very rewarding, they weren't very remunerative. I was single, with an income of only three hundred dollars a month—my expense allowance as a state senator. That was not enough to meet even my basic expenses.

By that time, my son, Billy, had joined the Navy. The only savings I had amounted to a thousand dollars. I was keeping that money to help him through school when he came home. His biological mother had promised to send money regularly to go into a trust fund for his education, but she hadn't done it. As it happened, when Billy came home he chose to take a job in a factory in Indiana rather than go to school. I gave him the money anyway, because, after all, I had saved it for him. He used the funds for a down payment on a car.

I knew I had to have more income. Either I'd have to go to work for someone else or go into business myself. About that time, Milton Hyman, the owner of the Little Palace Hamburger Shop on Twenty-eighth Street in Louisville, decided to sell the business and asked if I would be interested in buying it. This seemed like just the opportunity I needed. I borrowed seven thousand dollars from the Southern Music and Wagg Company through Kenny Young, got another loan from the Small Business Agency, and bought the Little Palace.

I knew nothing about running a restaurant, but Jim Powers did, so I sought his advice. We renamed the eatery "The Senator's Restaurant." Jim helped me choose the menu. We served a half-pound burger with a special sauce he made, calling it the "Senatorburger." Among the other things we featured were White Castle hamburgers, french fries, fried chicken, and a giblet stew which we made by the gallons. For dessert, there were homemade pies.

The restaurant opened on December 4, 1969. It was newly painted; everything was shiny and clean; the food was delicious. The white walls, black-and-white floors, chrome counter and black stools, the sun shining through the wide expanses of window glass, the jukebox playing the Jackson Five's "I'll Be There," the smell of Jim's sauce coming from the kitchen—these enticements all said, "Come on in!" to the public. "I hope they will," I murmured.

And they did. Customers filled the huge parking lot. When the Senate was not in session and my civil rights activities permitted, I spent time at the restaurant. Since I was single with no one at home, many times I slept during the day and spent my nights working. The business went well. I was making money. I bought a new 1970 Ford LTD from Summers-Herrman Ford, the dealership where Jim worked as a salesman.

When the General Assembly met in January 1970, I had to find someone to manage the restaurant while I was in Frankfort, so I hired my brother Bob. He was having problems on his job. International Harvester, his employer, was cutting back and, Bob was going to be demoted from his job as general foreman to foreman. His ego wouldn't let him accept this, so he retired. I thought he was making a mistake. However, since he was determined to leave International Harvester, I hired him to manage the restaurant.

Bob was dating Carrie Mae Parks, an elementary school principal. The three of us often went out together. Once a week, Jim Powers joined us to play bridge. In December 1970, his wife Gloria went home to Jamaica, and Jim and I were together frequently. Despite all the intervening events and years, our relationship had endured. Cheryl and Deborah, his daughters, were already on their own, and Carlton, the youngest child, was old enough to take care of himself.

We were planning a big celebration of my parents' fiftieth wedding anniversary on January 15, 1971. We rented the Masonic Temple for a reception, and Violet, my brother Lawrence's wife, decorated the hall with a flowered arch and a red carpet leading to two upholstered chairs where Mom and Pop would be seated while receiving guests. Friends and neighbors attended, along with dignitaries such as former Governor Bert Combs and his wife, Helen; Representative and Mrs. George Siemens; Representative Mae Street Kidd; Sam Ezelle, executive director of the Kentucky AFL-CIO, and his wife, Dorothy.

Jim spent the night before the reception at my house. The next morning he went home to get dressed. He was to meet me at the hall, but, within an hour, he was back at my house looking distraught.

"Georgia," he said. "I can't come to the reception. When I got home, Gloria was there!" She had returned from Jamaica without letting Jim know.

I was more than upset.

"I can't take this anymore," I said. "I can never count on you."

We had harsh words, and this time Jim said he was breaking off our relationship. That lasted five days. Even though we reconciled, however, the angry words we had spoken left a residue of bitterness and frustration. Still, neither of us could let go.

Sometimes we went to a bar in the Churchill Inn to hear Welton Lane sing and play the organ. He sang melancholy country songs such as "Help Me Make it Through the Night" and "I Just Got Tired of Being Poor," a recording that made the charts. Jim would follow me home after our evenings together to see that I got in safely.

One night at the Inn I was feeling despondent. I kept asking Welton to sing "Help Me Make It Through the Night." The more he sang that song, the more depressed I became. When I got home, I told Jim goodnight, locked my door, and began screaming and beating on the wall. I couldn't control myself. All the desire and frustration of my long, off and on relationship with Jim, and the riots and deaths of the past year blended together in my mind. I wept until I had no more tears. I went to bed, thinking I wanted to sleep forever. Instead I lay there, wide awake, for hours, feeling the depth of my despair and loneliness. Finally, I reached over and took out the gun I kept in the drawer of the night table by the bed.

"I'm going to shoot myself and end it all," I murmured. I stared at the gun and debated. Should I do it? I hesitated, then decided to call my father. I looked over at the clock; it was three in the morning, but Pop had always told me to call any time I needed him. I dialed the number not knowing what I was going to say. When he answered, I was crying so hard I could barely get out the words: "Pop, I'm so miserable."

"Do you want me to come, Georgia? I can be there in a few minutes."

"No, just talk with me a while," I said. "My life's going nowhere. I have my career, but that's not enough. I'm so lonely. This past year has been more than I can handle."

"Georgia, everything's going to be all right. Just be calm, and we'll talk to the Lord. He's the only one who can help you."

I listened as he poured out his heart full of love for me and asked God to help me throw off this awful despondency. As he prayed, I began to feel a peace that I hadn't known for a long time. My father had become a minister in the Holiness Church, and he believed in the power of healing by faith. People all over the world called and requested his prayers and comforting words. Now I knew why.

The next morning I realized how foolish I had been to even think about taking my own life. That was the first and last time I ever thought about suicide.

I returned to my life's work. Making an impact on race problems was difficult, but helping poor women proved even harder and more unpopular to do.

I killed a bill that would refuse mothers state aid for their third child and any other children born out of wedlock. There was a general feeling among legislators that most Aid to Families with Dependent Children recipients were slovenly, indolent Black women who had illegitimate babies to receive aid. Every time an AFDC bill came before my committee, I had testimony from White recipients from Eastern Kentucky and I pointed out that more than two-thirds of the AFDC recipients in Kentucky were White.

In 1970, my second Senate session, I was appointed to chair the Health and Welfare Committee. I had no experience in conducting a meeting according to parliamentary procedure and made many mistakes, but the members didn't embarrass me. After my first meeting, Senator Kelsey Friend stayed to give me some pointers on parliamentary procedure. I was given *Mason's Manual of Legislative Procedure* to study. With experience I improved and gradually became more confident of my ability to run a meeting.

I used my chairman position as leverage to pass my bills in the Senate. Before I brought up a legislator's bill in Health and Welfare, I would talk to him or her about supporting my bills. If I got no promise of support, I would shuffle that legislator's bill to the bottom of the stack until I got the commitment I needed. Being in the minority because of my race, sex, and the causes I was championing, I had to use any way I could find to get the right things accomplished.

As Chairman of the Senate Health and Welfare Committee, I was constantly fighting off those who wanted to penalize women who received funds from Aid to Families with Dependent Children. Most of my colleagues called it "welfare," and they repeatedly complained about how much money the state and federal governments were spending on the aid.

I would respond by saying, "Sir, do you realize we are subsidizing major corporations like the Lockheed Aircraft Company and others? The amount we spend on women who are trying to raise children is a drop in the bucket compared to what we give corporations. Why don't you complain about corporate subsidies? Why is public assistance called 'welfare' when it goes to individuals, and 'subsidies' when we give it to corporations?"

People in this country "strain at a gnat and swallow a camel," as the saying goes, when it comes to helping the poor. They can get outraged over someone receiving two hundred dollars a month and not working, but corporations and banks can rob the taxpayer of billions of dollars without any public outcry. Wealthy business people and politicians know this. I think they conspire to keep the public confused.

22

TAKING MY PLACE

In 1972 Jim Power's wife, Gloria, died suddenly, leaving him free. We moved in together.

A few months later, I introduced in the Senate an amendment to the Kentucky Civil Rights Act to extend the coverage of the Act to prohibit employment discrimination because of sex and age between forty and sixty-five. (Protection was extended to age seventy by a later amendment.) I also introduced amendments to remove exemptions in the original Act in the areas of public accommodations and housing, to provide even greater protection for the rights of citizens of the Commonwealth.

The original Kentucky Civil Rights Act had been enacted on January 27, 1966, two years before I was elected to the Senate. My amendment provided more efficient and less remote enforcement procedures than the federal law. The framers of the Kentucky Act based their law on a draft of a model act prepared by the National Conference of Commissioners on Uniform State Law. The 1968 Fair Housing Act, which I introduced during my first senate session, was also based on the model act.

Originally, intense opposition from barbers forced proponents of the law to compromise and exempt barbershops from coverage under the public accommodations law. Likewise, when the Fair Housing Act was passed, apartment buildings with four or fewer units where the owner lived in one of the units were exempted from coverage as a compromise to get the bill passed. My 1972 legislation removed the exemption for barbershops and changed the fair housing section to exempt only those buildings with two apartments where the owner lives in one of the apartments.

The Kentucky Civil Rights Act is enforced by the Kentucky Commission on Human Rights. I worked closely with the Commission's executive director, Galen Martin, to improve the law based on the Commission's experience in enforcing it. Kentucky's Civil Rights Act, as amended, is one of the most comprehensive civil rights laws in the nation. The Kentucky Act is strong because of its broad coverage and its effective enforcement procedures.

I felt proud of the progress I was making in bringing fair legislation for the poor and disenfranchised to Kentucky. At the same time I knew more had to be done.

Privately I made some hard decisions, too. After nine months of living together, I told Jim either we had to get married or he had to move out. We were married on August 17, 1973.

Our marriage was an easy, comfortable relationship from the very beginning. After what we had both experienced, it was good to be together without sneaking around. Years of living had taught us to respect each other and be tolerant of differences. He didn't resent my career and didn't try to tell me what to do. He was successful in his own right as a leading automobile salesman at Summers-Herrman Ford, at Third and Breckinridge Streets. He was becoming more and more successful. He had been hired by Ed Moore, the general manager, and was the only Black salesman. For the first year, he was told he could only sell to those who asked for him by name; he couldn't sell from the floor. After a few months, he requested floor time. Management agreed that Jim could sell to Blacks who came on the lot during his six-hour shift. Jim knew this was unfair, and he soon demanded to sell to any prospective buyer. The management gave in.

The first of each year, the Summers-Herrman manager gave each salesman a financial quota—everyone except Jim. Finally Jim asked for a quota, and they gave him one of $750 a month. By June, he had made his quota for the whole year. Jim knew the reason he was not given a quota was the prize that went with reaching or exceeding it. The reward was a trip that the winning salesmen and their wives took together. Ed Moore, the manager, warned Jim that "If you win, you will not be able to take the trip. The other salesmen and their wives would object."

"How much do you spend on each salesman on these trips?" Jim asked.

"About a thousand dollars," said Ed.

"Since my wife and I are not welcome to go, I expect you to give me the amount you spend, if I win," Jim said. Ed agreed to give him the money.

Little changed about the reality of these unfair employment practices during our first few years of marriage, but I continued to move Kentucky's legislation forward.

Kentucky was the second state to establish a holiday commemorating the birth of Dr. Martin Luther King Jr. The holiday was discretionary; it was not mandatory for businesses or state government to give employees a day off.

When I introduced the bill establishing the holiday in 1974, I said: "I feel it's important for the citizens of Kentucky to commemorate a holiday in honor of a Black person, but I am not asking you to support this bill simply because Martin Luther King Jr. was a Black man. His outstanding leadership transcended racial lines."

The bill passed and, at the signing ceremony, Governor Wendell Ford praised Dr. King. "The creed by which Dr. Martin Luther King Jr. lived can be found in Psalms Fourteen. 'Seek peace and pursue it.' This is what he believed. He advocated peace and nonviolence by dedicating his life to these goals," he said.

Although many attempts were made to make the King holiday mandatory, this was not achieved while I was in the Senate. I must admit I had ambivalent feelings about the question. While I knew it would give more status to the holiday, I resented giving state employees, many of whom didn't know or care about Dr. King or what he stood for, a day off with pay. Kentucky state government has never had more than 8 percent Black employees, and those Blacks who work for the state are mostly at the bottom of the ladder.

At the same time, those of us committed to the cause of equality for all people proposed civil rights legislation, those committed to hatred and bigotry also reacted. Court-ordered desegregation of Jefferson County schools in 1975 sparked some Ku Klux Klan activity in the south end of the county. In response to these racists hiding behind bedsheets, Galen Martin helped draft an anti-mask bill and I introduced it. My bill was an effort to pass a statewide law similar to the twenty-one local anti-mask ordinances already in effect.

Actually, this had a historical precedent. The first documented ordinance against wearing masks was passed in 1924 by the City of Danville. Owensboro also passed an anti-mask ordinance that year. The city of Pineville enacted a similar ordinance in this period, which was held to be constitutional by the Kentucky Court of Appeals in a 1927 case, *City of Pineville v. Marshall*. In an opinion on the constitutionality of such ordinances, six years later the Kentucky Attorney General cited the 1927 court of appeals opinion, which he said was directly on point.

Ku Klux Klan activity in the 1920s in Hazard, Pineville, and Middlesboro, among other Kentucky cities, had led to passage of those local ordinances. Interestingly, the demonstrations and cross burnings in southeastern Kentucky had been directed against the Irish and other Catholic populations, as well as against Jewish people.

Governor Julian Carroll, a lawyer from Paducah, served five terms in the Kentucky House of Representatives, and was Speaker of the House from 1968 to 1970. He was elected Lieutenant Governor in 1971, and when Governor Wendell Ford resigned in December of 1974 to run for the United States Senate, Carroll became Governor. He was elected to a full term as governor in 1975.

At the beginning of the 1976 session, Carroll called me aside and said, "Georgia, how would you like to be on the Senate Rules Committee? It's a powerful committee. As you know, it controls the flow of all the legislation that comes through the Senate." I knew if I accepted, I would have to give up my chairmanship of the Health and Welfare Committee. I was ready for a break from the strain of that committee; I think all the welfare clients in the state had my home telephone number and every time they had a personal problem, they would call me. I hesitated, then finally agreed. "Julian, I will try it for one session, and if I don't like it, I want another chairmanship."

I didn't like it. The Rules Committee was a steamroller

committee with everything decided before the committee even met. The chairman, Tom Garrett, would have a list of bills that he wanted to bring to the floor. He'd move to report a bill out, and one of his close associates would quickly second the motion, and Garrett would call for the vote. It was all over before I could even ask a question.

That session was my worst in terms of getting substantive legislation passed. Not just the leadership, but also the body of senators was more conservative, and I didn't have the power of my committee chairmanship to help me. Only two of my bills passed: one, to place a citizen member on professional and occupational licensing boards and commissions; and the other to require hotels to provide safety locks on all bedroom doors. Dismayed by this record, I resolved to give up the Rules Committee membership and seek chairmanship of another committee.

However, I kept up the good fight. In addition to strengthening the state's civil rights laws to give protection to individuals, I worked on many other race-related issues. In the early days of my time in the Senate, the governor had almost absolute power to decide what passed and what didn't. The legislature was not a separate, independent body. It usually adhered to the governor's wishes.

We were in the first session after Federal Judge James Gordon ordered Jefferson County to begin busing students for integration, when I argued with Governor Carroll over this issue. Jefferson County legislators Archie Romines, Dottie Priddy, Robert Hughes, and twenty other House members introduced a bill to prohibit the use of public funds to purchase vehicles used to transport public school children beyond the nearest school, buy fuel or maintain such vehicles, or pay the salaries of drivers. The bill passed the House by a substantial margin. When it came to the Senate, I had secured enough commitments to defeat it. When Governor Carroll realized this, he sent me a handwritten note:

Georgia,

While I can't ask you to vote for House Bill 168, I do want you to release your fellows committed against it.

We do not yet know the impact of Gordon's ruling today . . . it may require us to use 100% state funds to pay for busing. As I told you, we are trying to get the Court to allow use of Federal funds to pay for busing.

We plan an appeal, but need HB 168 if we ever expect to get federal funds to pay the cost of busing.

Julian

The members who were committed to me to vote against the bill came to me and said, "Senator, the Governor has called and asked me to vote for HB 168. I told him I had promised to vote against the bill because you asked me to."

I realized the kind of pressure the Governor was putting on them, so I said, "Just vote your conscience." One or two stuck with me, but most didn't, and the bill was passed and signed by the Governor.

Of course, the cost of busing was not the issue. I knew it, and Julian Carroll knew it. In his State of the Commonwealth address, he said, "Alternatives must be found to forced busing of children," while anti-busing demonstrators chanted and shouted outside the chamber.

When he denied a request for a supplemental appropriation of five hundred thousand dollars to the Jefferson County Board of Education, I spoke out:

"On busing, I think the Governor should have been up front from the beginning by stating that Kentucky would be a state that would abide by the law. He could have been a real leader, but I think he's becoming so obsessed by busing, he's sounding like a demagogue."

Helen Bland, speaking at a rally in support of integration of Jefferson County schools described the ludicrous position of those who say they are for equal opportunity, but against busing. She said it far better than I ever could:

> Lord, what is it with this bus? When I was growing up in rural Alabama, we weren't allowed to ride the bus. Rain or shine we had to walk five miles to school, and when the bus carrying the White children passed, we had to scramble up weed-filled banks to keep from having mud splashed all over us.
>
> Then, I moved to Montgomery and Blacks were boycotting the buses, so I still couldn't ride. Finally, I moved to Louisville where I raised my children and they again walked to school in the neighborhood, even though it was more than a mile—a long walk in bad weather. Then, along came the Court order, and they said my grandchildren had to ride the bus. They did, and they liked the bus, and got along well at the school they went to. Now, somebody's trying to turn back the clock and put them off the bus again.
>
> I said, "Lord, what is it with this bus? When's it gonna stop plaguing my life?"

I am a staunch supporter of school integration. My position has not wavered. Black and White students can't be educated in isolation. We live in this world together, we work together, and we need to go to school together. Busing is the only way Jefferson County schools can be integrated. It's ridiculous in this day and age when students travel miles in every direction to go to the doctor, to take dancing lessons, to play ball, and to do numerous other activities, to say that riding a bus a few miles to school is too great a hardship. The children are safer on the buses then they are on the sidewalks of Louisville walking to school. No, "it's not the bus, it's us," as the saying goes.

I am deeply concerned that some Blacks are willing to

resegregate our schools because there are still problems. There are problems, but we must work on them within the framework of a solid commitment to integration. A young minister who is vocal about his separatist views once said of me, "Senator Powers went to segregated schools and she did all right."

My answer to him was, "Yes, I went to segregated schools, and I became a state senator. But who knows what I could have become if I'd had the advantages provided by an integrated system? Maybe I could have been president of the United States."

During that same year I secured passage of a provision to allow the Commission on Human Rights to award damages for embarrassment and humiliation to a person discriminated against. The United States Justice Department called this provision "the strongest enforcement tool in the country," because it set no upper limits on the amount of damages that could be awarded.

23

IN
THE
FRAY

In 1978 Ray Crider, an officer of the Greater Louisville Labor Council, and other labor leaders recommended that the Senate Committee on Committees appoint me to chair the Labor and Industry Committee. Labor leaders had noted my favorable vote on labor issues and wanted me to head the committee. I was duly appointed and served as Labor and Industry Chairman until I retired.

Most of the legislators were from rural districts where organized labor had little clout. Business and industry could block any labor legislation they decided to. Their influence on the Kentucky legislature is so great, in my opinion, because of their heavy campaign contributions.

The main issues the Labor and Industry Committee dealt with were unemployment compensation, worker's compensation, minimum wage, and prevailing wage (requiring tax-funded projects to pay the prevailing union wage in the area of the project). I worked to increase the minimum wage, and also to require that prevailing wages be paid. Rural legislators didn't want prevailing wage because it was easy to get people to work for less. We passed a prevailing wage law, but it only applied to projects costing $275,000 or more. I was successful in passing legislation in 1983 to increase the minimum wage from $2.60 an hour to $3.35.

During my ten years as Labor and Industry Chairman, I stymied the repeated efforts of conservative forces to pass a "right-to-work" law. In many sessions an attempt was made to add Kentucky to the ranks of the twenty-six states that had such laws. Most Southern states have "right-to-work" legislation. In my opinion these laws do not guarantee a right to work; they allow employees in companies that have unions to reap the benefits of unionization without sharing the responsibilities by joining the union. When "right-to-work" legislation was referred to my committee, I wouldn't bring it up for a vote. In 1986, Joe Lane Travis of Glasgow, succeeded in getting enough votes to take a "right-to-work" bill away from my committee and send it to the Senate floor for a vote. The bill passed the Senate, but we managed to kill it in the House.

I was a seasoned politician now, or so I thought. After my first term, I felt I knew pretty well who the friends of Black people were, who their enemies were, and who was more or less neutral, meaning I could get their vote if I had something they wanted and it wouldn't cause them too much trouble back home.

However, to my distress, I was wrong. In 1978, I was betrayed by someone I counted as a friend to Black causes—Bill Kenton. Bill was a Lexington legislator who served as Speaker of the House from 1976 to 1980. He was progressive, energetic, and I respected him. Although he was White, much of his Lexington district was Black. In the 1978 session, he attached an amendment to a house bill to move ten predominantly White precincts from two other Lexington districts into his district. He had narrowly defeated Black challenger, Theodore Berry, in the 1977 primary election. A shrewd politician, he quietly redistricted ten precincts to preserve his seat.

He slipped the bill through the House by placing it on the Consent Calendar that is reserved for non-controversial bills. The three Blacks in the House—Aubrey Williams, Mae Street Kidd, and Carl Hines—voted for it. I think these legislators didn't realize what the bill did when they voted for it. I also think they trusted Bill Kenton. They didn't believe he would try to pass a law which would harm Black people, so they were caught off guard. It passed the House eighty votes to none and came to the Senate.

When Kenton's redistricting bill came to the Senate floor and I realized what he was doing, I spoke out. "This is gerrymandering in the worst sense," I said.

The Lexington-Herald blasted Kenton on its editorial page:

> The term for redrawing the boundaries of an election district for strictly political purposes, may be replaced in Lexington by another word—Kentonmandering. The original term was coined when the last name of Elbridge Gerry, a Massachusetts governor of the last century who used unfair redistricting practices to his party's advantage, was combined with a salamander, whose shape the rearranged districts resembled. Lexington's 75th will not resemble a salamander, but the method by which it was passed does seem to have something in common with that of a lowly amphibian—SLIMINESS.

Kenton had lined up too much support for his bill for me to have a chance to kill the redistricting provision. It passed the Senate twenty-six to eleven. After the vote was taken, I rushed out of the chamber and went to Kenton's office. "Bill, I have misjudged you," I said. "Were you so worried that you could not be re-elected that you would go this far to betray forty-five percent of your loyal supporters? The Black people in your district think you are here representing their best interests. I assure you I will let Mary Brown and Raymond Hampton (two Black leaders in Kenton's district who always worked hard to get out the vote for him) know what you have done!"

Bill had never seen me so upset and angry. "It's not racial, Georgia," he protested.

In one of the rare times I have used an off-color expression in public, I yelled, "Bullshit!" and strode out, slamming the door behind me. After this episode, I felt Bill Kenton was no better than the more conservative legislators I had to deal with—at least I knew where they stood.

Before I was able to work through my feelings and judge Bill and his record in a more objective way, he died suddenly of a heart attack. Jim and I went to his funeral in Lexington. I wanted to forget what he had done, but I couldn't get over my feeling of having been betrayed by a friend.

Though I was saddened by both Bill's actions and his death, there were other areas of life that were improving. The atmosphere of change also affected some of the practices at Jim's work place.

Jim had proved that he could compete with any White salesman in the business. According to Ed Moore, he was the first salesman in the history of the company to consecutively reach commissions of thirty thousand, thirty-five thousand, and forty thousand dollars a year.

Later that year Jim and I celebrated five years of marriage, and he won a cruise on the Carnival Cruise Lines. "We're going," I declared. We went to San Juan, Puerto Rico;

St. Thomas, Virgin Islands; and Saint Martin, West Indies. The other couples seemed proud to have us on board. They introduced me to strangers as "our Senator from Kentucky."

Jim was supportive of my son, Billy, and my grand-children. Billy had married a woman named Geraldine Jones after he returned from the Navy. They had three children: Don-Frederic Lamont, William Nicky Jr., and Artrice Nichelle. Artrice died of Sudden Infant Death Syndrome when she was only three months old. Billy and Geraldine's marriage lasted only eight years. After the divorce, I spent time with my grandsons, taking them on outings and listening to their problems. We went to the J.B. Speed Art Museum, and the Museum of Natural History. Picnicking and swimming—they taught me to swim—were two of our favorite activities.

I treated Jim's grandchild, Deborah's son Kebin, as one of my own. Kebin has cerebral palsy and is a very special child. I was happy and content with my personal life, and much of my attention was focused on the job I was trying to do in the Senate. When I wasn't in Frankfort, I was busy helping my constituents in the west end.

That was the same year I opposed Dottie Priddy, a fellow Jefferson County legislator, on a bill which promoted racism. Priddy introduced a bill to designate her community, Fairdale, as an "incorporated urban place." Dottie wanted the designation to make Fairdale eligible for state road funds. The preamble declared the mocking bird as the community's official bird, "We Shall Defend" as the motto, and adopted a special flag of five colors. The description of the flag read:

". . . red symbolizes the general term of rednecks by which the residents are proudly known, blue is for fidelity and because most of the area's residents are blue collar workers, and white is for purity and because over 95% of the area residents are God-fearing far right-wing conservatives."

The bill passed the House seventy-five votes to none. All three Black representatives—Carl Hines, Mae Street Kidd, and Aubrey Williams—not only voted for it, they co-sponsored it. I'm sure they didn't realize the language that was in it when they supported the bill.

When the bill came to the Senate, I read it and started pointing out the language to some of my colleagues. Senator Robert Martin, retired president of Eastern Kentucky University, immediately said, "Why, this is ridiculous! I'll speak against it."

"It reminds me of the White supremacy claims made in Nazi Germany," I said. I resented legislators inserting offensive language into the statutes, especially since we had just cleaned out many such words through a bill sponsored by Senator David Karem.

My tactic succeeded. I convinced Senator Martin of the racial and ethnic overtones of the legislation. I knew he could influence others to vote against it. Sometimes opposition was more effective coming from another legislator.

"If these people want to be known as rednecks, I see nothing wrong with it," said Senator Bill Quinlan, who was managing the bill on the floor.

Senator Robert Martin spoke eloquently against the bill and helped me convince other senators to vote against it. When the vote was taken, the tally was fifteen to fourteen, one short of the necessary sixteen votes to win passage.

Dottie, incensed and with blood in her eyes, immediately strode to the Senate floor. I told her exactly how I felt about the language in her bill and I wouldn't back down. Later that day, Senator John Berry came to me and asked if I objected to the bill on any grounds other than the preamble.

"No, as a matter of fact, I'll vote for it if that is deleted." The bill was amended to eliminate the preamble, and it passed easily.

I Shared the Dream

The next year, 1979, I had to fight a contested battle for my Senate seat. Gerald Neal, a Black attorney, and Mattie Jones, a civil rights activist, were running against me.

Neal was popular with young Blacks. He was president of the local chapter of the National Bar Association (which was for Black lawyers), had served as city safety director, and worked as hearing officer for the Workers' Compensation Board. Newspaper reports on the race said: "Party activists, who don't wish to be identified for fear of alienating Mrs. Powers or her opponents, say she will out-organize Neal and Jones. But they say Neal is not to be taken lightly."

I usually asked my father and friends like Darryl Owens to sign my filing papers. For this race I decided to ask Charles Roberts, my legislative chairman and the mayor's assistant, and Leonard Gray, legislative chairman of the adjoining district. I soon saw that the two of them were working both ends of the street. I found out they had also signed Neal's papers. They were playing a game with me and I knew it.

The newspaper quoted Neal as saying the top issue was leadership. "Mrs. Powers is a fine person, a capable person . . . but the issue is who is going to provide the most effective representation," he said.

I replied, "I'm not worried. I'm doing everything I know how to do in a political campaign."

On election day I went to the polls, shook hands with voters, and asked for their support. I visited all the precincts, then went home to rest and wait for the vote count.

As I walked into my house, however, something told me, "You are not through yet. Go to the corner to your precinct and shake some more hands." I freshened up and went back out. As I approached the polling place, Charlie Roberts, who had signed my papers and pledged his support to me, was laughing and talking with Gerald Neal. They gave me a condescending look as if to say, "You've lost today."

I politely spoke to them and then went over to the line where sixty or so constituents were waiting to vote. I shook each person's hand and gave him or her my card with my voting record on it. "I'd appreciate it if you'd vote for me," I said.

When the final count was in, I had won by only fifty-nine votes. I will always believe that I was led to go back to the polling place that day, and that those last hands I shook made the difference.

During the late fall of that year, my mother became ill.

On Christmas Eve, she lay on the couch as we all visited and exchanged gifts. We stayed until after midnight, laughing and talking. Mom seemed to be feeling better and enjoying the party. But the next day, Pop called while we were eating Christmas dinner.

"Georgia, I think you better come. Mom is very ill."

We took her to the hospital. Three days after she was admitted, her appendix ruptured. She died two days later, but not before we'd both been able to voice our love for each other for the first time.

Pop was lost without Mom, and when the Senate convened in 1980, I got him a job as assistant doorkeeper for the Senate chamber and took him to Frankfort with me. It was a special time for us both. He loved the work. When he would hear my voice over the hallway amplifiers, he'd come into the senate chamber and stand there, his face glowing with pride as he listened intently.

24

HATRED'S UGLY HEAD

Recurrence of Klan activity led many other communities to pass anti-mask ordinances, especially in 1980 and 1981. In March 1981, the State Commission on Human Rights reported in its publication, *Kentucky's Black Heritage*, "The Ku Klux Klan Can't Hide its face behind bedsheets in these Kentucky cities and counties." It also reported that there were twenty-one local ordinances in the state.

My bill was reported favorably out of the Senate Judiciary Committee. It prohibited wearing hoods, masks, and other disguises in public places—exempting certain things such as Halloween costumes—and prohibited cross burning. As I walked out of the committee meeting, the Grand Dragon of the Ku Klux Klan sauntered up and introduced himself, then said, "You know, the Klan once burned a man by dousing the bus he was on with gasoline."

He was trying to frighten me, and he succeeded. However, despite his words and my fear, I was determined to push the bill through. I kept a gun by the bed and put a chair under the lock of the door in the room of the motel where I stayed in Frankfort. Klansmen walked by my door in heavy boots, or drove by in pickup trucks with rifles hanging on a rack across their rear windows. A card with a picture of a Klansman wearing a robe and hood and riding on a horse rearing up on its hind legs was placed on my desk in the Senate chamber. On it were printed the words, "KNIGHTS OF THE KU KLUX KLAN ARE WATCHING YOU!" I knew they were already. I didn't have to be told.

Not only did the Klan threaten me, they also harassed my family. Pop said he had received calls saying, "Tell that nigger daughter of yours to lay off the Klan." The caller had only identified himself as "Jack Frost." Pop didn't know what it was all about, and I told him as little as possible, because I didn't want him to worry.

My bill had both support and opposition when it was introduced. "What's wrong with cross burning?" Senator Gus Sheehan of northern Kentucky asked me. "While it may be offensive to some, it's a free expression of speech."

"Let someone burn one in your front yard, and see how offensive it is," I replied. "See if you still think it's only a free expression of speech."

Many legislators told me how repugnant they thought the Klan was and how glad they were that someone had the courage to take them on. My gut told me I might be in danger, but I wouldn't back down. The bill passed the Senate thirty-three votes to none and went to the House, where a Black representative, Aubrey Williams, had agreed to manage it.

On the day the bill was to come up before the House Judiciary Committee, Williams told me it was not necessary for me to come over because, "he had everything under control." He obviously underestimated the efforts of the Klan. When they saw the sentiment of support in the Senate, they had stopped working there and begun working on House members—even before the bill was passed in the Senate and went to the House. The bill never made it out of the House Committee. We failed to get a statewide anti-mask law.

That same year, I also was a key player in a fight to stop the destruction of Kentucky State University as a four-year institution. The State Council on Higher Education was considering making Kentucky State a community college, closing it, or incorporating it into the University of Kentucky system. A subcommittee of the Council on Minority Affairs recommended that it be made a community college. Three members of the Minority Affairs Committee voted in favor of the change: Morton Holbrook, an attorney from Owensboro; and William Cox and William McCann, former legislators. Two voted against it: Raymond Burse, an attorney, Rhodes scholar, and later president of Kentucky State; and Donna Moloney, wife of Senator Mike Moloney.

Kentucky State University was the only traditionally Black education institution left in Kentucky. It was unconscionable to me that anyone would propose that it become a community college. The school had always been a "stepchild" in the higher education system, receiving only the crumbs. I thought it should be enhanced and integrated, not destroyed. When I first heard about the proposed change, I had only one week to act. As I worried and pondered, it suddenly came to me that the council might be responsive to the legislators, so I devised a plan to secure legislators' signatures on a petition to present to the council. I had to move fast. The prelegislative conference at Kentucky Dam Village Resort Park in the far western part of the state was scheduled for December 1. The meeting at which the council would vote on the future of Kentucky State University was scheduled for December 3.

After having spent much time and energy fighting to keep Kentucky State open, I addressed the council. "My primary reason for requesting to meet with you is to present this petition from legislators," I said, holding the petition up in the air. I read it aloud. "I am proud to announce that this petition was signed by both Democrats and Republicans, Blacks and Whites, men and women. It has a total of one hundred three signatures of legislators from all parts of Kentucky—eastern, western, northern, and the Bluegrass area," I said.

Continuing my plea to kill the vote, I said: "I do not believe that the internal problems of the institution should be mixed in with the federal requirements for enhancement. As Kentucky State Regent's Chairman Luska Twyman has said, other states have been able to solve similar problems without destroying the institution.

"I ask you as members of the Kentucky Council on Higher Education to present to the governor an enhancement plan which will help Kentucky continue to desegregate its higher education system in a manner which does not penalize the traditionally Black institution.

"We support a comprehensive plan for desegregation of all eight universities, but we are adamantly opposed to making Kentucky State the scapegoat for the past failures of public officials, including previous members of the Council on Higher Education, to devise a comprehensive desegregation plan including, but by no means limited to, Kentucky State University."

The Council members broke for lunch. When they reconvened, the room was filled with KSU supporters—students, alumni, and other friends of the school. There were others who spoke on behalf of the school, including civil rights leaders, ministers, members of KSU's Board of Regents, and the director of Franklin County's Chamber of

Commerce. The proposal to make KSU a community college was dropped.

Reporting on the Council's action and what had influenced the vote, the *Frankfort State-Journal* said, "Probably the most influential of all were the signatures of 103 of a possible 138 state legislators who said they favored keeping KSU a four-year school."

Two bills I introduced to help poor working women did not fare so well, however. I sponsored a bill to require retail stores, hotels, motels, and restaurants to pay time-and-a-half for hours worked over forty each week. The Kentucky Retail Federation defeated it. It wasn't even a contest.

It always upset me when a waitress received a tip for good service only to have her employer reduce her wage by an estimated amount of the tip. I introduced a bill to prevent employers from paying tipped employees less than the minimum wage. Again, I was no match for the Kentucky Retail Federation and their skillful lobbyists.

Nevertheless, I did achieve an important victory for women with the passage of my "displaced homemaker" bill. Many women stay home and raise the children only to have their husbands die prematurely or leave them for other women. These older women are then left with no income and no marketable skills for supporting themselves. My bill allowed the Department for Human Resources to provide training, counseling, and service programs for these displaced homemakers.

As a public figure, I felt I had to speak out about issues as they arose. Sometimes this was an agonizing experience. One such issue arose after David Richart, executive director of Kentucky Youth Advocates, brought a situation to my attention. Dominic Owens, a fourteen-year-old Black youth, died at a juvenile treatment center in one Kentucky town. Dominic was subjected to the so-called discipline of his peers through a technique called "grouping," which was practiced and sanctioned by the treatment center's staff at that time. Grouping meant that a group of residents of the department's facilities were allowed to harass another resident because of his behavior. Grouping supposedly included only verbal exchanges, but it often got out of hand. Peers sometimes used physical force on their victims.

In this instance, Dominic Owens was held to the floor by a group of fellow residents. He begged to be let up, but they held him until his eyes rolled back in his head and he became unconscious. The shocking fact about this inhuman behavior was that four college-educated and state-trained staff members working for the center stood by, watched, and did nothing to stop the cruelty.

Dominic was taken to a nearby hospital and then transferred to a Louisville hospital, where he was declared brain dead. He existed in this state for several days until his grandmother, who was his legal guardian, requested that life supports be withdrawn. The matter was not reported to the public for several days. From all I could learn, I felt there was a cover up of what had happened. The situation was eventually reported to Frankfort, where the Department for Social Services staff told higher officials that a routine death of a young resident had occurred during an asthma attack. The official in charge was told what allegedly really happened by an anonymous informant who knew of the group treatment.

I called a press conference and bitterly criticized the four social workers involved. The official fired these four from the treatment center and the commissioner and division director were removed from their posts. At the time I spoke out, the employees were appealing their dismissal to the State Personnel Board. They later won their appeal and were reinstated with back pay. At their hearing, the state coroner, Dr. George Nicholson, testified that Dominic Owens had a heart condition and probably "would have died anyway." Of course, we are all going to die some way. I don't dispute that. But should it be while being held down on the floor with publicly-paid professionals looking on and doing nothing? I don't think so. Thinking of the terror that Dominic must have experienced still gives me chills.

My speaking up did not influence the outcome of the hearing. the whole incident was just an example of how little the life of a poor, Black youth, who had problems living in society, was worth when it was measured against the careers of four middle-class "professionals." It still makes me sick to my stomach to think about it. One of the most nauseating of my memories is hearing the words of a Black social worker who lamented "the ruining of the staff people's lives." At least they still *had* lives. Dominic Owens didn't. After his death, the treatment center announced that it was discontinuing the practice of grouping in juvenile facilities. As far as I know, grouping no longer occurs.

I am proud of the part I played in giving Kentucky one of the best civil rights laws in the country. When the Civil Rights Act was first proposed, there was an extensive discussion among its proponents about who the best person to introduce the legislation would be. Commission on Human Rights director Galen Martin said in these discussions, "The best person to introduce this legislation is the person who is willing to introduce it this session." As a senator, I was always willing to not only introduce civil rights legislation, but also to work hard to get it passed.

During both the 1978 and 1980 sessions of the legislature, bills had been introduced to restructure the governments of Louisville and Jefferson County. Another bill to allow a merger of the two governments had been introduced in 1982. At first, I was opposed to this because I thought it would weaken the political power of Blacks. However, I didn't want to stand in the way of progress, either. I finally made up my mind to vote to get the bill out of committee. "This is the one of the most agonizing issues of my tenure," I said in explaining my vote. "I don't want to dilute the political strength of the Black community, but after seeing the City of Louisville deteriorate and unemployment rise, I've decided that whatever we're doing now must not be the right thing. Maybe it's time to try something else."

I later regretted my vote. Senator Eugene Stuart introduced an amendment to allow the ninety-five small incorporated cities in Jefferson County to remain independent. The bill, with Stuart's amendment, passed and was signed into law by the governor.

The legislation created a commission to draw up a charter for the merged government. I was one of five Blacks on the twenty-six-member commission. It was clear in the commission's discussions that the mayor and county judge, and the Board of Aldermen and Fiscal Court would be replaced by a single, stronger chief executive and one large legislative body elected by neighborhood districts. There was also talk of giving the new chief executive strong control over the independent boards, authorities, and commissions that oversee services ranging from planning, zoning, and health to public parks, the zoo, museum, and library.

The more the proposed charter was discussed, the more I was beginning to dislike it. It seemed to me that only one government was really being changed—the city of Louisville. All the ninety-five suburban cities were exempt. I thought the burden of taxes would fall on city residents. There were no assurances that Blacks would be included in the newly organized government. When the charter finally came up for a vote, seven of us voted against it and offered a minority report at a merger commission meeting.

"Senator, what are you going to do now?" a reporter asked as I left the meeting.

"I am forming a new organization, Volunteers Opposed to Enlargement, to fight the merger," I replied. Darryl Owens was standing nearby.

"How many members do you have?" asked the reporter.

"This is my first member," I said, putting my arms around Darryl.

The Louisville Fraternal Order of Police, whose members were opposed to a merger, gave Volunteers Opposed to Enlargement (VOTE) space for our headquarters. I moved in and organized all the community groups I felt would be most likely to oppose the merger. We ended up with twenty-nine very diversified groups. Blacks from the west end and the White anti-busing groups from the south end actually worked together. We raised less than twelve thousand dollars to fund our efforts, while the opposition raised two hundred thousand dollars. Members of the Chamber of Commerce, banks, businesses, the League of Women Voters, and other professionals favored the charter. Most of them lived in small cities that would not be affected.

The pro-merger forces had television spots and large newspaper ads; we could only afford radio spots in selected areas, but we distributed thousands of leaflets door to door.

Despite our small budget, we worked hard and I thought we would win. The pro-merger group was overconfident. Their votes came in first after the polls closed. Newsmen were pressing me to concede that we had lost. I continued to say, "We're going to win."

After four hours of returns, the numbers started to tilt in our favor. The facial expressions of the mayor and co judge told the story. The merger had been defeated by teen hundred votes.

"It was a fluke," proponents said. "We'll place it on the ballot next year."

"Yes," I said, "and next time we'll win with a bigger margin."

The following year, 1983, they kept their promise to put the merger on the ballot again. They raised over three hundred thousand dollars to sell the charter to the voters. Again, VOTE barely raised twelve thousand. However, the charter was soundly defeated, this time by eight thousand votes.

Taking unpopular stands on the Senate floor and in other public places was part of my job. Many times I stood alone. Nevertheless, I did it anyway—not because I enjoyed standing alone, but because my conscience just wouldn't let me off the hook. I was often discouraged that my colleagues wouldn't join with me, but there were two senators with whom I found common ground.

One was an unlikely cohort. My seat in the Senate chamber was close to Senator Mike Moloney from Lexington. "Good morning, Mike," I said one day. I got no reply.

"Mike, from now on when you want to speak, just let me know," I said.

Mike was a moody fellow. One day I heard Senator David Karem from Louisville, who sat next to me, ask him why he was so moody.

"I guess I'm just an ornery s.o.b.," Mike said. I didn't hold Mike's peculiar ways against him. As a matter of fact, I liked him. I trusted his judgment on most issues, and we voted together 98 percent of the time.

Senator Karem was another person I respected and counted on for support.

I agreed with his position on just about everything except abortion. I believe in the right of a woman to make her own reproductive choices.

Karem, Moloney, and I were labeled "liberals." I didn't like being tagged and prejudged about where I would stand on every issue. However, if I have to be called something, liberal is fine. My definition of a liberal is one who expects government to help those who can't help themselves. I define conservatives as those who expect people to pull themselves up by the bootstraps when they have no boots. By those definitions, I am, and will continue to be, a liberal.

25

PUBLIC SUCCESS, PRIVATE SORROW

My father suffered a stroke and was hospitalized in January of 1984. I had gone to church and was returning to the hospital when, at the end of a long corridor, I saw my four brothers and their wives. I knew it was bad news. John Albert spoke first. "Georgia, Pop has . . . "

I interrupted him. "He's dead, isn't he?"

"Yes, they have him in the anteroom waiting for you to see him."

I stood by Pop's body, staring at his face and repeating the Psalms. I touched his beautiful face with both hands, thinking of the past.

"Georgia, how long have you known Ben Montgomery?" Senator "Fibber" McGee had asked me one day when he saw me talking to Pop in the hall at the capitol, where Pop worked.

"All my life," I said. "He's my father."

"He's one prince of a man," McGee said. He had worked with Pop at American Standard in Louisville, but had not made the connection between Pop and me.

I thought of what McGee had said as I sat looking at Pop, his body still warm but lifeless. Yes, I had known him all my life and I had loved him all my life. Now he was gone. My heart hurt. It felt like a stake had been driven through it. We had been with Pop in the hospital around the clock for three days since his stroke. He couldn't talk, but when I took his hand and said, "Pop, you are not alone. God is with you," he squeezed my hand and I knew he understood and agreed.

I thought of how lovingly he took care of Mom when she was sick and dying. I remembered the Christmas Eve celebration just before she passed away. We all knew she was very sick, but Pop was determined to have us all at home to enjoy the big pot of soup beans and corn bread he cooked every year for the family gathering.

Mom and Pop both gone. How strange it felt. I remembered the night Pop had pulled me back from the brink of suicide with his prayers, and I understood now the power of his prayers which had brought me to my senses that night. Recently, I had gone to visit the Family Worship Center with a friend, Wilma Bowman. This church was started by Welton Lane, the singer Jim and I used to listen to at the Churchill Inn Lounge. He had given up his singing in order train for the ministry.

I began attending services at Family Worship Center, a non-denominational church, because I felt at home there. Black and White people were worshiping together. Everyone was on an equal footing. There was no status-seeking, just an atmosphere of love for God and love for each other. To the other members, I wasn't a senator—I was Sister Georgia. When I became a member, I felt I had returned to my roots, the simple faith espoused by my father in that shotgun house church long ago.

As I sat by Pop's body and thought of all this, I began to repeat the Psalm he so loved.

"The Lord is my shepherd, I shall not want . . . "

26

MOSES, THE ORATOR

Many adjectives are used to define Jesse Jackson: aggressive, arrogant, brilliant, erudite, and charismatic are just a few. Like most leaders, Jesse is a complex person. He has his detractors and his supporters. Both, I believe, agree that his oratory is powerful.

The first time I heard Jesse speak, I could feel his electrifying effect on the audience. Jesse had a meticulously trimmed, three-inch Afro, and was wearing a multi-colored Yoruban dashiki. With his high cheekbones and those big, dark eyes scanning the crowd, he reminded me of a black stallion poised on a hill.

He emerged out of a public housing project in Greenville, South Carolina, to fight discrimination and injustice. His work as a leader of the sit-ins in the 1960s was the beginning of his life in this civil rights movement. Dr. Martin

Luther King Jr. admired Jesse's youth and enthusiasm. As president of the Southern Christian Leadership Conference, Dr. King appointed Jesse national director of Operation Breadbasket, the economic arm of SCLC.

This position allowed him to travel across the country and converse with prominent Black leaders. In December 1971, after four years with Operation Breadbasket, Jesse resigned and joined with about seventy Black leaders to form People United to Serve Humanity (PUSH). The organization was launched in Chicago on Christmas Day. I believe that, after Dr. King's death, Jesse was disappointed with SCLC, which was then under the direction of Ralph Abernathy.

Some SCLC leaders felt betrayed by Jesse's move. I had once heard A.D. say to Dr. King, regarding Jackson's individuality, "Jesse wants to do his own thing." In his characteristic compassionate manner, Dr. King had answered, "Maybe it's better that he does."

Many SCLC board members saw Jesse as an opportunist who was using his position to propel himself to the forefront. They criticized him for moving too fast and leaving Operation Breadbasket impotent without his leadership. He was described as too aggressive and impatient in seeking power. I believe there was a good deal of jealousy in their judgmental statements—while they were talking, Jesse was producing.

Like many Black ministers in the civil rights movement, Jesse disregarded punctuality. He thought nothing of coming into a meeting or a rally two or more hours late. Once I asked A.D. King, "Do you ministers purposely come in late?"

"Yes," he said. "We like to let the crowd get settled and anticipate our appearance. We time it just right to get the most out of our entrance."

"You guys are such actors," I said. "Women would not

dare do that. It must be a male ego characteristic." A.D. laughed. He knew I spoke the truth.

I watched Jesse mature through the next two decades, leading up to his organizing the Rainbow Coalition, a multi-cultural, multi-racial coalition from which he launched his campaign to be chosen the Democratic nominee for the presidency. Blacks, Whites, Asians, Native Americans, Latinos, and the poor made up what Jesse called a "patchwork quilt."

"We are all separate patches of a quilt. Alone, we don't have an impact. Let's sew these patches together to make a beautiful quilt and win," he said.

He announced his candidacy on November 3, 1983. "The coalition will represent those who have traditionally lacked power and need a voice in government," he declared.

A national representative of the Jackson campaign, Lafayette Surney, came to Louisville in February 1984 to organize a local chapter of the Rainbow Coalition. Along with many others, I committed my support to Jesse's candidacy. The group selected me as state co-chairman, along with Reverend W. J. Hodge, who was a longtime civil rights activist, president of the local chapter of the NAACP, and pastor of the historic Fifth Street Baptist Church. Coordinators for the campaign across the state included Cheri B. Bryant, affirmative action director for the city of Louisville; Regina Thomas, a young, politically astute Black woman who worked as a researcher for the Kentucky Legislative Research Commission; Bill Allison, a White attorney who later won a lawsuit recovering millions of dollars for Black police officers who had been discriminated against by the city of Louisville; Theodore Berry, a Black Lexington attorney who had narrowly lost his legislative race against Speaker of the House Bill Kenton; and the Reverend Earl Mackey, of Lexington.

Enthusiasm ran high at our organizational meeting.

Reverend Hodge commented on those who criticized Jesse for taking an ego trip. "They say, 'Jesse is running for Jesse.' Who do they think Mondale is running for?" The group laughed. "This is a movement, not a campaign," he said.

Bill Allison said, "We should try to get White people to wake up to the fact that Jackson represents their best interests."

Mattie Jones, director of the local Alliance Against Racial and Political Repression, urged us to involve the people in Beecher Terrace and Southwick—two public housing projects.

As a practical politician, I talked about how we could get Kentucky delegates for Jesse.

"We must get as many Jackson delegates for the Democratic National Convention in San Francisco as we can," I said. "Kentucky does not have a primary system; we elect delegates in caucus. In order to get delegates sent to the Democratic Convention, we must elect them in the legislative district conventions and congressional districts."

When Jesse received the report of the meeting, he called me. "Sister Georgia, I am grateful for your support. We need your expertise and experience." I promised to do everything I could to get him delegates from Kentucky.

One thing I admired about Jesse was his willingness to break new ground in pursuit of his goals. He used obstacles as stepping stones. Two months after he announced his candidacy, he became a self-appointed international ambassador. He had no diplomatic experience or portfolio, but he negotiated with Syrian President Assad for the release of Lieutenant Robert Goodman, an American Air Force pilot. Later he repeated the same feat, accomplishing the release of forty-eight American and Cuban prisoners in negotiations with Fidel Castro.

After a month of organizing for Jackson in Kentucky, we planned a three-city appearance for him—Lexington,

Frankfort, and Louisville. Hundreds of supporters came to meet him at Lexington Bluegrass Airport. His entourage of assistants, newsmen, and supporters went in a motorcade to the Shiloh Baptist Church, pastored by Reverend T. H. Peeples. More than fifteen hundred people filled the church and lined the streets outside. Jesse began in a low, subdued voice. Soon, he had swung into a forty-five minute speech ringing out civil rights-era slogans with evangelistic zeal. Placard-waving supporters shouted, "Run, Jesse, run!" Several times they interrupted him in mid-sentence with applause and standing ovations. His reference to thoroughbred horses in Lexington evoked the most emotion.

"If we can get the same concern for people in Kentucky as we do for horses . . . ," he shouted. The audience went wild.

Time had gotten away from us that day, so we had to bypass Frankfort and drive on to Louisville for a rally at West Chestnut Street Baptist Church. Jesse knew the pastor, Reverend C. Mackey Daniels, who was also from South Carolina. During the seventy-eight-mile drive, Jesse and I discussed the campaign. He asked me how many delegates he could get out of Kentucky.

"I am hoping for ten, but it will be difficult because the largest concentration of Blacks is in Louisville, with Lexington next," I told him.

Although this was the first time I had been alone with Jesse since we were both at the Lorraine Hotel in Memphis where I had heard him talking to Dr. King on the balcony just before King was killed, neither of us brought up Martin or the early days of the civil rights movement. At that point, the memories were still too painful. We purposely concentrated on discussing his political campaign.

We continued our fight for more delegates by appealing to the Credentials Committee of the Democratic National Convention. Bill Allison filed our complaint. A representative was appointed to make recommendations to resolve the dispute. After a day-long hearing, he recommended that our challenge be denied. He did admit, however, that there had been many mistakes made during the lengthy delegate selection process.

"There is no evidence that those mistakes cost Jackson any delegates he might otherwise have had," he said.

At the first Kentucky caucus in San Francisco, I tried, without success, to get delegates to support four of Jackson's planks for the platform: affirmative action, reduction in the military budget, voting rights, and a commitment against the first use of nuclear weapons.

After much heated debate and compromise, the Democratic National Convention adopted a thirty-five thousand-word platform. Governor Mario Cuomo of New York delivered the strong keynote address and set the tone for the Convention. Cuomo, a street-smart intellectual, told the delegates in a memorable speech, "We are a family needing only the courage of our convictions to win."

The following evening Jackson spoke to the full Democratic Convention for fifty minutes. He said that he needed the party and the party needed him. Unfortunately, in a private conversation, Jackson had called Jewish people "Hymies" and referred to New York as "Hymietown." In a manner uncharacteristic of him, and in contrast to his evasiveness about and nonadmission of the error, he lifted the audience with an extraordinary plea for forgiveness. He said, "If in my low moments in word, deed, or attitude, through some error of temper, taste, or tone, I have caused anyone discomfort, created pain, or revived someone's fears, please forgive me." His stirring message was interrupted thirty-four times by applause.

Jackson said, "I would rather have Roosevelt [Franklin D.] in a wheelchair than Reagan on a horse!"

One Black delegate from another state exclaimed, "My God, he's Moses, the orator!" as Jackson's voice flooded the hall.

I supported Jackson's candidacy for the Democratic nomination for president again in 1988, though, admittedly, not with the same enthusiasm and time I had committed to it in 1984. I was working hard to pass an affirmative action bill, and the time I had to give to the campaign was limited.

I did, however, join the "Women for Jackson in 1988" forces to bring out the women's vote for Jesse. In that campaign, when we got to Hazard, two thousand people, mostly Whites, jammed the Hazard Memorial Gymnasium to hear Jesse speak. He used his quilt analogy to ask for their support.

"Unemployed coal miners, and those whose land has been stripped, face problems similar to those Iowans who have lost their farms to debt, [as well as problems similar to those of] laid-off auto workers in Wisconsin and displaced homemakers in New Hampshire. If we unite, we can make a beautiful quilt," he told the crowd.

In the current political environment there are those who say that Jesse Jackson is neither radical enough for the Louis Farrakhans, nor conservative enough for the Vernon Jordans—and sometimes I don't agree with him myself—but I view Jesse with respect, admiration, and affection.

27

THE
LAST FEW PLAYS

When I went to Frankfort for the 1988 session, I knew
it would be my last, but I didn't tell right away. Even though
these were my final days in politics, I continued to work hard
to pass the legislation I thought important. I introduced a bill
to affirm the executive order, first issued by Governor
Martha Layne Collins, that requires all state agencies, including boards and commissions, to have affirmative action plans
to ensure equal employment opportunity. Governor Collins,
a native of Shelbyville, Kentucky, had served as lieutenant
governor from 1979 to 1982, and was elected governor in
1983, the first woman to be elected to that office in Kentucky.
While Governor Collins was in office, her employment
opportunity policies resulted in the employment of Blacks in
state government rising to a record 7.9 percent, even though
many of the Blacks were in entry-level jobs. My friend and

supporter, Raoul Cunningham was hired by Governor Collins as Deputy Personnel Commissioner in the last year of her administration, and he stayed in that post under Governor Wilkinson. With the passage of my bill, the requirement became law, eliminating the need to convince each succeeding governor to continue it.

I also tried to get a bill enacted to let judges consider the value of a married person's efforts to help a spouse through school when dividing marital property in a divorce settlement. My male colleagues in the Senate wouldn't support it.

Another bill I tried to pass in that last session was one to cap the interest rate that leading institutions can charge on credit card balances. My bill proposed that interest rates be capped at 5 percent above the prime rate at the beginning of each cycle. Four senators on the Banking and Insurance Committee promised to vote to report the bill out, but bank executives, and even credit union officials, came to Frankfort in droves to fight my bill. The committee room was full when the vote was taken. The financiers had done their work well; I had only three votes, not enough to report it out. I hated to lose, but I also despised the actions of some of my colleagues who belittled me in the committee. One legislator asked me to define the word "consummate" in the bill, while the others snickered. I kept a stone face; I would not dignify their immature behavior with any visible reaction.

The bankers argued that rates had to be kept high to cover their losses from credit card holders who defaulted. How did these defaulting customers get their cards? For a very long time, banks and other institutions were pushing credit cards at people like candy. They tried to get everybody, even those who were bad risks, hooked on plastic. Then they defended their exorbitant rates on the grounds of covering their losses.

I made my retirement announcement to my fellow senators on February 12, 1988—my mother's birthday, my grandson Nicky's birthday, and Abraham Lincoln's birthday.

"The chair recognizes the lady from Jefferson Thirty-three," said Lieutenant Governor Brereton Jones.

"Today is a special day for me and one I want to share with you. I have decided not to seek reelection to another term to this august body, and so, in December, having been here twenty-one years, I will say goodbye."

As I spoke those words, I felt both relief and sadness at the thought of closing this chapter of my life. Relief because there were other things I wanted to do, and sadness because I would miss my colleagues and the excitement of each session. However, I would be sixty-five when this term was over, and I thought it was time to go—time to give an opportunity to a younger person.

I spoke about the past. "In 1968, the first bill I introduced in this body was Senate Bill 264 [open housing]. Many thought it had no chance of passing. It did pass twenty-seven to three and became law without Governor Louis Nunn's signature."

I summed up my service in this way. "In twenty-one years I have had some successes and some failures. As a double minority, it has not been easy, but it has been a challenge. There has never been any doubt about who I was here to represent."

That assessment was affirmed by *The Courier-Journal* in its editorial three days later.

Georgia Davis Powers was often a lonely voice in the Kentucky Senate . . . she was the chamber's conscience . . . she went to the Senate—its first Black and first female member—to make a difference, and she did.

She guided fair housing legislation into law in her very first session in 1968. It made Kentucky the first state below the Ohio

River to outlaw discrimination in housing. That a newcomer should be the moving force behind such highly controversial legislation was a tribute to her legislative skills.

That set the tone for her long tenure, which will end with her retirement at the end of the year . . . Her leadership of two successful fights against [a] city-county merger earlier this decade put her at cross-purposes with the community's establishment and the Courier-Journal, but she was standing up for what she perceived was her constituents' interest. On that, as on most legislative matters, Senator Powers left no doubt where she stood.

I knew a retirement party was being planned for me. Raoul Cunningham had talked with me about it and we agreed that it would be held on my sixty-fifth birthday.

I bought a special dress for the party. It was a long, teal-colored, chiffon gown which had a silver beaded neckline and a jacket to match. As Jim and I entered the ballroom of the Executive Inn West, the sound of Ray Charles singing "Georgia" began to echo through the room, and seven hundred friends, relatives, and state and national political figures rose to their feet.

My son, Billy, who was living in Louisville and working for the Water Company, was there.

My brothers and their wives were there: Joseph Ben (Jay) and his wife, Verna, had come from their home in Gary, Indiana. Jay had transferred from the U.S. Post Office in Louisville to the Gary Post Office, working there thirty-five years before he retired.

Robert, who had become the first Black foreman at International Harvester, and later became a deputy sheriff in Jefferson County, was there.

John Albert was there with his wife and childhood sweetheart, Laurine Jones Calbert. They lived in Cincinnati, where John Albert had worked as an inspector at the Cincinnati Water Company. He was now retired.

Phillip and his wife, Rose, also came. He had retired from his job as vice-principal of Scott Detrick Vocational School in Louisville. He had earned his bachelor's and his master of science degrees while teaching vocational education and raising a family with his wife.

Lawrence Franklin was there with Violet Coatley, whom he had married after they graduated from high school. He had been the manager of the Postal Employee Development Center of the U.S. Post Office in Louisville, and was the youngest Grandmaster of the Prince Hall Grand Lodge of Kentucky, having served from 1976 to 1978.

James Isaac and his wife, Marie Ann Josey, attended. He had also retired as manager of five different stations in Louisville. He followed Lawrence as Grandmaster of the Prince Hall Grand Lodge of Kentucky, having served from 1990 to 1994.

My husband Jim's sister, Clementine, had come from Cleveland along with his brother, John, and his brother's wife, Earnestine. His sister Ruth, another sister, Ann, and her husband, Sam, from New Jersey were there. My longtime friend, Marlene Tentman, a teacher in the public school system who was now married to Marion Samuels, came from Cleveland. Inez Gillings from Costa Rica, my friend for more than forty years, was also there.

While I treasured those who were present, I missed those who had passed away—Pop, Mom, and my brothers Rudy and Carl. We have been a close, strong family, and as long as any of us live, we will stay close to each other.

As I looked out at all my relatives, friends, and supporters, I thought about my life. I had received many honors. During my last session in the senate, Yvonne Easton had called and invited me to be a part of a national photographic exhibit, *Portraits of Black Women Who Changed America*, upon which a book would be based. The book title was from a Langston Hughes poem, "I Dream A World." Easton was on loan from *Life Magazine* to help Brian Lanker, the Pulitzer Prize-wining photographer, assemble the exhibit, which was being financed by Eastman Kodak.

Lanker came to Louisville on May 18, 1988 to take photographs. He first drove around the community to choose the settings and selected Western Parkway, a tree-lined street a few blocks from my home, for the first shots. After that, we went to Shawnee Park, where he photographed me sitting on the grass leaning against a tree. At my house he photographed me on the front porch, looking west as the sun was setting. In the living room, I was photographed sitting in front of the fireplace with candles burning in a candelabra. In all, we worked ten hours, took 250 shots, and I changed outfits four times. Afterwards, I was quite sure I would never like having a full-time job as a model.

The exhibition opened at the Corcoran Gallery in Washington, DC on February 8, 1989. Jim and I were there along with the other honorees: Oprah Winfrey, the popular talk show host; Congresswoman Maxine Waters from California's Twenty-ninth District; Johnetta Cole, President of Spellman College in Atlanta; Leontyne Price, the Metropolitan Opera diva; Beah Richards, actress, poet and playwright; Rachel Robinson, the widow of Jackie Robinson; Dr. Betty Shabazz, the widow of Malcolm X; and many other distinguished Black women.

Among the other honors I received, there were some that were exceptionally special to me. The University of Kentucky conferred an honorary doctor of law degree upon me, and the University of Louisville gave me an honorary doctor of humane letters degree. These schools from which I would have been barred as a young woman were now honoring me. Those were sweet moments.

All these thoughts ran through my mind as I looked

out at the crowd. Governors, senators, educators, local officials—they had come to pay their respects to me, the once-impatient young woman from the west end of Louisville. Telegrams and phone calls came from world leaders. The many tributes from such leaders touched me, but, above all, I valued the recognition and respect I had earned from my constituents—the people of Jefferson County Senatorial District Thirty-three. I couldn't ask for more. As I listened, I wanted to laugh and cry at the same time.

"How had I come to this place?" I asked myself—and the answer came. From my humble birth in Washington County, I had traveled an uncharted road that eventually brought me recognition and respect from my state and nation. In so doing, I had suffered the pain of my mistakes, and rejoiced in the triumph of my successes.

EPILOGUE

One of the first things I did after retiring was to purchase a great many books by Black authors: *I Know Why the Caged Bird Sings*, by Maya Angelou; *Ain't I A Woman? Black Women and Feminism*, by Bell Hooks; *You Can't Keep a Good Woman Down: Stories*, by Alice Walker; and *Their Eyes Were Watching God*, by Zora Neale Hurston. I wanted to learn more about Black culture, as I had been shortchanged in learning about my own people while in school. At first I had time to read and relax, but, five months after my retirement, Jim began to have health problems. Subsequently, he had five heart bypass operations. Much of my time was spent caring for him.

In the winter of 1990, on a Sunday afternoon after church, I went to visit my elderly cousin, who was eighty, widowed, and childless. William Ray was living in a nursing home; I was saddened by his lonely state.

Billy, as we called him, was sitting in a wheel chair. His chin rested on his chest and he was sleeping. As I moved closer to him, I saw his hair was uncombed and growing over his ears; his pajamas were stained; the sheets on his bed were soiled; the floor was dirty and dusty. Food droppings were scattered about the room. Horrified, I went to the desk and asked the attendant, "Why is Mr. Ray in this condition at two-thirty on a Sunday afternoon?" My angry attitude and loud voice conveyed my displeasure. The woman stopped what she was doing and jumped from her chair to investigate. I followed her, saying, "Is this the way patients are neglected here?" After seeing my cousin, she summoned the aides and housekeepers to come to his room and take care of him.

Meanwhile, I walked down the long hall to look into the other rooms. I wanted to see if the other residents were also being neglected. Only the rooms with visitors in them were bright and clean, with the residents dressed. Obviously those with visitors received better care and attention than those who were alone. After I left, the residents' lonely plight began to weigh on me. At first, I tried to push it away, but I couldn't.

One morning, I went down into my basement and dug out files on an organization I'd started in 1981 to bring visitors to nursing home residents. I'd been too busy with my Senate work to continue it, but now I made plans to reactivate the group. This time I decided to try to match up churches with nursing homes to provide volunteers who would form friendships with the residents. Later, explaining my idea, I emphasized that the residents needed one-on-one contact. I didn't mean just going to visit once a month for a religious service; some of the churches were already doing that. I was talking about getting to know the residents and providing the kind of support that friends everywhere give each other.

Since there are twelve hundred churches in the Louisville area and about forty nursing homes, my objective was to get five hundred volunteers to visit the nursing homes each week. I drew up the by-laws for the organization and formed a board, serving as president.

Going to see Jefferson County Judge Executive David Armstrong, I explained my plans and the services I wanted this organization to provide in the community. I told him that we needed a one-time-only grant to pay for a part-time director. In addition, we needed office space, office equipment, access to a computer system, a telephone, mailing privileges, and office furniture. He was excited about the program and arranged a meeting with the director of the Jefferson County Department of Human Resources, Katherine M. Schneider. She, too, was willing to help. Armstrong, Commissioner Darryl Owens, Irv Maze, and Chris Gorman placed a grant of over fifteen thousand dollars in the budget. The total budget of Friends of Nursing Home Residents, Incorporated (FONHRI) for the first year was $27,638, including in-kind services. After the first year, funds were raised from the private sector.

"Friends" are making a difference in Jefferson County's nursing homes. Staff and residents have come to depend on their visits; they welcome the sight of the large pink badges the volunteers wear, proclaiming that they are there as a "friend." The relationships formed have enriched both the lives of the nursing home residents and the volunteers. "This is simply the most rewarding activity I have ever been involved in," one volunteer said to me.

By October of 1994, forty-five nursing homes had been adopted by churches and other groups; the number of volunteers had grown to more than five hundred.

For a time, the nursing home project was my only public endeavor. However, magazines and newspapers continued to contact me for statements on current issues. Many groups asked me to serve on their boards and to speak to them, but I accepted few engagements. When constituents would call me for help I usually advised them to contact my successor, Senator Gerald Neal.

"He is your Senator now, and you should look to him to lead," I would tell them.

On September 21, 1991, however, Jefferson County School Superintendent Donald Ingwerson announced his intention to end busing for school desegregation, claiming that it was necessary to implement the 1990 Kentucky Education Reform Act (KERA). There had been rumors about such a move, but school officials were sworn to secrecy about what was planned.

I was appalled when Don Ingwerson unveiled the sketchy details of his plan and announced that it would be voted on by the school board on October 23. He planned to end sixteen years of busing and embark on a plan of "voluntary" busing for desegregation with only one month's notice and *no* public discussion.

What Ingwerson proposed was essentially the final dismantling of the busing plan that was implemented in 1975 and amended in 1984. Louisville and Jefferson County were recognized nationally as having the most desegregated system in the nation, according to a National School Boards Association study in 1989. In an article on January 16, 1991, *The New York Times* referred to "places like Louisville, Kentucky where research shows that school desegregation resulted in more Blacks and Whites living side by side."

Impatient as always, I waited for someone to speak out publicly against Ingwerson's proposed plan. Eighty-five-year-old Lyman T. Johnson, a retired teacher and assistant principal, the first Black admitted to the University of Kentucky by court order, and a plaintiff in the 1975 federal lawsuit resulting in the sweeping busing plan issued by Judge Gordon, was the first. But *all* he did was speak. There needed to be organized opposition.

The next morning I made up my mind. Someone had to take the lead—and soon. I couldn't wait any longer. This was a disaster to our community. I had to speak out.

I called C. Mackey Daniels, a former school board member and pastor of West Chestnut Street Baptist Church, saying to him, "We need to have a public forum to organize opposition to the plan to end school desegregation."

"Yes, we need to, and as soon as possible," he responded.

"Can we have a rally at your church?" I asked.

"Yes," he said, "just name the time."

"Sunday afternoon—when we can get the biggest crowd," I said decisively. I wanted to have the rally at the church, because it was centrally located and not too far into the predominantly-Black west end. White people needed to feel comfortable attending. I held a press conference announcing my opposition to the plan and scheduling a mass meeting open to others who also opposed it. I mailed over 250 letters to pastors and various groups, inviting them and their congregations and members to the meeting. I left no doubt where I stood. "I am unalterably opposed to any plan which will resegregate our schools. My whole life experience tells me that the Supreme Court was right when it said that segregation is inherently unequal," I stated.

The school board, in my opinion, was using KERA as a smoke screen to resegregate Black children. My public stand galvanized a host of other people who believed in desegregated schools, but also solidified support for Don Ingwerson from those who were willing to risk a return to a segregated system, including some in the Black community.

In an emotional meeting, I arranged what the *Courier-Journal* said, "often took on the tenor of a tent revival. A series of speakers—black and white, young and old, lashed out at the proposed student assignment plan that would end involuntary busing for desegregation in Jefferson county."

There were twelve speakers, including three pastors of major churches, Black and White: W.J. Hodge of the Fifth Street Baptist Church and president of Simmons Bible college; Richard Beale, White pastor of First Unitarian Church; and James Chatham, White pastor of prestigious Highland Presbyterian Church. Jim Hill, a Black attorney who was a student during the first year of busing and a graduate of the University of Kentucky, said, "My heart is sad and filled with pain, for again the forces of evil and division have found a tool fashioned to reshackle our community. Let there be no doubt that the national trend toward rolling back the clock has come to plague our community."

After the successful rally, I suggested that community leaders and groups coalesce into an organization to monitor and keep abreast of what the school board was doing. The group was called QUEST (Quality Education for All Students).

QUEST was incorporated on October 11, 1994. I am listed as the incorporator. QUEST members attended school board meetings, contacted newspaper editors, held rallies, worked with the business community, and brought in national experts on school integration. I relinquished the position of chairing the group after two years. Dr. Madeline Maupin Hicks, a former teacher who later became a dentist, and Dr. James Chatham accepted the co-chairmanship.

Our efforts made a difference. Ingwerson was forced to abandon the strategy of a quick implementation of his plan. He announced "public" meetings around the county to discuss his plan for voluntary integration. The meetings were shams as far as I was concerned,.

The school board finally adopted a plan for voluntary desegregation of schools in December of 1991, but the plan mandated that guidelines for desegregation be maintained. If they are not, the board has promised that students will return to busing as a means of ensuring desegregation. It is my position, and the position of QUEST, that a segregated education is not, and cannot be, a quality education. Although QUEST did not succeed in killing the superintendent's plan altogether, it did awaken the community to the danger and mobilize citizens to monitor the system closely, not only for adherence to integration guidelines, but for other shortcomings.

"We will not go back to sleep," I said. "We will stay organized. We are concerned about segregation within the schools. We are concerned abut discipline problems. We are concerned about dropouts. We are concerned about recruiting more Black teachers. We are demanding that our schools serve all our children according to their needs and society's needs. Nothing is more important to this community.

In the middle of this school desegregation struggle, I began to have pain in my knees that became so severe I had to have surgery. Walking the marble halls of Frankfort had taken its toll, resulting in severe osteoarthritis. My knees had bowed and I had lost two inches in height. In April of 1992, I had bilateral total knee replacements. After a year, I completely recovered, gained my two inches back, and resumed a normal schedule.

Now I am active and busy, but I no longer feel the responsibility of the community on my shoulders. I continue to work with QUEST and FONHRI, but limit my participation in new causes to letters to the editor and speaking out on issues when I need to. It is time for others to take up the mantle and begin to solve some of this world's problems—of which there are many.

My greatest concerns for this country are the continued battles to be fought against discrimination—because of race, gender, ethnic origin, and economic status. America continues to pay the price for allowing poverty to fester and racial divisions to grow. We need a new covenant of justice, in which everyone—regardless of circumstances—has access to adequate health care, quality education, decent housing, and, most important of all, a job paying livable wages.

In the 1960s, and for a time thereafter, African Americans had the Federal Judiciary as an ally in fighting for civil rights and economic justice. However, in the last two decades, rulings by conservative judges have eroded many previous gains. *University of California v. Bakke* (a 1978 case in which Bakke's denial of admission to medical school was ruled "reverse discrimination") is an example of the Supreme Court's regressive rulings. When racial discrimination in America is eliminated so that everyone is on an even playing field, then we can talk about reverse discrimination. Until then, there is no such thing.

I think back to the Kerner Commission's prediction twenty-five years ago that "America is becoming two societies—separate, unequal, and racially divided." There are times when I ask myself the question, "Were all the anxieties, the long hours, the sleepless nights, and dangers I faced worth it?"

I have to answer, "Yes." To do otherwise would be to accept that the the struggles I have participated in are hopeless, and they are not. There have been gains. Blacks and women are in corporate boardrooms, heading successful businesses. Educational opportunities are available. And many Blacks and women are holding elective offices—though not nearly enough.

I feel strongly about the need for job training to put young men who are heads of households to work. It is a dichotomy when politicians cry out that family values need enhancing and then vote against programs that will help strengthen the family. In the current welfare system, an out-of-work father too often has to abandon his family so that his wife can get the resources needed for the family to survive.

I am greatly concerned about public education. Changes are needed, but those changes must be made within the framework of integrated systems. The Federal courts are making it easier for school districts to abandon desegregation through devious methods. In 1994, many African-American students are returning to the same separate, unequal schools that existed when I was a young person—before 1954 and *Brown v. Board of Education of Topeka*, which held that state-provided public school segregation was a violation of the equal protection clause of the Fourteenth Amendment of the United States Constitution.

In this epilogue to my autobiography, I refer to race by different labels. In my life I have been referred to as colored, Negro, Black, and African-American—which is prevalent today. I prefer just to be called an American, because that is what I am. I am more interested in how I am treated than in what I am called.

Now, as always, I share the dream that we all shall be free!